The Founding of New Acadia

D1243658

The Founding of

New Acadia

THE BEGINNINGS OF ACADIAN
LIFE IN LOUISIANA, 1765–1803

Carl A. Brasseaux

Louisiana State University Press
Baton Rouge and London

Designer: Diane B. Didier
Typeface: Linotron Palatino
Typesetter: G & S Typesetters, Inc.
Printer: Thomson-Shore, Inc.
Binder: John Dekker & Sons, Inc.

10 9 8 7 6 5 4 3 2

Library of Congress Cataloging-in-Publication Data
Brasseaux, Carl A.
    The founding of New Acadia.

    Bibliography: p.
    Includes index.
    1. Cajuns—History.   2. Cajuns—Social life and
customs.   3. Louisiana—History—To 1803.   I. Title.
F380.A2B72   1987   976.3'0042   86-20099
ISBN 0-8071-1296-8

To Ryan André and David Marc Brasseaux,
ninth-generation residents of New Acadia

You can tell a Cajun a mile off,
but you can't tell him
a damned thing up close.

—Antoine Bourque

Contents

Illustrations

Preface and Acknowledgments

I am a Cajun, a direct descendant of an Acadian exiled from Grand Pré to Maryland in 1755. Like most Cajuns of my acquaintance, I have been intrigued since childhood with Acadian history. The printed sources that I consulted, however, not only contained contradictory information, but also portrayed rural south Louisiana's francophones in a light that I knew from personal observation to be incorrect. My initial skepticism regarding Acadian historiography was reinforced by my research endeavors in the mid–1970s. While preparing a master's thesis on the career of French colonial bureaucrat Denis-Nicolas Foucault, I encountered much primary source material regarding the first Acadian influx to Louisiana. Upon closer scrutiny, I discovered that these documents contained the framework for an accurate account of the Acadian migration, which had hitherto been shrouded in speculation and myth. I therefore began to collect notes from these manuscripts simply to reconstruct the story of my family's arrival in the Pelican State.

In 1977, my modest investigation blossomed into a full-blown research project with acquisition by the Center for Louisiana Studies of the colony's commandants' reports in microfilm, from the Papeles Procedentes de Cuba. As curator of the Colonial Records Collection, I began to compile a calendar of the new collection's component materials and soon discovered that the reports provided a wealth of information regarding Acadian arrival and settlement in the lower Mississippi Valley. The result of my expanded investigation was a dissertation that was revised and developed to become this book.

In the process, I enjoyed the advice and assistance of several friends and colleagues. Nicholas Spitzer and Alan Lomax read the manuscript and offered timely advice. I am also deeply indebted to James H. Dormon for valuable suggestions. My major professor, Geneviève Fabre, merits special appreciation for giving freely of her time and knowledge. Last, but certainly not least, are my wife and sons, whom I thank for their forbearance, support, and understanding during the many, many months of my preoccupation with this project.

Writing *The Founding of New Acadia* was a labor of love, but because of my close personal connection to the subject, I have made every effort to provide an unbiased account of the Acadian migration. In an effort to stamp out partisanship, I recruited Claudia Domingues and Brenda Hobbs, for whose time and perceptive insights I extend my heartfelt thanks.

Despite all efforts to anticipate and remove this work's deficiencies, I am painfully aware that perfection lies beyond my grasp. I therefore freely acknowledge all remaining errors of fact or interpretation as my own.

Abbreviations

AC   Archives des colonies, in Archives Nationales, Paris
        B Ordres du roi (accompanying numbers provide volume and folio)
        C 9b Saint-Domingue, Correspondance générale (accompanying numbers provide volume and folio)
        C 11d Acadie, Correspondance générale (accompanying numbers provide volume and folio)
        C 13a Louisiane, Correspondance générale (accompanying numbers provide volume and folio)

AE   Archives du Ministère des Affaires Etrangères Political Correspondence Series Angleterre, Archives Nationales, Paris (accompanying numbers provide volume and folio)

APOA Ascension Parish Original Acts

ASD   Audiencia de Santo Domingo, in Archivo General de Indies, Seville (accompanying numbers provide legajo and folio)

CO   Colonial Office, Public Record Office, London (accompanying numbers provide record group and folio)

PPC   Papeles Procedentes de Cuba, in Archivo General de Indias, Seville (accompanying numbers provide legajo and folio)

SJOA St. James Parish Original Acts

SMOA St. Martin Parish Original Acts

The Founding of New Acadia

1

Children of the Frontier

[The Acadians live] in a manner from hand to mouth, and provided they have a good field of Cabbages and bread enough for their families with what fodder is sufficient for their Cattle they seldome look for much further improvement.
—Lieutenant Governor Paul Mascarene, 1720

In a landmark ruling on the case of *James Roach* v. *Dresser Industries* (July, 1980), Judge Edwin F. Hunter classified Louisiana's 500,000 Acadians as a national minority. The plaintiff, Calvin J. Roach, who claimed Acadian descent through his maternal line (Leger), allegedly was fired by an oil-field service business when he objected to his Texan supervisor's repeated use of the pejorative term "coonass" in referring to Louisiana Cajuns. Roach consequently filed suit against his former employer for discrimination banned by the Equal Employment Opportunity Act. Despite the defendant's argument that Acadia had never been an independent country and thus was incapable of producing a national minority, Judge Hunter ruled on July 17, 1980, that Louisiana's Acadians are of "foreign descent" and thus entitled to the full protection of the aforementioned federal legislation.[1]

Judge Hunter's decision was merely the federal government's belated recognition of the persistence of a francophone culture forged in the North American wilderness in the seventeenth century and tempered by foreign domination, dispersal, and subjugation, and, finally, by adaptation to life in an alien land. The remarkable longevity of Acadian culture can be attributed to group cohesiveness and insularity. These social mechanisms, developed in the earliest days of French colonization in Acadia as a response to Maritime Canada's harsh climate and intercultural rivalry, permitted the Acadians to

1. "Cajuns Can Claim Status Under Equal Job Act," Lafayette *Daily Advertiser*, August 10, 1980, p. 17.

1

preserve their core values and ethnic identity while simultaneously adapting their culture to a succession of new physical and social environments—a process that has persisted to the present.[2]

The significant role of the frontier in the development of new, distinctly North American societies such as Acadia has been the subject of intense interest among American and Canadian historians since Frederick Jackson Turner's pioneer study of 1893. Though American frontier historiography has focused primarily upon Anglo-American colonies, the small body of scholarly literature on colonial Acadia suggests that environmental factors played an equally important role in shaping Acadian society.[3]

As elsewhere in North America, European colonists in Acadia quickly molded their life-style to suit the demands of the Canadian wilderness and, in doing so, created a society far different from that of their French cousins. By 1671, the Acadians had become a distinctive people, a frontier nation; yet, the course of this society's rapid sociocultural development differed significantly not only from the Anglo-American experience but also from that of French colonists in the neighboring St. Lawrence Valley.[4]

Like their French counterparts in the St. Lawrence Valley and their English neighbors in New England, the Acadians were initially overwhelmed by their new environment. In order to survive, the colony's European settlers were forced to acquire new skills, thereby changing the face of their colonial society. This metamorphosis being a universal phenomenon in North America's early colonial settlements, the Acadian pioneers shared with their opposite numbers in New France and New England the following characteristics: individualism, adapt-

2. Glenn R. Conrad, "The Acadians: Myths and Realities," in *The Cajuns: Essays on Their History and Culture*, ed. Glenn R. Conrad (Lafayette, La., 1978), 1–20; Mathé Allain, "Twentieth-Century Acadians," in *ibid.*, 129–41.

3. Frederick Jackson Turner, "The Significance of the Frontier in American History," *Annual Report of the American Historical Association for the Year 1893* (Washington, D.C., 1894), 199–277; Morris Zaslow, "The Frontier Hypothesis in Recent Canadian Historiography," *Canadian Historical Review*, XXIX (1948), 153–67; Andrew Hill Clark, *Acadia: The Geography of Early Nova Scotia to 1760* (Madison, 1968); François-Edmé Rameau de St-Père, *Une Colonie féodale en Amérique: L'Acadie, 1604–1881* (2 vols.; Paris, 1889); Naomi Griffiths, *The Acadians: Creation of a People* (New York, 1973); Emile Lauvrière, *La Tragédie d'un peuple: Histoire du peuple acadien de ses origines à nos jours* (2 vols.; Paris, 1886); John B. Brebner, *New England's Outpost: Acadia Before the Conquest of Canada* (New York, 1927).

4. Clark, *Acadia*, 4–5; Geneviève Massignon, *Les Parlers français d'Acadie, enquête linguistique* (2 vols.; Paris, 1962), I, 70–75.

ability, pragmatism, industriousness, equalitarian principles, and the ability to close ranks in the face of a general threat.

These shared traits, however, masked the underlying cultural differences responsible for the divergent evolution of the three neighboring colonial societies. The early Acadians, for example, maintained an extended kinship system—unlike the transplanted Englishmen at Plymouth and Jamestown and the Normans and Picards in the St. Lawrence Valley; distinctive language and speech patterns; a more uniform socioeconomic background; and a far greater degree of social equality. When coupled with a common North American identity, these characteristics set them apart from their neighbors and provided the elements of social cohesion necessary to forge a nationalistic identity.

The development of an Acadian identity was accelerated significantly by the colony's geographic isolation, by its chronic neglect by the mother country, and by the peasant background of its settlers. Effectively shielded from the outside world by geography and deprived of cultural contacts and economic support by the motherland's benign neglect, the early Acadians were almost completely isolated in the Maritime Canadian wilderness. In order to survive, the colonists were compelled to adapt quite rapidly to their new surroundings, exploiting virgin forests and meadows as sources of food, clothing, and shelter. Completely immersed in this environment, the Acadian pioneers developed a frontier mentality.

In the tiny settlements punctuating the wilderness, French peasants were transformed in one generation into independent and self-sufficient pioneers. The woods and meadows in remote areas of the colony insulated them from the feudalistic bonds with which the peasants had been shackled in France. In the frontier's social vacuum, individual talents and industry soon supplanted inherited social position as the measure of a man's worth. The resulting equalitarian spirit, so pervasive in the early Acadian community, encouraged endogamy, which in turn fostered a common group identity.

Group cohesiveness, coupled with the spirit of independence engendered by landownership and the self-sufficiency demanded by the environment, interacted to produce a rapidly maturing colonial mentality. The psychological evolution from French peasant to Acadian yeoman was accelerated by the dissolution of cultural ties with the motherland through France's chronic neglect of the colony and the Acadian settlers' subsequent transposition of a characteristically French affinity for their home provinces to the new homeland. This sense of group identity, based on shared experiences and later reinforced by blood ties, crystallized a century before that of their counterparts in New France and New England.

The circumstances of its birth thus left a lasting impression on Acadian society. Flexibility and pragmatism demanded by frontier life permitted the settlers to adapt their survival skills—the basic life-supporting processes—to new environments, but these necessary changes were never permitted to alter fundamentally the colonists' common values and expectations. With rare exceptions, the Acadians were drawn from peasant stock, usually in the Centre-Ouest provinces, and their socioeconomic background provided the foundation upon which their colonial society was built. These former peasants had shared a rather difficult existence in France, where rising agricultural levies by their landlords had resulted in a steadily declining standard of living. Oppression by the noble landholding class had made the first colonists suspicious of persons in positions of authority, and it is hardly surprising that the transplanted peasants would come to view their provincial administrators with the same mixture of fear and contempt they had felt for their French landlords. The growing avarice of the French landholders had also made the former peasants very protective of their belongings, and, to the land-poor farmers, the ultimate prize was farmland. Landownership was the key to the settlers' modest social and economic aspirations. Products of a precapitalistic environment, they sought neither prestige nor affluence through land acquisition, but rather economic independence and a comfortable existence patterned upon their former agrarian life-style.

Preservation of their agrarian way of life was not only a matter of choice but also an economic necessity, because France's neglect forced the colonists to be self-sufficient. Moreover, as French peasants, they had regularly participated in communal harvests of crops in adjoining fields. This tradition would serve the Acadian pioneers well in the young colony, where large cooperative labor pools were essential to agriculture and thus to survival.

The establishment of communal labor pools was facilitated by an extensive kinship system. The French peasantry had been essentially a patriarchal society placing great importance upon the extended family. The significance of these sociological units was enhanced by the great number of endogamous marriages called for by the rigid caste structure in France. Thus, a propensity for social cohesion was a prominent part of the cultural baggage carried to America by the Acadian pioneers.

The blending of such traditional peasant values with the changes in life-style demanded by environmental factors produced a distinctive society. The physical environment was not the only stimulus for change. Local political, economic, and sociological factors were also instrumental in changing the character of early Acadian society. Particularly significant was the internal and external political turmoil of the seventeenth and eighteenth centuries, which prevented the establishment of an effective provincial government, thereby preserving the physical, cultural, and social isolation of the early Acadian settlements. From the very outset, Acadia was plagued by governmental instability, stemming from the rapid turnover in colonial administrators through death or the proprietors' financial difficulties, from the absence of a cohesive French policy regarding the development of Acadia, from English invasions, and ultimately from the appearance of rival economic interest groups, each seeking to control the colony. The seeds of chaos were sown by the collapse of the first Acadian administration.

Acadia was established in 1604 as a proprietary colony by Pierre Duguay, sieur de Monts, who, one year earlier, had acquired a ten-year monopoly over the region's fur trade and fisheries. After a nearly disastrous winter at Ile St. Croix (present-day Dorchet Island, Maine), during which 36 of the 125 settlers died of scurvy, De Monts transferred the colony to present-day Port Royal, Nova Scotia, where he erected a trading post and established amicable relations with the neighboring Micmac Indians. As a result of the growing Indian desire for French trade goods, the Port Royal fur trade soon expanded and, in 1605, De Monts returned to France with a small cargo of pelts. Upon arrival in the mother country, however, the colonial proprietor discovered that his monopoly had been revoked, necessitating the evacuation of Port Royal in June, 1607.[5]

In 1610, however, Port Royal was reoccupied by Jean de Biencourt de Poutrincourt, who had previously acted as governor of Acadia

5. Rameau de St-Père, *Une Colonie féodale*, I, 20–25, 39–41; Lauvrière, *Tragédie*, I, 10–14.

during the ill-fated De Monts' proprietorship. Although his colony consisted of only twenty-five men, Poutrincourt and his son and governmental successor, Charles de Biencourt de St. Just, laid the foundation for a permanent settlement. The fur trade was reestablished, crops were sown, and large concessions—many with overlapping boundaries—were established among the settlers. The French presence in Acadia nevertheless remained tenuous at best, particularly after the destruction of Port Royal by English privateer Samuel Argall in 1613. The colony never fully recovered from Argall's raid, and after Biencourt's death in 1623, the small band of French adventurers became so demoralized that they were unable to prevent the colonization of Scottish Calvinists at Port Royal in 1628–1629 by Sir William Alexander, who in 1621 had been granted proprietary rights to "Nova Scotia" by James I of England. Though driven from Port Royal by Scottish invaders during the colony's brief encounter with the Thirty Years' War and though virtually abandoned by the French government, the French settlers continued their fur-trading operations from Cape Sable under the leadership of acting governor Charles de St. Etienne de La Tour, thus maintaining French claims to the region.[6]

With the restoration of French dominion over Acadia by the Treaty of St. Germain-en-Laye in 1632, the French government, through the Company of New France, reversed its long-standing neglect of the colony by reinforcing its vulnerable outpost and by encouraging increased colonial revenues through expansion of the local fur trade. In July, 1632, three hundred French settlers, commanded by newly appointed Governor Isaac de Razilly, landed at the mouth of La Hève River. Organized into military units, the colonists reoccupied Port Royal in early September and expelled all but a handful of the resident Scots.[7]

The restoration of the colonial capital to French rule seemed to augur a new era of peace and intracolonial stability. But while Razilly

6. Rameau de St-Père, *Une Colonie féodale*, I, 44–46, 49; Griffiths, *Creation of a People*, 6–8, 10; Clark, *Acadia*, 81–82; Brebner, *New England's Outpost*, 20, 22–24; George Folsom (ed.), "Expedition of Capt. Samuel Argall . . . to the French Settlements in Acadia . . . 1613," New York Historical Society *Collections*, Ser. 2, I (1841), 335–42; Lauvrière, *Tragédie*, Vol. I; Gustave Lanctot, *Histoire du Canada* (3 vols.; Montreal, 1960–63), Vol. I.

7. Clark, *Acadia*, 85; Brebner, *New England's Outpost*, 20–29; Griffiths, *Creation of a People*, 12.

was reestablishing the monarchy's authority over the colony, Cardinal Richelieu, architect of French absolutism, was undermining the power of the colonial governor, who managed the company's fur-trapping operations in Acadia. Indeed, in a classic example of Richelieu's policy of protecting the crown's interests by placing colonial figures of authority in competitive situations, the French government awarded La Tour large seigneuries at Cape Sable, Pentagouet, and the St. John River Valley—prime fur-trapping areas.[8]

The concessions sparked a bitter confrontation between the fur-trading interests represented by La Tour and Razilly. Tensions between the rival firms were heightened by Razilly's death in 1635 and the resulting power vacuum in the colony. The result was fifteen years of open warfare between La Tour's *engagés* and those of the company, commanded by Razilly's former lieutenant, Charles Menou d'Aulnay. Rival fur trappers frequently engaged in "skirmishes, blockades, fort-storming, and the capture and recapture of [trading] posts." Fighting ceased only in 1650, when La Tour entered into a *marriage de convenance* with the widow of his former adversary, who had drowned in a boating accident only weeks before.[9]

The intracolonial tranquillity following the cessation of the colony's economic warfare was short-lived. In 1654, the British government, capitalizing on France's preoccupation with the war of the Fronde, seized Acadia, and the colony remained in British hands for sixteen years.[10]

The British occupation brought to a close the turbulent half-century in which Acadian society assumed its national character. The power vacuum existing within the colony during the early seventeenth century and the resulting civil war taught the colonists to think and act in their own best interests. For example, from 1655 to 1755, the century before the Grand Dérangement (as the Acadian dispersal is popularly known), the Acadians did not hesitate to protest the actions of local administrators and clergymen to higher authorities in Quebec and France. When appeals proved ineffective, the colonists resorted to procrastination, subterfuge, and other forms of passive resistance to foil unpopular administrative policies. While closing

8. Griffiths, *Creation of a People*, 12.
9. *Ibid.*; Clark, *Acadia*, 92.
10. James B. Perkins, *France Under Mazarin* (2 vols.; New York, 1886), I, 377–446; Brebner, *New England's Outpost*, 31–33.

ranks to oppose individuals or policies perceived as detrimental to the group, the Acadians engaged in constant in-fighting, inundating colonial magistrates with petty civil suits, usually involving disputed boundary lines. Though paradoxical on the surface, Acadian contentiousness clearly reflects the eagerness of the frontiersmen to protect their newly acquired and highly prized personal liberties from encroachment on any level.[11]

The rugged individualism of the early settlers was tempered by a strong sense of group identity and loyalty, particularly within the Aulnay faction. Many of the families brought to Acadia by Razilly in 1632 were bound together by blood and cultural ties. Establishing themselves in the Port Royal area after the deportation of the Scottish invaders, these related families effectively constituted a clan; the boundaries of the sociological units, however, were quite fluid, and the Loudunais group quickly absorbed through intermarriage most of the French bachelors who subsequently entered the colony as *engagés,* or indentured servants.[12]

The assimilation of French immigrants did not compromise the integrity of the mother culture. On the contrary, because Aulnay's chief colonial recruiter, notary Vincent Landry, was stationed at the Poitevin town of La Chausée, approximately 55 percent of Acadia's "first families" were drawn from France's Centre-Ouest provinces (Poitou, Aunis, Angoumois, and Saintonge), while at least 47 percent of the early seventeenth-century immigrants were former residents of the La Chausée area of Poitou alone. In addition, it is apparent that throughout the early seventeenth century the *engagés* were drawn consistently from a particular stratum of rural French society—the peasant class—and were destined to serve as laborers in the New World. Most early French settlers in Acadia thus shared not only the same subregional culture and language, but also the same agrarian background and nonmaterialistic values.[13]

---

11. Griffiths, *Creation of a People,* 13.

12. *Ibid.,* 14, 18; Massignon, *Les Parlers français d'Acadie,* I, 70–72. For the identity of these families, as well as the background and occupational skills of the early Acadian settlers, consult Nicole T. Bujold and Maurice Caillebeau, *Les Origines des premières familles acadiennes: Le Sud-Loudunais* (Poitiers, 1979); Griffiths, *Creation of a People,* 18; Massignon, *Les Parlers français d'Acadie,* I, 70–72; Rameau de St-Père, *Une Colonie féodale,* I, 167.

13. Of the eighteen Acadian men whom Bujold and Caillebeau identify as being of

Though the assimilation process preserved the core values of the immigrants from western France, environmental factors and the nature of their employment necessitated significant changes in their life-style. Indeed, the role of the frontier as a catalyst in transforming European subcultures into a distinctly American synthesis was nowhere more evident than in the early Acadian settlements, where the French colonists were thrown into the wilderness for extended periods through their employment as fur trappers. Legally bound to one of Acadia's fur-trading companies for five years, *engagés* (who were consistently experienced farmers) were compelled by the demands of the colonial frontier to adopt the seminomadic life-style and seasonal occupations of the neighboring Micmac Indians. Like the Micmac, and often in conjunction with them, Acadians entered the woods of the Nova Scotian interior in the bitterly cold months of January and February to hunt deer and moose. In addition, the French hunter-trappers acquired additional furs through barter with the local Indians, who by the mid-seventeenth century had become quite dependent upon French trade goods.[14]

Most Acadian colonists maintained their newly acquired frontier way of life long after the termination of their employment with the colony's fur-trading companies. Neglect of the colony by France throughout the seventeenth century, and particularly during the intracolonial civil war and the periods of English occupation, forced the Acadian pioneers to utilize their skills as backwoodsmen to support themselves. Thus, though the typical Acadian settler engaged in subsistence agriculture, as he had in France, a great deal of his time was devoted to nonagricultural pursuits: gathering shellfish in spring, small-scale fishing in summer, and hunting and trapping in winter. The fruits of the pioneer's labors were complemented by cottage industries employing men and women. During the long winter months, Acadian women produced woolen and linen fabric and

---

Loudunais extraction in 1644, ten (56 percent) were laborers drawn from the peasant class, and of the remaining eight Aulnay employees, only one claimed to be an artisan. Bujold and Caillebeau, *Les Origines*, 11–33; Massignon, *Les Parlers français d'Acadie*, I, 70–72.

14. Frederick Jackson Turner, *The Frontier in American History* (New York, 1920), 4; Rameau de St-Père, *Une Colonie féodale*, I, 147, 152, 172–73; Bujold and Caillebeau, *Les Origines*, 29, 31–32, 40; Griffiths, *Creation of a People*, 6–7; Clark, *Acadia*, 59, 60, 67–70, 94–98, 158; Lauvrière, *Tragédie*, I, 179.

clothing, as well as soap and candles. The men made maple syrup, brewed beer with spruce buds, and made wooden furniture and agricultural tools and implements. The combination of these indoor and outdoor pursuits made the frontier households largely self-sufficient.[15]

Self-sufficiency was absolutely vital to survival on the Acadian frontier in the early seventeenth century. Though of strategic importance to North America's emerging colonial powers, France and England, Acadia was nevertheless far removed from the heavily traveled sea-lanes to Quebec and Boston. The colony also lacked both trade goods and specie to attract many merchants. Throughout the seventeenth and early eighteenth centuries, Acadia consequently remained an economic backwater.[16]

The role of geographic isolation in creating, molding, and nurturing early Acadian society cannot be overemphasized. Chronic isolation enhanced the impact of the frontier on the transplanted Frenchmen, for it dictated not only the need for economic self-sufficiency, but also for a clannish, self-contained society, able and willing to carve a new life far from other European outposts in North America. Such independence was absolutely essential in the Acadian settlements whose lines of communication with the outside world were often tenuous at best. While not impossible, overland communications with the St. Lawrence Valley, via the St. John River, were quite difficult, requiring a minimum of twelve days and at least a dozen major portages. Travel to neighboring New England settlements was even more inconvenient, owing to the absence of a major arterial waterway. Finally, even transportation within the Nova Scotian peninsula was arduous because the coastal lowlands were ringed by salt marshes and plagued by exceptionally high tides, and the glacially scarred coastal uplands were heavily wooded and laced with numerous creeks, lakes, and bogs. The Acadians were thus almost completely insulated against the mainstream of cultural evolution, both in the Old World and in the neighboring colonial capitals.[17]

The absence of sociocultural imperatives for change was partially

15. Lauvrière, *Tragédie*, I, 179, 182; Clark, *Acadie*, 158, 231; Rameau de St-Père, *Une Colonie féodale*, I, 154, 156.

16. Clark, *Acadia*, 4.

17. *Ibid.*, 63, 378; Griffiths, *Creation of a People*, 18; Rameau de St-Père, *Une Colonie féodale*, I, 143, 154–57, II, 10.

offset by environmental factors necessitating change for survival. Facing a harsh climate in which median temperatures for January and February were fifteen to twenty degrees colder than their counterparts in western France, the Acadian settlers experienced initial difficulty in producing certain European crops, such as rye. Acadian agriculture was also restricted to reclaimed coastal marshland, which, because of its salinity, remained unsuitable to cultivation for three years after draining. The early colonists, particularly the Aulnay *engagés* at Port Royal, thus were compelled by necessity to rely upon their recently acquired trapping and hunting skills as alternative means of subsistence.[18]

The resulting diversified economy was merely one facet of the Acadians' socioeconomic and cultural evolution on the Nova Scotian frontier. Dyking and draining the very fertile sea marsh above Port Royal (begun sometime after 1630), construction of homes and barns, cultivation and harvesting of crops, and hunting expeditions were activities based on communal labor pools, which, drawing upon Centre-Ouest traditions, were synonymous with tightly knit extended families. Large extended families served as unifying agents, contributing greatly to the growing Acadian sense of sociocultural unity in the mid- and late seventeenth century.[19]

Acadian group identity initially was an outgrowth of the 1632 immigrants' common sociocultural background, which permitted the Loudunais settlers of the Aulnay faction to close ranks against the challenges of frontier isolation, the feuding economic powers, and the frequent changes of European domination. Moreover, the British occupation of Acadia from 1654 to 1670 served as a catalyst to unify the formerly factionalized population against a common foe, thereby facilitating the assimilation of the former La Tour employees by their more numerous and more prolific Aulnay counterparts. Group identity was reinforced also by the necessity of presenting a united front to defend their interests against the provisional English authorities.

This solidarity persisted after the withdrawal of the English garrison in 1670, despite the fact that the external military threat had

18. Clark, *Acadia*, 31, 34, 86, 162; Griffiths, *Creation of a People*, 10; Rameau de St-Père, *Une Colonie féodale*, I, 152.

19. Clark, *Acadie*, 103, 161–62; Philippe Erlanger, *La Vie quotidienne sous Henri IV* (Paris, 1958), 137–45; Edmond-René LaBande (ed.), *Histoire du Poitou, du Limousin et des Pays Charentais* (Toulouse, 1976), 292–300.

been its principal raison d'etre. This phenomenon can be attributed to the fact that extensive blood ties soon strengthened sociocultural bonds forged during the English occupation. Following the restoration of French rule in 1670, many young Acadians, who obviously viewed with dismay the development of all prime arable land at Port Royal, sought opportunities at the newly founded Upper Bay of Fundy settlements—Mines, Pisiquid, and Beaubassin. In most instances, pioneers persuaded numerous relatives to relocate in such outposts, and the frontier settlements frequently became little more than adjoining clusters of five or ten interrelated family units. Once established, the young bachelors sought wives either in their respective outpost or in Port Royal. Neighboring families within the posts were allied by marriage, and social bonds were similarly established between the posts and the colonial capital. As the Acadian social fabric became increasingly intricate, the acclimated frontiersmen became "a clan, a body of people united by blood ties, common beliefs and common aims for the group as a whole."[20]

The strengthening of social bonds within the Acadian community was particularly significant in the twilight years of the seventeenth century when rapid development of the Bay of Fundy's northern littoral spawned heated land disputes. Seigneurs, most of whom had received large coastal fiefdoms before 1650, were quite eager to develop their properties after 1670 and offered concessions to immigrants as inducements for settlement. In their enthusiasm, and frequently through unfamiliarity with their own *seigneuries,* the colonial seigneurs often issued land grants with overlapping boundaries, leading inevitably to disputes. Though frequently involving members of different families, the individual confrontations were resolved peaceably, apparently through social pressure or, less frequently, by the normal channels of the French colonial judiciary. Thus, potentially explosive situations did not escalate into intracolonial warfare, as they had in the early days of colonization, when extensive social bonds were nonexistent.[21]

20. Griffiths, *Creation of a People,* 18; L. U. Fontaine (ed.), *Voyage du Sieur de Dièreville en Acadie* (Quebec, 1885), 44; Rameau de St-Père, *Une Colonie féodale,* I, 195–99; Clark, *Acadia,* 202–204.

21. Clark, *Acadia,* 113–21, 238; Rameau de St-Père, *Une Colonie féodale,* I, 46, 181–96; Brebner, *New England's Outpost,* 139–49; 239–40.

Acadian group solidarity was intact when the nascent society again faced the threat of foreign domination during the War of the Spanish Succession. In 1710, Port Royal fell into English hands, and in the following two years, the Acadians at Mines and Beaubassin successfully engaged in guerrilla warfare against the invaders. Indeed, in 1712, Acadian partisans conducted an abortive siege of the provincial capital. Tensions within the colony were consequently quite strained in 1713 when France ceded Acadia to Britain through the Treaty of Utrecht.[22]

Under the terms of the treaty, the Acadians were permitted to leave the colony within one year and to transport their movable property to "any other place they shall think fit." Those remaining under British rule, however, were guaranteed freedom of religion and, under the terms of Queen Anne's proclamation of June 23, 1713, full title to their lands and movable possessions.[23]

Refusing to submit to English rule, many young Acadians migrated from Port Royal to Beaubassin and Chepody (Shepody), which, despite the vague terms of the treaty, were widely considered to be French possessions. The vast majority of the established colonists, however, preferred to reach an accommodation with the new colonial government before abandoning their now well-developed farms. As early as 1710 the Acadians had refused to take an unconditional oath of allegiance offered by the new colonial administration, and it was not until 1717 that the former French subjects agreed upon terms under which they would accept British rule. The Acadians generally believed that the colony's destiny had not been definitely resolved by the Treaty of Utrecht, that the English occupation of the colony would be of short duration, as in the mid-seventeenth century, and that French rule would ultimately be restored. Given the perceived weakness of the British position, the Acadians agreed to pledge their loyalty to England and to remain in the colony, which the English renamed Nova Scotia, under the following conditions: freedom to exercise their Catholic faith; guaranteed neutrality in the inevitable future Franco-English colonial wars in order to avoid retributive raids by local French-allied Indians; and recognition by

22. Rameau de St-Père, *Une Colonie féodale*, II, 5, 8, 20–25.
23. Griffiths, *Creation of a People*, 20.

the colonial government that the Acadians were, in fact, a distinct community.[24]

The Acadian demands placed the colonists in direct confrontation with the newly appointed provincial governor, Richard Philipps. Compelled to govern a hostile population of 2,500 with a garrison of only 500 men, divided between the widely separated posts of Annapolis-Royal (formerly Port Royal) and Canso Island (the Grand Banks fishing center of the northeastern extremity of the Nova Scotian mainland), Philipps was understandably anxious to impose an unconditional oath of allegiance upon the settlers. Lacking the necessary military force to compel submission, however, and fully cognizant that an Acadian exodus would deprive the garrison of its principal source of supplies, the chief executive wisely deferred judgment. In fact, he abruptly terminated Anglo-Acadian negotiations by sailing for England in 1723.[25]

As a result of Philipps' departure and of an Indian uprising in Nova Scotia, the question of Acadian loyalty, and thus of continued Acadian occupation of the Bay of Fundy settlements, lay dormant until the summer of 1726, when Lieutenant Governor Lawrence Armstrong, Philipps' surrogate, demanded an unconditional oath of allegiance from the francophone population. Armstrong's action precipitated a small wave of emigration to the French-held areas of Cape Breton Island and Ile St. Jean (present-day Prince Edward Island). But once again the overwhelming majority of Acadians closed ranks to present a united front to their principal antagonist. Once more the French frontiersmen adamantly rejected the unconditional oath and responded with a counterproposal including guarantees of Acadian neutrality, property rights, and freedom of religion.[26]

The resulting diplomatic impasse prompted Philipps' return to Annapolis-Royal in late 1729. In the ensuing months, the chief executive achieved through chicanery the success that had proved elusive for twenty years. In negotiating with the Acadian represen-

24. *Ibid.*, 21, 23, 26; Rameau de St-Père, *Une Colonie féodale*, II, 8; Brebner, *New England's Outpost*, 76.

25. David E. Henige (comp.), *Colonial Governors from the Fifteenth Century to the Present* (Madison, 1970), 155; Rameau de St-Père, *Une Colonie féodale*, I, 14; II, 10; Brebner, *New England's Outpost*, 80.

26. Rameau de St-Père, *Une Colonie féodale*, II, 38–39, 44–47, 50, 52–53; Griffiths, *Creation of a People*, 25; Lauvrière, *Tragédie*, I, 250.

tatives, Philipps assured the intransigent colonists that the British government had approved their demand for neutrality in the event of Franco-English hostilities. On the basis of these verbal assurances, the Acadians subscribed to the unconditional oath. Armed with their signatures, the erstwhile chief executive returned to England. In presenting the rolls of oath-takers to the Board of Trade, however, Philipps, under intense pressure from his superiors, notified the Lords of Trade that his mission had been a complete success and that the Acadians had abandoned their claims to neutrality. Thus, through the so-called "conventions of 1730," the Nova Scotian governor managed simultaneously to please and deceive all parties to the escalating controversy over the unconditional oath of allegiance, thereby laying the groundwork for future Anglo-Acadian confrontations. By 1731, both parties believed that the dispute had been settled to their satisfaction; tensions eased, and life returned to normal.[27]

The Acadians quickly adjusted to the new political realities. Although the absence of military support effectively restricted the colonial government's sphere of control to Annapolis-Royal, the British administrators in Nova Scotia made token efforts, between 1730 and 1749, to control the Acadian population. For example, the chief executives consistently rejected requests by Annapolis River Valley residents to relocate along the Bay of Fundy's northern littoral, where British authority was nonexistent. The governors also went through the motions of regulating the residents of the outlying posts, but despite the presence of a small garrison at Mines, their missives fell generally upon deaf ears.[28]

English rule thus meant little if any change in the Acadians' daily lives. In practice, the francophone colonists continued to "regulate a considerable amount of their day-to-day affairs themselves." Furthermore, the Acadians consistently viewed the English colonial government as an instrument to serve their needs, particularly in the areas of judicial and notarial services, and not as an arbiter of their lives and properties. Thus, when the governor at Port Royal, or his representative at Mines (a notary usually of Acadian descent) placed

27. Rameau de St-Père, *Une Colonie féodale*, II, 61; Griffiths, *Creation of a People*, 27.
28. Rameau de St-Père, *Une Colonie féodale*, II, 63–65; Griffiths, *Creation of a People*, 21–22, 32.

demands upon the "French Neutrals" to survey lands, build roads, quarter troops, or furnish firewood and provisions to the garrison, the colonists quickly joined ranks to oppose these levies and, through procrastination or the arguments of their shrewd representatives, often succeeded in foiling the chief executives' designs. This is particularly true of the English governors' efforts to survey Acadian landholdings and to supply the occupational forces with locally grown grain and meat. The Acadians, speaking through their elected delegates, as they had since 1710, managed to delay the surveys and reduce the agricultural quotas, apparently under the pretext of poor harvests. At the same time, they were smuggling their not inconsiderable agricultural surplus to Boston merchants at Baie Verte and to the poorly supplied French fortress of Louisbourg on Cape Breton Island. While the specter of famine frequently hovered over the English garrison, the French Neutrals obtained much-needed specie and manufactured goods, both chronically scarce, to satisfy their own needs.[29]

The Acadians' fierce independence, as manifested in their smuggling activities, earned them the scorn of their provincial administrators, who labeled the French Neutrals "ungovernable," "a bunch of republicans," and a score of other equally uncomplimentary epithets. Indeed, writing in late 1732, Lieutenant Governor Armstrong lamented the "insubordination" of the Acadians who "behave[d] themselves in most respects as independent of any Government" and "treated with so much contempt" the English authorities who ruled over them. The Acadians, nevertheless, wisely avoided direct confrontations with the local officials and their inevitable consequence of military clashes. The majority of francophone colonists also strictly observed the 1730 oath of neutrality, for, in the Acadians' eyes, the neighboring French lacked the means of wresting the colony from English hands, while the British were incapable of protecting the colonists from Franco-Indian incursions. Even when Annapolis was twice attacked by French-Canadians, and an intrepid band of French-Canadians captured the English garrison at Mines in

29. Griffiths, *Creation of a People*, 9, 21–22, 25, 32, 34; Brebner, *New England's Outpost*, 38, 50, 61, 67, 89, 91, 99, 100, 144–49, 152–54, 162–64; Thomas B. Akins (ed.), *Acadia and Nova Scotia: Documents Relating to the Acadian French and the First British Colonization of the Province, 1714–1758* (2nd ed.; Cottonport, La., 1972), 89–91, 93, 99–100, 114, 137, 152; Lauvrière, *Tragédie*, I, 190, 213, 220, 222–28, 242–56, 263; Clark, *Acadia*, 176, 189–90, 230–31.

February, 1747, the overwhelming majority of local residents refused to aid the raiders.[30]

The military situation, upon which Acadian neutrality was based, changed drastically after the cessation of intercolonial hostilities in 1748. Establishment of the fortified English port of Halifax in 1749, as well as construction of French and English fortresses at strategic points in the Chignecto Peninsula in 1750, demonstrated renewed interest by the European powers in the neglected colony. The Acadians, however, failing to perceive the gravity of the escalating intercolonial tensions, maintained their traditional noncommittal stance. Neutrality became not only increasingly difficult to maintain but also increasingly dangerous. Acting in cooperation with the French governor of Louisbourg, Abbé Louis Joseph de Le Loutre, a missionary who had worked among the Micmac Indians since 1738, attempted to force the Beaubassin settlers into the French camp by ordering his ecclesiastical flock to destroy the Acadian village. The razing of Beaubassin by French-allied Indians and the resulting defection of between two thousand and four thousand French Neutrals into French-held territory promoted reciprocal, albeit peaceful measures by Nova Scotian officials to maintain control over the Acadian population.[31]

In 1750, Governor Edward Cornwallis of Nova Scotia revived the long-dormant issue of an unconditional Acadian oath of fidelity to Britain and proposed to the Board of Trade numerous means of controlling the nonpartisan population. The Acadians flatly refused the proffered oath, demanding instead the right to renew the "conventions of 1730." When the chief executive rejected the existing agreement as "illegal and unacceptable," from two thousand to four thousand colonists secured British passports for the French-held Shediak Peninsula and Ile St. Jean, abandoned their family farms, and fled the specter of English regulation of their lives.[32]

The issuance of passports to the disgruntled Acadians by Cornwallis represents an important change in English policy toward Nova

30. Akins (ed.), *Acadia and Nova Scotia*, 89, 90, 99, 100, 140–63; Griffiths, *Creation of a People*, 21, 44–49; Lauvrière, *Tragédie*, I, 256; Rameau de St-Père, *Une Colonie féodale*, I, 118–31; Brebner, *New England's Outpost*, 115–19; Edouard Richard, *Acadia: Missing Links of a Lost Chapter in American History* (2 vols.; New York, 1895), I, 201–16.

31. Clark, *Acadia*, 221, 331, 334–39, 349, 350, 364; Brebner, *New England's Outpost*, 115–17; Akins (ed.), *Acadia and Nova Scotia*, 250–300; Griffiths, *Creation of a People*, 42–44; Rameau de St-Père, *Une Colonie féodale*, II, 147–48.

32. Brebner, *New England's Outpost*, 166, 179–80; Richard, *Acadia*, I, 236–47; Rameau de St-Père, *Une Colonie féodale*, I, 141.

Scotia's large French Neutral population. Prior to the founding of Halifax, the presence of a stable, agrarian Acadian population was vitally important to the security of the poorly supplied garrison. In the absence of a real French military threat to the colonial borders, Acadian recalcitrance regarding an unconditional oath of allegiance was viewed by colonial officials as a mere annoyance that did not jeopardize England's tenuous military position in the area. With the establishment of Halifax, however, the Acadians were no longer a vital cog in the garrison's chain of supply, and British attitudes toward their reluctant subjects consequently changed dramatically, particularly when destructive, French-inspired Indian raids on Acadian border settlements in 1750 awakened the French Neutrals to the potential consequences of their continuing allegiance to England. The Acadians thus became even more reluctant to pledge their unconditional loyalty to George III, while the British were never more adamant about the necessity of such a commitment.

Fully cognizant of the strategic importance of Nova Scotia and France's continuing designs upon the region, the British Board of Trade had determined in 1749 to hold the colony at all costs. Forts were built, internal communications were improved, and a large number of Protestant colonists were established in Nova Scotia. With the transformation of the colony into a vast military complex came the emergence of a siege mentality among the British leadership. Ignoring the French Neutrals' demonstrations of neutrality during the War of the Austrian Succession, Nova Scotia's English administrators began to view them more and more as a potentially dangerous "foreign" population. They thus interpreted the Acadian rejection of the oath of allegiance as a demonstration of pro-French sympathy.[33]

The Acadians failed to perceive this significant shift in British policy. Moreover, following Cornwallis' departure in 1752, the Acadians were lulled into complacency by the tranquil but brief administration (1752–1753) of Peregrin Hopson, a conciliator by temperament who attempted to heal the rift between the colonial government and the French Neutral population. Hopson's appeasement policies deluded the Acadians into believing that there had been no real change in English policy since 1749, particularly as Cornwallis and his suc-

33. Richard, *Acadia*, I, 235.

cessor had abandoned the quest for a reaffirmation of loyalty to Britain in the face of stubborn Acadian resistance. The French Neutrals thus anticipated the reestablishment of the advantageous relationship with the colonial government, in which the Acadians could be cooperative only when they wished to be. Life under English rule was considered preferable to French domination, for many Acadian refugees complained bitterly to relatives of the oppression they encountered at Cape Breton Island and Ile St. Jean. Moreover, despite England's efforts to expand its colonial war machine through large-scale colonization at Halifax and subsequent attempts to establish German Protestants at Lunenburg, the French Neutrals viewed the Anglo-French struggle for the area as being at a stalemate; thus, when Hopson was compelled by failing health to return to England in 1753, "the Acadians had no reason to suspect a radical alteration of their lives." Their unwarranted optimism would soon have tragic results.[34]

34. Brebner, *New England's Outpost*, 48, 175–76, 188–89; Griffiths, *Creation of a People*, 45, 48–49; Clark, *Acadia*, 339–43.

2

Dispersal and Survival

By unswerving adherence to the "conventions of 1730," the Acadians in 1750 had foiled a concerted British effort to undermine their semiautonomous political status and wed them firmly to the British nation, a move that, according to many eighteenth-century colonial officials and observers, was to have constituted the first step toward their assimilation into the Anglo-Protestant mainstream. Thus, though their struggle with the colonial administration was couched in political terms, the French Neutrals were actually fighting to preserve their way of life, a unique blend of French and Indian folkways forged on the seventeenth-century Acadian frontier. Acadian society enjoyed a temporary reprieve under the Hopson administration, but as the English Empire marshaled its forces for intercolonial warfare in the mid–1750s, the colonial regime, succumbing to a cresting wave of francophobia, redoubled its efforts to subjugate Nova Scotia's Acadians and thus present a united front to the French-Canadians. Unlike their predecessors, the newly appointed colonial officials displayed a grim determination to expel from the colony all elements of resistance within the Acadian community—the entire francophone population if necessary.[1]

The fate of the Acadians lay with the Nova Scotian governor and colonial council, in whom all authority was vested by the colonial charter. The chief executive played a pivotal role in shaping the British response to the recently resurrected Acadian problem.[2] The leg-

---

1. Richard, *Acadia*, I, 220–24, 319; Brebner, *New England's Outpost*, 127; Griffiths, *Creation of a People*, 50.
2. Brebner, *New England's Outpost*, 73, 134–36, 138, 208, 239; Griffiths, *Creation of a People*, 53–56.

acy of Cornwallis' firm albeit unsuccessful stand regarding the unconditional oath of allegiance endured beyond his administration.
Indeed, even the conciliatory measures of Cornwallis' successor,
Peregrin Hopson, failed to eradicate the growing francophobia of the
ruling English oligarchy. Thus it is hardly surprising that when Hopson retired and was succeeded by Major Charles Lawrence in 1754,
the colonial government resumed its hostile stance toward the Acadian population.[3]

The sudden shift in administrative policy can be attributed to Lawrence's military training and experience on Nova Scotia's poorly defended borders. A professional soldier formerly entrusted with the
establishment of fortifications on the Isthmus of Chignecto, Lawrence was preoccupied with the growing French military presence in
the neighboring French territories and the corresponding vulnerability of the colony he now commanded.[4] Like Cornwallis, he was
most anxious to secure an unqualified commitment of support from
the colony's large French-speaking population, but unlike his predecessor, Lawrence would brook no opposition. The Acadians, who
consistently manifested no interest in linking their interests with
those of the British Empire, were viewed by the colonial administration as subversives whose continued presence jeopardized British
security. In addition, the rapid expansion of the Acadian population,
from between 300 and 350 people in 1654 to between 12,000 and
18,000 in 1755, despite a 50 percent child-mortality rate, indicated all
too clearly that the perceived threat to the Empire would increase
geometrically each year if left unchecked. The problem defied easy
solution: the occupation by the francophones of the region's choicest
farmlands, plus their ability to absorb all rival cultures, discouraged
Anglo-Protestant immigration, thereby frustrating English designs
to anglicize the French Neutrals.[5] Nova Scotia's Acadian problem
consequently held the promise of long duration; yet the colony's escalating border war with French Canada demanded, in Lawrence's
eyes, a speedy resolution of the colonial government's crisis of au-

3. Lauvrière, *Tragédie*, I, 387–89, 414–15; Clark, *Acadia*, 341; Winthrop Bell, *The
"Foreign Protestants" and the Settlement of Nova Scotia* (Toronto, 1961), 450–68; Griffiths,
Creation of a People, 49.

4. Griffiths, *Creation of a People*, 46, 49–51; Brebner, *New England's Outpost*, 176,
183; Richard, *Acadia*, I, 355–56.

5. Brebner, *New England's Outpost*, 175–77, 208–209; Griffiths, *Creation of a People*,
14, 18; Clark, *Acadia*, 99–100, 121–31, 201–12; Richard, *Acadia*, I, 197–200.

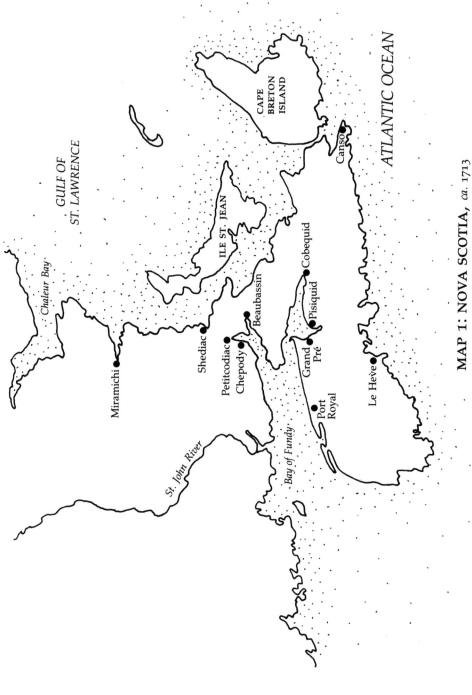

MAP 1: NOVA SCOTIA, *ca.* 1713

thority—either full integration of the semiautonomous Acadian population into the English colony or deportation of the recalcitrant French Neutrals.[6]

Lawrence lacked both means and legal justification for driving thousands of nominally British subjects from their traditional homeland. Nevertheless, as early as November, 1754—three months after his appointment as lieutenant governor, Major Lawrence conspired with Governor William Shirley, commander-in-chief of British forces in New England and an outspoken proponent of English colonial supremacy in America, to remove all Acadians from the Bay of Fundy coast.[7] False rumors of an impending French raid on Fort Lawrence, an English outpost near Beaubassin, provided the conspirators with the pretext for massing British troops in Nova Scotia. In addition, as 1,800 British soldiers sailed from New England for the Isthmus of Chignecto in late spring, 1755, Lawrence coerced the French Neutrals into surrendering their arms. Finally, in June, 1755, the Nova Scotian governor ordered a successful assault on Fort Beauséjour, a French fortress commanding the heights around Beaubassin, thereby securing the area against French-Canadian incursions and preventing the flow of Acadian refugees—potential French soldiers—into Quebec.[8]

With the fall of Fort Beauséjour, the Acadians' fate was sealed. Deprived of their weapons and barred from escape, they were completely at the mercy of the colonial government, and Lawrence quickly capitalized upon their vulnerability. Using the capture of three hundred Acadian conscripts at Fort Beauséjour as a pretext for reviving the long-dormant issue of the oath, Lawrence in late June summoned to Halifax representatives of the major Acadian settlements, ostensibly to discuss the return of firearms. Appearing before the governor and colonial council on July 3, the Mines delegation was ordered to accept, on behalf of their constituency, an

6. Akins (ed.), *Acadia and Nova Scotia*, 212–14.

7. Lauvrière, *Tragédie*, I, 307–13, 387–95; Akins (ed.), *Acadia and Nova Scotia*, 229, 235–376, 391; Brebner, *New England's Outpost*, 209; Richard, *Acadia*, I, 217–26.

8. Lauvrière, *Tragédie*, I, 396–97, 399–408, 410; Akins (ed.), *Acadia and Nova Scotia*, 214, 405, 408–409; Judge Charles Morris, Papers on the Causes of the War in 1755 and the History of the Acadians, July, 1755, folios 31–38, in Brown Manuscript Collection, Add. MSS 19072, British Museum, London, England; Rameau de St-Père, *Une Colonie féodale*, II, 8, 14, 38–39.

unconditional oath of allegiance. When they reiterated their long-standing commitment to neutrality, the representatives were summarily imprisoned to serve as an example to the intractable Acadian population. The colonial council then ordered Nova Scotia's French Neutrals to swear allegiance under pain of deportation.[9]

Lawrence's decision to rid the colony of its "perfidious subjects," vindicated by the colonial council, was reaffirmed by Admiral Edward Boscawen's approval of the council's aforementioned decree in mid-July. The ruling oligarchy's rampant francophobia was heightened by the reports on July 23 of General Edward Braddock's defeat in the Battle of the Wilderness and the onset of the French and Indian War. As a consequence, when new Acadian delegations reached Halifax in late July and refused to alter the "conventions of 1730," the colonial government showed no flexibility, on July 31 ordering the Acadians' forcible removal from the Bay of Fundy settlements.[10]

In order to effect the removal as expeditiously and as cheaply as possible, Lawrence devised a diabolically clever scheme for assuring the Acadians' peaceable submission. Drawing upon engineer Charles Morris' hitherto neglected memorandum on Acadian deportation, Lawrence directed the English commandants at Beaubassin, Pisiquid, and Annapolis-Royal to lure the local Acadian males into their respective posts.[11] There, the unsuspecting victims would be arrested and detained until the arrival of transports which would carry them into exile. The detention of male hostages would ensure that the local women and children remained home with the possessions and livestock, thus expediting their removal from the colony. Finally, all Acadian property was to be confiscated to reimburse the English government for the cost of their removal, and all Acadian homes and boats were to be destroyed.[12]

Lawrence's directives were promptly and efficiently executed by his military subordinates. At Fort Cumberland (formerly Fort Beauséjour) on August 9, Colonel Robert Monckton captured between

9. Griffiths, *Creation of a People*, 52; Lauvrière, *Tragédie*, I, 401, 414; Akins (ed.), *Acadia and Nova Scotia*, 248–56.

10. Griffiths, *Creation of a People*, 54; Akins (ed.), *Acadia and Nova Scotia*, 258, 263–68.

11. Lauvrière, *Tragédie*, I, 396–97, 446, 455–56, 484.

12. Akins (ed.), *Acadia and Nova Scotia*, 267–69.

250 and 400 local Acadians, summoned to the post ostensibly for an important gubernatorial decree regarding their lands. The use of subterfuge and the element of surprise also worked to the English government's advantage at Minas Basin. Fresh from the English success at Beaubassin, Monckton's chief subordinate, Lieutenant Colonel John Winslow, in mid-August led approximately 400 New England militiamen to Grand Pré, the largest settlement in the Minas Basin area, established his headquarters in the presbytery of the local Catholic church, and prepared to ensnare the area's male population. On September 5, a total of 418 Acadian men and teenage boys, answering Winslow's summons, were summarily arrested as enemies of the crown. Five days later, the prisoners and their wives and children, divided into groups by sex and age, were escorted under heavy guard to the waiting English transports. Demoralized by the removal of the Grand Pré settlers and intimidated by large English patrols, the neighboring villages succumbed to Lawrence's Acadian-eradication program, and by mid-October most of the French Neutrals had been deported from the Minas Basin area.[13]

Winslow's efficiency in uprooting the Grand Pré and Beaubassin Acadians contrasts sharply with the incompetence of his counterpart at Annapolis-Royal, Major John Handfield. Apparently unable to lie convincingly, Handfield failed to lure some 100 Acadian males into a snare; indeed, suspecting a trap, all of the local French Neutrals fled into the woods, where they remained for several weeks. Captured in late November by English patrols, however, the Annapolis-Royal Acadians ultimately shared the fate of their northern neighbors. By December 9, a total of 1,664 residents of the former colonial capital and its environs had boarded British transports.[14]

The Acadians taken prisoner at Annapolis-Royal, Mines, and Beaubassin—approximately 5,400 individuals—were either distributed among Britain's Atlantic seaboard colonies or sent to England. The deportation marked the end of the first phase of the English campaign to remove from Nova Scotia an ethnic group that the colonial government considered a potential internal military threat and that, because of its cohesiveness, promised to remain an unassimi-

13. Lauvrière, *Tragédie*, I, 448–49, 456–59, 464, 471–83.
14. *Ibid.*, I, 484–93.

lable bastion of "French popery" for generations to come. Thus, through using social fragmentation and immersing the Acadians in a predominantly anglophone society, the British government hoped to reduce Acadian society to an unpleasant memory. The Acadian deportation opened the fertile and now fully developed Fundy Basin farmlands to colonization by New Englanders, "good Protestant subjects" who, it was hoped, would destroy all trace of their predecessors.[15]

Yet, except for approximately 100 Beaubassin men whose spouses chose to resist deportation, members of Acadian nuclear families generally were not separated—contrary to the Evangeline myth—and though extended families were disrupted by the Grand Dérangement, each English transport usually carried passengers from only one Acadian settlement. Upon reaching their destination, the exiles found themselves surrounded with cousins and other relatives. Acadian solidarity consequently remained intact, helping the deportees to endure the rigors of exile. Group cohesiveness proved most significant to the expatriates who suddenly found themselves unwelcome guests of the British empire.[16]

This impulse was shared by somewhere between seven thousand and ten thousand Acadians who escaped the first wave of deportations, but unlike their brothers in exile, these survivors in the Bay of Fundy area chose to oppose English oppression more vigorously. Their bellicosity was a necessary response to changing British strategy. Encountering stiffening Acadian resolve to remain in Maritime Canada after the fall of 1755, the colonial government abandoned its policy of eradicating by deportation for one of exterminating pockets of French Neutral resistance.[17]

The Acadian resistance movement was centered in present-day New Brunswick, where at least 3,500 residents in the areas of Beaubassin and Cobequid sought refuge after many local men fell into Monckton's trap at Fort Cumberland. The refugees, including many

15. In 1755, between October and December, 5,364 Acadians were deported to New England. *Ibid.*, I, 479, 480, 485; Akins (ed.), *Acadia and Nova Scotia*, 421.

16. Lauvrière, *Tragédie*, I, 453; Griffiths, *Creation of a People*, 71. Only those colonies from which large numbers of exiles migrated to Louisiana will be examined in subsequent chapters.

17. Clark, *Acadia*, 211–12; Akins (ed.), *Acadia and Nova Scotia*, 297–99, 308–10; Lauvrière, *Tragédie*, II, 79–85.

wives and children of the captives, were established along the Lower Miramichi River by Abbé Le Guerne.[18] Smaller groups of refugees relocated along the Petite Restigouche River, and approximately 250 Annapolis-Royal residents, who seized possession of their Boston-bound English transport, settled along the Upper St. John River. Finally, small groups of exiles sought refuge along the Chepody and Petitcodiac rivers.[19]

Having withdrawn from Nova Scotia proper, the refugees felt sufficiently secure to begin life anew. These displaced Acadians were not only generally unarmed, but they were also preoccupied with the demands of adapting to the forbidding wilderness in which they now found themselves. Yet the British high command felt sufficiently threatened by them (eager as they were to return to their confiscated farms) to harass continuously and ultimately destroy their settlements. Between 1756 and 1758, in fact, the Nova Scotian government placed bounties on all Acadian prisoners and, unofficially, on their scalps.[20]

As a result of British military raids, the patrolling of the coastline by English warships, and the lengthy and arduous flight to freedom, the refugees were unable to cultivate their traditional crops or to fish the coastal waters, and thus hundreds of displaced Acadians were reduced to starvation in the winter of 1756–1757. Forced to subsist upon their leather moccasins, carrion, and spoiled meat, the Miramichi Acadians died of malnutrition and its attendant diseases "in great numbers." Suffering was only slightly less severe in the other refugee camps.[21]

The trials of the winter months and the unrelenting British military pressure forced the survivors to reevaluate their tenuous position and to adopt, on an individual basis, any of several options that appeared most conducive to survival. First, the refugees could remain at Miramichi, clear the land, and begin life anew. Second, the Miramichi Acadians could relocate either in less forbidding sections

18. Lauvrière, *Tragédie*, I, 453, II, 75–78; C. O. Gagnon (ed.), *Lettre de M. l'abbe Le Guerne, missionnaire de l'Acadie* (Quebec, 1889).
19. Lauvrière, *Tragédie*, I, 486, II, 69; Akins (ed.), *Acadia and Nova Scotia*, 297.
20. Abbe Le Guerne to (?), March 10, 1756, quoted in Lauvrière, *Tragédie*, I, 75; Akins (ed.), *Acadia and Nova Scotia*, 297–300.
21. Lauvrière, *Tragédie*, II, 73–80.

of present-day New Brunswick or in Quebec. Finally, the displaced French Neutrals could surrender to British authorities and entrust their lives to a demonstrably hostile and devious Nova Scotian administration. As the last option was initially unacceptable, many Acadians dissatisfied with the deplorable conditions at Miramichi settled upon the second choice.

The result was a second dispersal. Dislodged by English Rangers, many French Neutrals on the Upper St. John River, as well as hundreds of starving refugees from Miramichi, sought asylum, in 1757–1758, in neighboring Quebec which, though beleaguered, remained in French hands until 1759. Hundreds of additional Acadians—perhaps as many as a thousand—migrated northward to the Chaleur Bay area and the Lower Restigouche Valley, establishing the communities of Petit Rochelle and Tracadièche.[22] Not all of the Miramichi Acadians, however, abandoned their ill-starred first encampment; indeed, despite the camp's destruction by British marines in 1758, Miramichi in 1761 rivaled Restigouche as the largest Acadian settlement along the Gulf of St. Lawrence coast.[23]

Like the Miramichi Acadians, the pioneer families and the more recently established Beaubassin and Chepody refugees along the Petitcodiac and Memramcook rivers determined to maintain possession of their homes and properties despite intensifying British efforts to dislodge them. Unlike their northern cousins, however, these Acadians had not been disarmed by the British in 1755 and were capable of mounting a viable resistance movement.[24] Led by former militia captain Joseph Broussard *dit* Beausoleil, the Petitcodiac settlers organized a highly effective guerrilla unit, which, with the occasional assistance of Lieutenant Charles Deschamps de Boishébert's small French force in the neighboring St. John River Valley, successfully

22. *Ibid.*, II, 74, 76, 77, 83. By 1758, between 1,600 and 2,000 Acadians had sought refuge at Quebec. Bona Arsenault, *History of the Acadians* (Montreal, 1978), 165. The settlement of Petit Rochelle contained 750 refugees. Lauvrière, *Tragédie*, II, 77–78.

23. W. F. Ganong (ed.), "The Official Account of the Destruction of Burnt Church," *Collections of the New Brunswick Historical Society*, No. 7 (1907), 301–306; Clark, *Acadia*, 351; William O. Raymond, "The North Shore: Incidents in the Early History of Eastern and Northern New Brunswick," *Collections of the New Brunswick Historical Society*, No. 4 (1899), 91.

24. Akins (ed.), *Acadia and Nova Scotia*, 247–67, 298, 299, 302, 304, 427; Lauvrière, *Tragédie*, I, 410, 452; Esther C. Wright, *The Petitcodiac: A Study of the New Brunswick River and of the People Who Settled It* (Sackville, N.B., 1945), 14–15.

defended Acadian homes against British incursions until 1758.[25] Broussard's guerrillas also frequently harassed British patrols in the eastern Chignecto area. In fact, the unit was so effective that in 1757 fifty members of the Acadian resistance successfully raided English positions as far east as Pisiquid. Activities of the Acadian resistance, often aided by local francophile Indians, were so effective that until 1758 British troops at Fort Cumberland ventured from the post's protective walls only rarely. Military success on land was matched by the guerrillas' achievements at sea, as Broussard and a handful of other Acadian resistance leaders preyed upon coastal shipping and fishing vessels in privateers commissioned by Canadian Governor Pierre Rigaud de Vaudreuil in 1755.[26]

The small-scale victories enjoyed by the Acadian guerrillas and privateers between 1755 and 1758 undoubtedly boosted the refugees' flagging morale. In the long run, however, these triumphs proved counterproductive—continually reminding British military authorities of the Acadian presence—and ultimately generated more misery for the displaced French Neutrals. Preoccupied with Indian raids along the Appalachian Mountains and with the 1758 siege of the French stronghold at Louisbourg, the British high command was unable to devote much attention to the activities of the Acadian raiders in such a backwater of the French and Indian War.[27] But with the capture of Louisbourg in July 1758, British commander-in-chief Sir Jeffrey Amherst turned his attention toward French Quebec. Because the extended English supply lines in the projected campaign would lie dangerously close to the refugee camps, the Acadian problem was viewed with renewed interest by British military leaders in

25. Charles J. d'Entremont, "Joseph Brossard (Broussard) *dit* Beausoleil," in *Dictionnaire biographique du Canada*, eds. George W. Brown *et al.* (10 vols.; Quebec, 1966–72), III, 92–93, hereinafter cited as "Joseph Broussard"; Akins (ed.), *Acadia and Nova Scotia*, 311; Lauvrière, *Tragédie*, I, 453; Barbara M. Schmeisser, "La Vallée de Memramcook et la continuité du peuplement acadien," *Les Cahiers de la Société historique acadienne*, XII (1981), 143–46.

26. Lauvrière, *Tragédie*, I, 452–53; II, 75; James Hannay, *History of New Brunswick* (2 vols.; St. John, N.B., 1909), I, 55; "Joseph Broussard," 93; Akins (ed.), *Acadia and Nova Scotia*, 307–308, 316.

27. Akins (ed.), *Acadia and Nova Scotia*, 296–308; William J. Eccles, *France in America* (New York, 1972), 181–94; Guy Frégault, *La Guerre de la conquête, 1754–1760* (Montreal, 1955), 17–277. Vol. IX of *Histoire de la Nouvelle France*, 9 vols.; George Stanley, *New France: The Last Phase, 1744–1760* (Toronto, 1968), 60–100.

North America. As a consequence, in the fall of 1758, Amherst ordered the destruction of Miramichi, Restigouche, and the refugee settlements in the Petitcodiac and St. John River valleys.[28]

Though demoralized by unexpected raids and disheartened by the seizure of many Acadians (usually women and children) as well as the destruction of their new homes and crops, the French Neutrals in what is now New Brunswick remained firm in their determination to resist English domination.[29] But when Quebec, the last French stronghold in Canada, fell to the British in 1759, most Acadians realized that continued resistance was futile. On November 16, 1759, Alexandre Broussard, Simon Martin, Jean Basque, and Joseph Broussard, elected delegates for 190 Acadians in the Petitcodiac and Memramcook districts, arrived at Fort Cumberland to surrender unconditionally and to beg provisions for their starving comrades. These delegates were joined eight days later by Pierre Suretz, Jean Bourque, and Michel Bourque, representatives of seven hundred refugees at Miramichi, Richibouctou, and Bouctouche, who in declaring their submission to England also requested material assistance.[30]

Accepting the capitulation of these last pockets of Acadian resistance, Fort Cumberland's commandant, Colonel Frye, graciously agreed to support until spring small numbers of refugees facing death through starvation in the harsh winter months. Their less destitute comrades, on the other hand, were directed to present themselves to colonial authorities after the spring thaw.[31]

In compliance with Frye's orders, "between three and four hundred" French Neutrals gathered at Fort Cumberland in late spring and early summer, 1760. The able-bodied members of this group were compelled by the colonial government to march in August to Halifax, where they were detained in "open Barracks." Unlike their predecessors, these captives were not deported, apparently because the Nova Scotian government lacked the necessary resources during the English invasion of lower Canada. Also, there was opposition from Britain's other seaboard colonies. The Anglo-Saxon and German immigrants who occupied the deserted French Neutral farms within weeks of the Grand Dérangement could not utilize effectively

28. Lauvrière, *Tragédie*, II, 78–87.
29. *Ibid.*, II, 89; Akins (ed.), *Acadia and Nova Scotia*, 311; Clark, *Acadia*, 351; Raymond, "The North Shore," 91.
30. Akins (ed.), *Acadia and Nova Scotia*, 311.
31. *Ibid.*, 311–12.

the complex Acadian dike system protecting their lands against the Bay of Fundy's mighty tidal surges and desperately required the captives' services. Bowing to this pressure, the colonial government, despite oft-stated misgivings about the continuing Acadian presence, not only maintained the captives in Halifax at governmental expense, but also allowed the French Neutrals to work on the dike system at "high wages."[32]

Even while working for their captors in order to supplement "the provisions they receive[d] on the military list," the Acadian prisoners' will to resist remained intense. Indeed, when news of Spain's belated entrance into the Seven Years' War as a French ally reached Nova Scotia in February, 1761, "they assumed fresh courage, and began to be insolent to the Settlers in the Townships where they were at work, telling them that they would soon regain possession of their lands and cut every one of their throats."[33]

The Acadians' intemperate remarks, coinciding with growing Indian unrest in Nova Scotia, terrorized the new Anglo settlers on the "forfeited" French Neutral lands, prompting the colonial government to revive the issue of a second massive deportation. When the French occupation of St. John's, Newfoundland, precipitated a strong outburst of Acadian "insolence," Acadian prisoners from throughout the colony were assembled at Halifax, placed aboard five English transports, and in August, 1762, deported to Boston. The Massachusetts government, however, "refused [them] permission to land" and ordered the transports to return to Halifax.[34] Thwarted in their second attempt to resolve the thorny Acadian problem by exiling the captives to their southern neighbor, Nova Scotia's governor and colonial council were unable to select a suitable, alternate destination— although several Canadian sites were proposed—for the 1,700 prisoners remaining in the colony. The issue of massive deportation thus lingered until the Treaty of Paris (1763) established the framework for final resolution of the Acadian problem.[35]

Through Article IV of the treaty, the Acadians were granted a period of eighteen months to abandon England's North American colo-

32. *Ibid.*, 307, 314, 316, 318–20, 332–37, 702, 704.

33. *Ibid.*, 316, 318–20.

34. *Ibid.*, 316–18, 322–38, 344, 702, 704; Julian S. Corbett, *England in the Seven Years' War: A Study of Combined Strategy* (2 vols.; London, 1907), II, 323–25; Lauvrière, *Tragédie*, II, 299–301.

35. Akins (ed.), *Acadia and Nova Scotia*, 331, 338–41, 344, 348, 352.

nies for any French possession. Because of the colonial government's persistent refusal to grant the Acadians permanent status within Nova Scotia and also of the captives' burning enmity toward their English oppressors, many French Neutrals developed great interest in going to the French West Indies. Notified by exiled relatives in late 1763 that the French ambassador was secretly negotiating their release and transfer to France, many Acadian prisoners in Halifax eagerly anticipated deliverance in the hands of Louis XV. In December, 1763, seventy-six Acadian families petitioned the French government for provisions and vessels for the transatlantic crossing. No French assistance was forthcoming, however, because the French crown had assured the British government that it would not interfere in Nova Scotia's internal affairs.[36]

The Acadians in Nova Scotia, and particularly those in Halifax, were confronted with the choice of either remaining under English rule and facing a proposed scheme of intracolonial dispersal and the possibility of rapid assimilation, or utilizing their own hard-earned financial resources to flee British tyranny. A significant minority of the French Neutral prisoners wished to depart their native land, but the avenues of escape were quite limited.[37] First, the French government was quite interested in bolstering through immigration the porous defenses of the French Antilles. To this end, the governor of Saint-Domingue (present-day Haiti) invited the Acadian dissidents in the summer of 1764 to relocate in that prosperous sugar island; the invitation, however, was accompanied by reports of heavy mortality among the Acadians who had sought refuge there after years of exile in Philadelphia.[38]

As Saint-Domingue was an undesirable settlement site, the Halifax Acadians turned their sights toward Quebec, where the climate closely resembled that of Nova Scotia and the large francophone population faced no immediate threat of assimilation. In 1761 the Quebec and Nova Scotian governments had actually discussed possible transfer of French Neutral captives to the St. Lawrence Valley. Such a resettlement plan held little appeal. The captives generally

36. *Ibid.*, 314, 342–49.
37. *Ibid.*, 347–51.
38. *Ibid.*, 349; Jacqueline K. Voorhies (trans.), "The Promised Land? The Acadians in the Antilles, 1763–1764," *Attakapas Gazette*, XI (1976), 81–94.

believed that during the Seven Years' War the Acadian refugees in Quebec had been "not only treated with the utmost neglect, but also with contempt and disdain by the Canadians." Finally, the Board of Trade banned Acadian migration to Quebec to ensure the captives' acceptance of the unconditional oath of allegiance and their submission to dispersal within Nova Scotia.[39]

The French Neutrals detained at Halifax would have no part of the English scheme, which they saw as designed to fragment and ultimately to assimilate Acadian society, and they consequently forged their own plan of escape. Relying upon secret communications from the Acadian expatriate community at Cap Français, many Halifax Acadians apparently attempted to coordinate their own resettlement efforts with those of the disgruntled exiles in Saint-Domingue. As early as March, 1764, hundreds of Saint-Domingue Acadians attempted to reach Quebec via Louisiana and the Mississippi River, but their plans were foiled by the Saint-Domingue government's refusal to underwrite the intercolonial transportation costs.[40] The French Neutrals detained in Halifax nevertheless went ahead with their efforts to reach Canada or at least the Upper Mississippi Valley. As Governor Wilmot reported in early November, 1764, "I apprehend that all those people [Acadians] who live in and about this Town [Halifax], have so peremptorily refused to take the Oath of Allegiance, by the best information I can obtain of their purposes, they intend going directly to Cape Francois [sic], from thence to the Mississippi and finally to the Country of the Illinois and there to make a settlement."[41]

In order to reduce the staggering cost of so lengthy a voyage, Halifax's Acadian community petitioned the colonial council in November, 1764 to subsidize their voyage to the French Antilles. The council refused on the grounds that the former prisoners had "amassed a considerable sum of money from the profits of their labor, purchased at a high price, during the last four years." The co-

39. Akins (ed.), *Acadia and Nova Scotia*, 339, 345, 348.

40. *Ibid.*, 349–50; Governor d'Estaing's Journal, March 1–23, 1764, in Series C 9b (Saint-Domingue, Correspondance générale), Volume 116, nonpaginated, Archives des Colonies, Archives Nationales, Paris, France, microfilm copy on deposit at Center for Louisiana Studies, University of Southwestern Louisiana; hereinafter cited as AC, C 9b, with volume and folio numbers.

41. Akins (ed.), *Acadia and Nova Scotia*, 349–50.

lonial legislators made no further effort to hinder their departure, for these French "partisans" continued to be viewed as a viable military threat to Nova Scotia's internal security. Moreover, whereas legal obstructionism would inevitably have driven the rebellious Halifax Acadians into surreptitious flight to the neighboring French possessions of St. Pierre and Miquelon, the captives' removal to distant Saint-Domingue not only extinguished their potential threat but doomed the migrants to certain death in the Antilles' tropical climate.[42]

Free to execute their designs, approximately six hundred Acadians, led by Joseph Broussard *dit* Beausoleil, charted "Vessels at their own Expense" and, in late November or early December, 1764, began the first segment of their roundabout voyage to Illinois. Unable to complete their preparations before the onset of winter, however, numerous other Acadians, "amounting to as many more, in different parts of the Province," made ready to depart for "the same destination" in the early spring of 1765.[43]

The exodus of hundreds of Acadian "survivors" from postexpulsion Nova Scotia signaled not the final chapter for a frontier-spawned culture, but the beginning of a major experiment in cultural transplantation. Unwilling to abandon their ethnic identity for the privilege of becoming proper British Protestants and for continued servitude to the oppressive colonial regime, most, though not all, of the Acadians captured in the Seven Years' War preferred to carve out a new life in an alien land rather than to face the insidious death of assimilation. Undeterred by the challenge, the emigrés readily faced the task of rebuilding their lives and reuniting their large extended families in a stable, francophone environment.

42. *Ibid.*, 349–51.
43. *Ibid.*

3

Acadians in the Middle Atlantic Colonies

The Halifax-Acadian migration to the lower Mississippi Valley alerted French Neutrals exiled in English seaboard colonies to the existence of an accessible though distant refuge populated by other Catholic francophones. Because of the distance and expense involved in traveling to Louisiana, only persons in desperate circumstances, faced with even bleaker prospects, actually would consider such a voyage. It is thus significant that the vast majority of Acadians exiled to Maryland and Pennsylvania abandoned the comparative security of these now familiar surroundings for the wilderness along the banks of the Mississippi River.

Of all the English seaboard colonies, Maryland and Pennsylvania—long recognized by historians for religious tolerance and humanitarianism—should have proved the most hospitable to the homeless French Neutrals. Maryland, established as a refuge for persecuted English Catholics in particular, might have been expected to provide a more congenial environment for the downtrodden "papists" than its solidly Protestant counterparts. The exiles, however, encountered only oppression in this former haven for the oppressed.

Upon arrival in Maryland, the Acadian colonists found the colony inflamed by anti-Catholic agitation and rampant francophobia, spawned by the British Empire's escalating border war with France's North American possessions. As French-speaking prisoners of war detained in an area vulnerable to French attack, the exiles collectively became a scapegoat for the fear, frustration, and vulnerability so pervasive in Maryland society following British military reverses in the Appalachian Mountains.

Once again, the Acadians were caught in a crossfire between the continent's major colonial powers as they mobilized their forces to struggle once more for imperial domination. The focal point of this military activity in the English Middle Colonies was the disputed but French-held Ohio River Valley. In 1749, shortly after the conclusion of the War of the Austrian Succession, the French and English empires began preparing for a confrontation to determine European hegemony over the North American interior. Since Maryland's security was directly threatened by the French presence in the eastern Ohio Valley, the resulting francophobia was fueled by an intensive propaganda campaign conducted by the sole provincial newspaper, the Annapolis *Maryland Gazette*. Among editor Jonas Green's favorite targets was Acadia's French population. The average Marylander's perception of the Acadians was colored by Green's jingoistic reports, suggesting that the undisputed French presence along the Nova Scotian border spelled a "fatal consequence to the Eastern Parts of New England, as well as to the Province of Nova Scotia." The only solution to this dilemma, according to Green, was a preemptive attack by the British navy on the threatening French installations and immediate subjugation of Nova Scotia's "30,000 French inhabitants," whose continuing presence jeopardized English control.

Subsequent commentaries on Nova Scotia not only perpetuated the image of a seditious francophile population and repeated the grossly exaggerated estimates of size and military significance of the French Neutral population but also lauded the region's agricultural potential and rich cod fisheries.[1] It is hardly surprising that the British government capitalized on the resulting fear and land lust among the Anglo-Americans to justify dispersal of Nova Scotia's Acadians. A typical English report appeared in the September 11, 1755, issue of the *Maryland Gazette*, the official printer for the provincial government.

1. "Extract of a Letter from a Gentleman at Halifax, in Nova Scotia, to His Friend in London, Dated July 31, 1753," Annapolis *Maryland Gazette*, January 24, 1754. See also the issues of October 10, 1754, and May 22, 1755.

We are now upon the great and noble Scheme of sending the Neutral French out of this Province [Nova Scotia], who have always been secret Enemies, and have encouraged our Savages to cut our Throats. If we effect their Expulsion, it will be one of the greatest Things that ever the English did in America; for by all the Accounts, that Part of the Country they possess, is as good Land as any in the World: In case therefore we could get some good English farmers in their Room, this Province would abound with all Kinds of Provisions.

The anti-Acadian propaganda campaign coincided with the onset of Anglo-French hostilities in the eastern Ohio Valley and the emergence of its attendant nationalism and francophobia. In early October, 1754, months after the initial clash between rival colonial forces, Jonas Green depicted Frenchmen as "the most ignorant slavish Herd of Bigots," displaying a remarkable proclivity for looting, homicide, arson, and rape. This antipathy toward the French was intensified by a wave of paranoia that swept the colony following General Edward Braddock's humiliating defeat by outnumbered French forces at the Battle of the Wilderness on July 9, 1755, and the subsequent commencement of Indian raids on English frontier settlements. The resulting reign of terror in Maryland during the summer and fall of 1755 unleashed latent anti-Catholicism among the province's Protestant majority. On August 15, Governor Horatio Sharpe, with the concurrence of the Provincial Council, directed all county magistrates to arrest "papists" falsely rumored to be inciting the colonial slave population to insurrection in order to assist their Gallic coreligionists.[2]

The Acadians were exiled to Maryland just as the waves of francophobia and anti-Catholicism crested. Between November 20 and 30, four dreadfully overcrowded British transports carrying 913 Acadians—493 from Pisiquid and 420 from Grand Pré—cast anchor at Annapolis, the provincial capital. Because of overcrowding and the necessity of seeking refuge at Boston from severe winter storms, the ships' stores were depleted, thus compelling the city to support

2. Annapolis *Maryland Gazette*, October 10, 1754, July 10, 1755. Contemporary estimates indicate that Maryland Catholics constituted one-twelfth of the provincial population. William Hand Browne, Bernard Steiner, and J. Hall Pleasants (eds.), *Archives of Maryland* (59 vols.; Baltimore, 1883–1953), VI, 497, XXXI, 72.

the displaced Frenchmen.[3] As Jonas Green lamented: "While they have lain in this Port, the Town has been at considerable charge in supporting them, as they appear very needy, and quite exhausted in Provisions; and it cannot be expected that the charge or Burden of maintaining such a Multitude can be supported by the Inhabitants of Annapolis . . . it will be necessary soon to disperse them to different Parts of the Province."[4]

Green's words were prophetic. Benjamin Tasker, president of the Provincial Council and acting chief executive in the absence of Horatio Sharpe (who was en route to Maryland from a governors' conference at New York), hastily convoked a session of the Council to determine a course of action regarding the Acadians. Apparently acquiescing to Green's cry for relief, the assembly adopted a resolution ordering three of the transports to the "Patuxent River, another to the Choptank, and a third to Wicomico, there to [await] the Orders of his Excellency our Governor." The *Leopard's* complement of 170 French Neutrals, however, was directed to remain at the provincial capital.[5]

Once deposited on the Chesapeake's shores, the Acadians were compelled to build a new life. As they were legally British subjects, the provincial government initially viewed them merely as immigrants, affording them no special assistance. The Acadians, on the other hand, had been expelled from their homeland by force of arms and viewed themselves as prisoners of war and, consequently, wards of the state. According to one contemporary account, "The simple French at Annapolis . . . call themselves prisoners of war. They did likewise here [Oxford] at first; but when one considers that they were treated as prisoners of war by Governor [Charles] Lawrence . . . they might have thought themselves not only in duty bound to declare themselves prisoners, but also in that character to be entitled to better treatment than they have met with as faithful subjects."[6]

3. Annapolis *Maryland Gazette*, November 20, December 4, 1755; Akins (ed.), *Acadia and Nova Scotia*, 42–44; Lauvrière, *Tragédie*, II, 103.

4. Annapolis *Maryland Gazette*, December 4, 1755.

5. *Ibid.*, December 4, 11, 1755; January 1, 1756; Browne et al. (eds.), *Archives of Maryland*, VI, 280–325; William D. Hoyt, Jr. (ed.), "A Contemporary View of the Acadian Arrival in Maryland, 1755," *William and Mary Quarterly*, 3rd Ser., V (1948), 572.

6. Henry Callister to Governor Horatio Sharpe, quoted in John Thomas Scharf, *History of Maryland from Earliest Times to the Present Day* (3 vols.; Baltimore, 1879), I, 476.

When no public assistance materialized, however, the exiles were compelled to rely heavily upon private aid. As Maryland's Catholic minority was enjoined from assisting the destitute immigrants, the Acadians were at the mercy of the region's openly hostile Protestant majority. Some assistance was provided by a few philanthropic individuals, but because of the broad range of basic services required by the exiles and the correspondingly heavy financial burden entailed, these good samaritans were soon compelled to abandon their wards. Forced to make their own way, the Acadians grudgingly accepted the low-paying and often degrading jobs offered by their reluctant hosts and gradually improved their lot, though never rising above the poverty level.[7]

This evolutionary process is best exemplified by the Acadians exiled to Baltimore. In December, 1755, Andrew Stygar carted an undetermined number of Acadians and their belongings from "Philpot's Point to Baltimore Town," where he maintained the exiles at personal expense for eleven days. When Stygar's assistance was terminated, however, only a few exiles could find lodging in private homes. The remaining Acadians were forced to congregate in an unfinished, abandoned two-story house built by Edward Fotterell.[8] Shunned by the population, they drew upon their own resources and abilities for survival. Utilizing their experience with small fishing vessels, some Acadian men found employment as sailors, while others apparently worked as longshoremen. By means of their "extraordinary industry and frugality," the exiles gradually improved their standard of living, and by 1763 most Acadians had abandoned their original, overcrowded quarters for "cabins or huts of mud and mortar," erected on lots lining South Charles Street.[9]

The experience of the Baltimore Acadians was shared by their confreres throughout Maryland, but the economic opportunities afforded most Acadians, particularly those exiled to tobacco plantation areas, were far more limited than those enjoyed by exiles residing near the province's thriving ports. The more fortunate French Neu-

7. Scharf, *History of Maryland*, I, 477; Gregory A. Wood, *The French Presence in Maryland, 1524–1800* (Baltimore, 1978), 77; Basil Sollers, "The Acadians (French Neutrals) Transported to Maryland," *Maryland Historical Magazine*, III (1908), 14.

8. Baltimore County Court Records, March, 1756, quoted in Sollers, "The Acadians," 12, 18; Scharf, *History of Maryland*, I, 479.

9. Lauvrière, *Tragédie*, II, 102; Griffith quoted in Sollers, "The Acadians," 19.

trals in the rural counties found employment as day laborers on plantations, while many others, debilitated by age, disease, or malnutrition, were driven to beggary.[10]

In some areas, the plight of these people attracted the interest of compassionate individuals. At Oxford, for instance, Henry Callister, a local tobacco factor and a staunch supporter of Acadian dispersal, was motivated by humanitarian interests to assist them. On Christmas Day, 1755, Callister drafted, on the Acadians' behalf, a petition for relief and redress to George III. Callister also provided the Frenchmen with substantial monetary assistance for the acquisition of badly needed provisions and clothing at the Cunliffe Brothers Store at Oxford.[11] In fact, Callister's expenditures were so heavy as to precipitate the collapse of his once prosperous business; but such charitable donations were unavoidable, Callister confided to business associate Anthony Bacon of London in December, 1755, because "these poor wretches have been here ever since the 8th current, and nothing yet has been done for them by the public. . . . Nobody knows what to do; and few have charity on them. I see no one interested for them but myself. . . . There's a number of them now about me in tears, craving relief for their sick, &c."[12]

Despite "potent opposition and much difficulty," the Anglo-American humanitarian managed to place "almost every [Acadian] family" in "good houses for the winter," at Oxford and in the Wye River area, to which Callister had sent over sixty exiles at personal expense.[13]

Callister's humanitarian crusade was consistently opposed by Colonel Edward Lloyd, a prominent Talbot County planter. Lloyd, who despised the Acadians because of their Catholicism and feared them as a threat to internal security, had vociferously opposed the

10. Memoir on the Acadians, February, 1763, in Series C 11d (Acadie, Correspondance générale), Volume 8, folios 242–51, Archives des Colonies, Archives Nationales, Paris, France, microfilm copy on deposit at Center for Louisiana Studies, University of Southwestern Louisiana; hereinafter cited as AC, C 11d, with volume and folio numbers.

11. Scharf, History of Maryland, I, 475–76; Lawrence C. Wroth (ed.), "A Maryland Merchant and His Friends in 1750," Maryland Historical Magazine, VI (1911), 237.

12. Callister to Anthony Bacon, December 25, 1756, quoted in Scharf, History of Maryland, I, 475–76.

13. Ibid.; Hoyt (ed.), "Contemporary View," 574.

Council's decision to disperse them throughout Maryland. Writing to a friend, he complained that "as Enemies they came here, and as such must certainly remain, because they are all rigid Roman Catholicks, and so attach'd to the French King, that sooner than deny his power over them, they have quitted all that they had in the World."[14] Subsequent comments, however, betray the source of Lloyd's fears.

> He [Callister] has sent me . . . 8 or 9 [Acadians] that were left with Mattw. Tilghman & Phil Halbleton, and order'd them to be Landed on me; which will subject me to the expense of at least 12 a week, beside making me liable to a great deal of Danger by their corrupting mine & other Negroe Slaves on this River, of which there is at least the num: of 300 that may be call'd Roman Catholicks: who, being, by some very late practices and declarations, dangerous in themselves . . . because some of my Slaves have lately said, They expect that the French . . . wou'd soon set them Free.[15]

Lloyd's sentiments accurately reflect the prevailing attitude toward the exiles. With the exception of a handful of humanitarians in Baltimore, Annapolis, and Oxford, Maryland, Protestants watched Acadian "papists" die of exposure and malnutrition without offering assistance. In Somerset County, for example, the exiles were compelled to "betake themselves for shelter to the swamps, now and for a long time full of snow, where they sicken and die."[16]

The Maryland provincial government also closed its eyes to the Acadians' plight. Addressing the provincial legislature March 16, 1756, Governor Horatio Sharpe indicated that the exiles had been afforded only private aid, despite a formal Acadian petition for assistance and urged the solons to "provide for their support as you shall judge proper." When the legislators demonstrated little interest in such a program, Sharpe again encouraged them to provide relief for the exiles in conformity with a bill recently adopted by the Pennsylvania assembly, but coupled his plea for aid with a strong appeal for termination of the Acadians' freedom of movement. The French Neutrals, he advised, should not be permitted to leave the counties

14. Hoyt (ed.), "Contemporary View," 572–73.
15. *Ibid.*, 575.
16. Callister to Bacon, December 25, 1755, quoted in Scharf, *History of Maryland,* I, 476.

to which they had been assigned; he also counseled the assembly to provide stringent penalties for "such of them as may presume to travel to, or be discovered near our Western Frontiers," attempting to escape to French territory.[17]

On April 23, the legislature responded with "An Act to Empower the Justices of the Several County Courts, to Make Provision for the Late Inhabitants of Nova Scotia, and for Regulating Their Conduct." The bill, reflecting the prevailing public revulsion for the French-Catholic immigrants, ordered the exiles, who were characterized as insolent and obstinate, to rely upon "their own Labor and Industry to procure a comfortable subsistence for themselves."[18] By providing relief to the province's Protestant humanitiarians and by simultaneously denying any responsibility for the truly needy wards of the state, the provincial assembly legislated the demands of the most vocal detractors. In cases where French Neutral parents were deemed incapable—for whatever reason—of supporting their children, county magistrates were empowered to "bind out" the children to local farmers and artisans "upon the best terms they can make . . . for the ease of the County." Moreover, after June 1, all able-bodied Acadians accused of wandering, loitering, or refusing to work for reasonable wages were to be incarcerated until they manifested a desire to find gainful employment. To ensure that the exiles could secure jobs, counties with Acadian populations exceeding legislated allotments were permitted to transport the surpluses into any less densely populated area of the colony except Frederick County, whose western frontier formed the boundary between French and English territory.[19]

The April 23 act also furnished the magistrates with administrative machinery for preventing the exiles from reaching the western border, where British troops were under gubernatorial orders to "destroy without hesitation any of them that may be seen in that Part of the Province."[20] All Acadians wishing to travel more than ten miles from their residences were required to secure passports from

17. Horatio Sharpe's address to the Maryland legislature, quoted in Sollers, "The Acadians," 12, 13.
18. "An Act to Empower the Justices . . . ," quoted in *ibid.*, 14.
19. Browne *et al.* (eds.), *Archives of Maryland*, LII, 542–44.
20. *Ibid.*, XXX, 103.

the local justice of the peace. Violators were subject to citizen's arrest, five-day imprisonment, and subsequent forcible removal to a place of residence to be determined by census schedules that would be taken by the county magistrates in August, 1756.[21]

The Acadians' freedom of movement was further restricted by Maryland's militia regulations. On May 22, 1756, through "An Act for Regulating the Militia of the Province of Maryland," French Neutrals were banned from militia training sessions; failure to comply with the prohibition would inevitably result in detention "out of View of the Said Place of Training until Sun Set that day."[22]

During the two years in which it was in force (1756–1758), the act effectively reduced Acadian mobility; in late August, 1756, Horatio Sharpe could assure Governor Charles Lawrence of Nova Scotia that "none of the French who were imported into this Province last year from Nova Scotia have been suffered either by Land or Water to return . . . thither."[23] But, when the act expired in 1758, the Acadians were no closer to economic self-sufficiency than they had been in 1756. As indicated by the following petition of the freeholders of Talbot County to their elected representatives, published in the February 10, 1757, issue of the *Maryland Gazette*, the exiles' position had become desperate.

> The wretched Acadians, in a manner Quarter'd upon us, are become a Grievance, inasmuch as we are not at present in a Situation, and in Circumstances, capable of seconding their own fruitless Endeavors to support their numerous Families, as a People plunder'd of their Effects: For tho' our Magistrates have taxed us, perhaps sufficient to feed such of them as cannot feed themselves, they cannot find Houses, Clothing, and other Comforts, in their Condition needful, without going from House to House Begging, whereby they are become a Nuisance.[24]

Nor had the Acadians' economic position improved by the end of the decade. Writing to his son on January 9, 1759, Charles Carroll indicated that the exiles had been reduced to a "state of . . . Misery, Poverty, and Rags." He subsequently reported that native Mary-

21. Sollers, "The Acadians," 12.
22. Browne *et al.* (eds.), *Archives of Maryland*, LII, 450.
23. *Ibid.*, VI, 471.
24. Annapolis *Maryland Gazette*, February 10, 1757.

landers were growing increasingly dissatisfied with supporting the French Neutrals through charity. In fact, the Maryland planter confided, he himself had provided the exiles more than "2,800 *livres*" in assistance.[25]

The aid provided by Carroll and other humanitarians fell far short of the exiles' needs. The persistent economic deprivation faced by the Acadians, as well as the resulting inadequacies of diet and lodging, produced a dangerous side effect—susceptibility to disease. Not only were the exiles stricken by an unidentified disease—probably pneumonia—in the swamps of Somerset County during the winter of 1756, but they were also hit by a smallpox epidemic on the western shore in the spring and summer of 1757. Though demographic information is scanty, it is certain that the death toll was heavy; the Acadian population shrank from 913 in December, 1755, to 667 at the conclusion of the Seven Years' War (1763).[26]

The high death rate, the squalor in which they were forced to live, and the fall of strategic French bases in Canada overwhelmed the usually buoyant Acadian spirit. During the first three years of the war, the exiles had openly anticipated a French military victory that would not only have humbled their captors but also permitted their repatriation. They took no pains to conceal their delight at reports of English defeats. The final years of the conflict brought the Acadians few opportunities to rejoice, and the decisive British victories of the late 1750s broke Acadian morale, signaling the irretrievable loss of their homeland.[27]

By 1760, the Acadians seemed destined to remain in Maryland, where their cultural institutions and their ethnic identity were doomed to extinction within a generation. Though most Acadians recoiled from the thought of assimilation by their oppressors, the social and governmental pressures for amalgamation with the dominant

25. Charles Carroll to Charles Carroll of Carrollton, January 9, 1759, quoted in Sollers, "The Acadians," 18.

26. Annapolis *Maryland Gazette*, July 21, 1767; Callister to Bacon, December 25, 1755, quoted in Scharf, *History of Maryland*, I, 476; "The Humble Petition of the Neutral Settlers of Acadia Detained in the Province of Maryland, July 7, 1763," in Political Correspondence, Series Angleterre, Volume 450, folios 438–44, Archives du Ministère des Affaires Etrangères, Archives Nationales, Paris, France, microfilm copy on deposit at Center for Louisiana Studies, University of Southwestern Louisiana; hereinafter cited as AE, with volume and folio numbers.

27. Annapolis *Maryland Gazette*, February 10, 1757; Charles Carroll to Charles Carroll of Carrollton, August 13, 1759, quoted in Sollers, "The Acadians," 18.

Anglo-American community were irresistible. Parents watched with dismay as their children gradually adopted English as their primary language. In Baltimore, families blessed with mercantile skills entered the local anglophone business community and quickly shed much of their cultural baggage.[28] Sensing that the group's socio-cultural sense of itself was being rapidly undermined, Acadian leaders desperately sought refuge for their embattled culture, but their liberation seemed remote if not impossible, as the war lingered and France's military fortunes waned.

Just when it appeared that the Acadians were to be perpetually exiled in Maryland, political developments in Europe offered faint hope for escape. During the final negotiations leading to the Treaty of Paris (1763), which ended the Seven Years' War, Louis Jules Barbon Mancini Mazarini, duc de Nivernois, the French minister plenipotentiary to the English court, sought to end Acadian internment in England and the Anglo-American colonies. While negotiating the exiles' release, the French diplomat entrusted his personal secretary, M. de la Rochette, with a secret dispatch to the Acadians incarcerated in England, promising them King Louis XV's protection. Copies of this communiqúe were subsequently smuggled by the French Neutrals to friends and relatives in the thirteen English seaboard colonies, including Maryland.[29]

The Nivernois letter prompted an immediate and positive response from Maryland Acadians. In a letter to the French ambassador, dated July 7, 1763, the "neutral settlers of Acadia detained in Maryland" expressed their fervent longing for "deliverance."[30] But freedom was not yet within their grasp, for though the British government reluctantly permitted the Acadians to depart for any French possession within eighteen months of the treaty's ratification, the Acadians lacked the means of securing passage aboard local merchantmen. The exiles preferred resettlement in Canada to life in the French Antilles, which were notoriously unhealthy and where the prevailing slave economy held as little opportunity as Maryland for Acadian economic independence.

28. See an exile's reminiscences in G. P. Wellington (ed.), "The Journal of Dr. John Sibley, June-October, 1802," *Louisiana Historical Quarterly*, X (1927), 477.
29. Oscar W. Winzerling, *Acadian Odyssey* (Baton Rouge, 1955), 25–49; "The Humble Petition, July 7, 1763." AE, 450:438–38vo.
30. "The Humble Petition, July 7, 1763," AE, 450:438–38vo.

The Acadians sought financial assistance from the Maryland government for their migration to Canada. In late spring, 1765, one Landry (probably Joseph Landry, who had previously represented the Acadians before Governor Sharpe and the Maryland legislature) addressed a petition to Governor Sharpe on behalf of the exiles detained in Maryland and Pennsylvania, requesting "a Settlement . . . be given them in Nova Scotia or Canada, either on the Bay of Gaspé, or Chaleur . . . [because] the Climate agrees with them."[31] On June 20, Maryland's chief executive referred the Acadian spokesman to General Thomas Gage, governor of New York and commander-in-chief of British forces in North America, to secure a determination of the exiles' request. Gage favored approval but refused to rule on the matter until he had consulted with the governors of Canada and Nova Scotia, as well as with the British secretary of state—officials adamantly opposed to Acadian repatriation.

Frustrated in their efforts to reach their native Canada, the exiles turned their eyes toward Louisiana. Despite reports of the French colony's partition and transfer to England and Spain, Louisiana proved appealing to the French Neutrals because of its francophone population and, more important, because of correspondence from the Broussard-led Acadians urging them to relocate in the lower Mississippi Valley.[32] The Maryland exiles, once again acting in conjunction with their ethnic kinsmen in neighboring Pennsylvania, now organized successive waves of emigration to New Orleans.

Departure of the Acadians from the Middle Atlantic colonies was apparently facilitated by the respective colonial governments. The vast majority of the exiles were destitute and continued to require public assistance. As indicated above, their British captors had long since tired of supporting "papists." In order to rid the colony of them for once and for all, colonial officials seized the opportunity to assist them in chartering ships for Louisiana. In late March, 1767, for example, the Cecil County justice of the peace, responding to a petition from Isabelle Brasseux (Veuve Cosme Brasseux), Ignace Hebert,

31. Browne et al. (eds.), Archives of Maryland, III, 246, 362, XIV, 2111; Lauvrière, Tragédie, II, 104.

32. Lawrence Kinnaird (ed.), Spain in the Mississippi Valley, 1765–94: Translations of Materials from the Spanish Archives in the Bancroft Library, Annual Report of the American Historical Association for the Year 1945, Vols. II–IV (Washington, D.C., 1946), II, 36–37.

Ignace Granger, and Joseph Hebert, provided the "destitute" petitioners with passage to "the French Settlements on the River Mississippi" aboard the *Virgin*. Such governmental assistance helped to swell the ranks of the refugees. Between 1766 and 1770, at least 782—some 90 percent—of the Maryland and Pennsylvania Acadians boarded Louisiana-bound English merchantmen at Chesapeake Bay ports.[33]

The Pennsylvania Acadians who joined in the journey to the "Mississippi's shores" were fleeing a hellish existence in the Keystone Colony. In fact, the banishment to Pennsylvania constitutes one of the bleakest chapters in Acadian history. As in Maryland, the exiles faced social ostracism, governmental oppression, and the threat of assimilation. By closing ranks against these common threats, the Acadians preserved their cultural integrity; but by vigorously defending their group boundaries, the exiles further aroused their already hostile neighbors.

The Pennsylvania Acadians, like their Maryland counterparts, faced severe economic deprivation. Bowing to public opinion, the provincial government chronically neglected the exiles. Denied adequate administrative support and lacking the skills and resources to compete individually in the local economy, the exiles were forced to seek employment from area businessmen. Few jobs were proffered by Pennsylvania merchants, and the Acadian population was reduced to a miserable existence in which starvation and epidemic diseases were commonplace. Emigration was their only salvation.

As in Maryland, the poor treatment endured by the Acadians in the Quaker colony, which prided itself on religious tolerance, was a direct outgrowth of the francophobia and anti-Catholic sentiment that engulfed the colony at the outset of the Seven Years' War. The wave of anti-French and anti-Catholic sentiment in Pennsylvania was swelling as the British sloops *Hannah, Three Friends,* and *Swan* arrived in the Delaware River on November 18 and 20, 1755, with 454 Acadian exiles. As the western Pennsylvania borders had recently been subjected to raids by French soldiers and their Indian allies

---

33. Petition by Isabelle Brasseux, Ignace Hebert, Ignace Granger, and Joseph Hebert, quoted in Sollers, "The Acadians," 19–20; "The Humble Petition, July 7, 1763," AE, 450:438–38vo; Wilton Paul Ledet, "Acadian Exiles in Pennsylvania," *Pennsylvania History*, X (1942), 125.

following the defeat of General Edward Braddock's British army, native Pennsylvanians were understandably unenthusiastic about the exiles' sudden appearance. Of particular concern to Pennsylvania were initially unfounded rumors that the Acadians would either escape into the trans-Allegheny region and assist their French brethren in prosecuting the war or, remaining within the province, incite to rebellion Philadelphia's significant Irish- and German-Catholic minorities.[34]

These popular fears were reflected in the actions of Governor Robert H. Morris, who placed the Acadians under guard aboard the British sloops until the convocation of a special session of the provincial assembly. Morris also ordered newly recruited provincial troops to remain under arms in Philadelphia to protect the colonial capital from the alleged Acadian threat.[35] Efforts to maintain the Acadians in isolation quickly proved untenable. On November 24, 1755, Governor Morris, acting upon a physician's report regarding deplorable health conditions as well as the outbreak of disease aboard the ships, urged the colonial legislators to provide temporary quarters for the French Neutrals. The assembly responded on the same day by directing the sloops' commanders to land their human cargoes at Province Island, where the exiles would be housed and fed at public expense. The assembly adjourned on November 25 after reimbursing Anthony Benezet, descendant of French Huguenots, for "blankets, shirts, stockings, and other necessities" given the exiles, at the request of several assemblymen, during the detention period aboard the sloop.[36]

The Pennsylvania assembly again took up the matter of the Acadians during its regular session of February, 1756. As the detention and support of the Acadians on Province Island had proved costly— totaling in excess of a thousand pounds—the legislators directed James Pemberton, a leading Quaker, to draft legislation providing for the exiles' dispersal throughout the easternmost counties—Philadelphia, Bucks, Lancaster, and Chester. The act, signed into law

34. *Pennsylvania Gazette*, November 20, 1755; *Pennsylvania Colonial Records: Minutes of the Provincial Council of Pennsylvania* (16 vols.; Philadelphia, 1838–53), VI, 711–13, 740, 751; Ledet, "Acadian Exiles," 120.

35. *Pennsylvania Colonial Records*, VI, 712.

36. Ledet, "Acadian Exiles," 120.

by Governor Morris on March 5, 1756, directed four Philadelphia Huguenots sympathetic to the Acadians' plight to supervise the dispersal, placing one per county township on condition that township wardens of the poor accepted them.[37] Land was to be rented for Acadian farmers, who were to be given a maximum of ten pounds' worth of agricultural implements and livestock. Widows, orphans, and other Acadians incapable of providing for themselves were to be supported at public expense. The overseers, who were to report the Acadians' conduct regularly to the assembly, would tabulate the cost of settling the exiles; the provincial legislature would, in turn, divert funds raised for the king's war chest to extinguish these expenses. The act was effective for one year.[38]

Although the foregoing legislation theoretically resolved Pennsylvania's Acadian problem to the satisfaction of both parties, the act failed wretchedly in practice. First, many rural townships in Philadelphia County refused to accept the French-speaking immigrants. Second, the Acadians themselves not only refused to be dispersed but also declined to support themselves, on the grounds that they were prisoners of war and thus entitled to public support. Because of unanticipated resistance to the Acadian resettlement plan, the Pennsylvania government was compelled to maintain the exiles on the public dole, and by late 1756, the sum of £2,285 had been spent on their behalf.[39]

Public funds for the Acadians' support were exhausted by September, 1756. On September 2, Acadian representatives addressed a memorial to the assembly reporting that their daily ration of one-half pound of meat and one pound of bread had been suspended. They begged the legislature to "give us leave to depart from hence, or be pleased to send us to our nation [Nova Scotia] or anywhere to join our countrymen; but if you cannot grant us these favors, we desire that provision may be made for our subsistence so long as we are detained here. If this, our humble request, should be refused, and our

37. The four Huguenots were Jacob Duché, Thomas Say, Abraham de Normandie, and Samuel Lefebvre. William Reed, "The French Neutrals in Pennsylvania," *Pennsylvania Historical Society Memoirs*, VI (1858), 297–98.

38. *Pennsylvania Colonial Records*, VI, 55–58.

39. Lawrence Henry Gipson, *The British Empire Before the American Revolution* (15 vols.; New York, 1946–70), VI, 312; Reed, "French Neutrals," 298–300; Ledet, "Acadian Exiles," 122.

wives and children be suffered to perish before our eyes, how griev-
ous will this be!—had we not better have died in our native land?"[40]
The memorial concluded on a defiant note, stating, "We shall never
freely consent to settle in this province."

The provincial assembly was clearly stunned by the memorial. Unable to resolve the perplexing problem of the Acadians' legal status,
the legislators placed the matter in the hands of Governor Morris'
successor, William Denny. Denny responded with a forceful rebuttal
to the exiles' claim that they were prisoners of war. With the concurrence of the provincial council, Denny recommended that the assembly disperse them, settling them "as far from the Frontiers
as possible." Deprived of public support, the Acadians were con-
demned to abject poverty. In a report to the provincial assembly in
October, 1756, Quaker William Griffith, a newly appointed commissioner, indicated that the exiles had been reduced to "a starving condition." Acadian men had searched for work unsuccessfully in Philadelphia because of the prevailing "prejudice against the foreigners."
Able-bodied exiles in Philadelphia subsequently resorted to the traditional Acadian home industries: manufacturing *sabots*, or wooden
shoes, and reconstructing fabric from "discarded pieces of cloth and
even rags gathered from the streets." As there was no market for
these items in Philadelphia, many exiles, Griffith reported, "had neither meat nor bread for many weeks together, and were necessitated
to pilfer and steal for the support of life." Disease was the hand-
maiden of malnutrition, and an undetermined number of Acadians
died of fevers and of smallpox in the fall of 1756.[41]

Moved by Griffith's report, the colonial assembly reinstated public
relief, and on November 9, 1756, appointed a committee to draft legislation permanently providing for the maintenance of the exiles in
Pennsylvania. This legislation was forthcoming in January, 1757.
Signed into law on January 18, the measure required Acadian parents to apprentice their children to local artisans to ensure their support. While thus engaged until age twenty-one for boys and eighteen for girls, the Acadian children were to attain literacy in English.

40. Memorial of September 2, 1756, quoted in Reed, "French Neutrals," 300.
41. *Ibid.*; Gipson, *The British Empire,* VI, 313; Reed, "French Neutrals," 300–301;
*Pennsylvania Archives: Votes and Proceedings of the House of Representatives of the Province
of Pennsylvania,* 8th Ser. (8 vols.; Philadelphia, 1931–35), VI, 4408; Ledet, "Acadian
Exiles," 126.

Finally, the aged, handicapped, and infirm were to be supported by public funds.[42]

Three weeks after the bill's enactment, the Acadians bitterly denounced their captors' effort to disperse families which were the very cornerstone of the close-knit society. In a remonstrance, dated February 8, the exiles demanded to know whether they were "Subjects, Prisoners, Slaves, or Freemen."[43] In addition, they sought permission to leave the colony, offering, if public funds were unavailable, to sell the few household articles and clothing that they had brought with them from Acadia to secure passage to another colony. The assembly refused to consider the remonstrance.

The Acadians reacted by publicly denouncing the colonial government and the British crown. In early March, 1757, for example, Lord Loudoun, commander-in-chief of British forces in North America, who was touring the colony, ordered the arrest of five Acadian leaders for openly defaming King George: Charles LeBlanc and Jean-Baptiste Galerme of Philadelphia; Philippe Melancon of Frankford; Paul Bujaud of Chester; and Jean Landry of Darby.[44] According to Loudoun:

> the French Neutrals there [Pennsylvania] had been very mutinous, and had threatened to leave the women and children to go over to join the French in the back country; they sent me a Memorial in French setting forth their grievances. I returned it and said I could receive no memorial from the King's subjects but in English, on which they had a general meeting at which they determined they would give no Memorial but in French, and . . . I am informed they come to this resolution from looking on themselves entirely as French subjects.[45]

Infuriated by the Acadians' intransigence, Loudoun contacted an exile who had been a spy for Governor Charles Lawrence of Nova Scotia. The spy, in turn, informed Loudoun that the five Acadian leaders had urged their countrymen not only to join the French forces, but to resist submission to governmental regulation of their lives, particularly the "binding out" of their children to English

42. Ledet, "Acadian Exiles," 123; *Pennsylvania Archives*, VI, 4491–92.
43. *Pennsylvania Archives*, VI, 4509.
44. David Hawke, *The Colonial Experience* (Indianapolis, 1966), 391; Reed, "French Neutrals," 304.
45. Lord Loudoun to William Pitt, April 25, 1757, quoted in Reed, "French Neutrals," 305.

households. Acting upon this report, the British commander ordered the arrest and incarceration of the alleged "ringleaders" aboard the HMS *Sutherland,* a warship bound for England. They were "subsequently acquitted and released," however, returning to Philadelphia in 1758.[46]

Deprived of their spokesmen, the Acadian population grew silent but continued to resist British efforts to assimilate them by indenturing Acadian children to (and educating them in) Protestant English homes. In 1761 an investigative governmental committee—appointed for the purpose of reducing public expenditures for the exiles—discovered that most Acadian parents had refused to part with their children. In fact, the exiles informed the committee that they had petitioned George III for permission to emigrate from the colony as a means of preventing the dispersal of their families.[47]

Though the committee urged strict enforcement of the statute requiring the indenturing of Acadian children, the provincial government closed its eyes to the problem, refusing also to act upon the investigators' conclusion that the exiles' living conditions were deplorable. As a consequence, the Acadians were again ravaged by diseases, especially smallpox. Epidemics were especially severe in Philadelphia, where philanthropist Anthony Benezet and other Huguenot sympathizers had furnished the exiles one-story frame houses on the north side of Pine Street, between Fifth and Sixth streets.[48]

The mortality rate was appalling. In a memorial to George III in 1760, the exiles claimed that they had "already seen in this Province of Pennsylvania two hundred and fifty of . . . [their] people, which is more than half the number that were landed here, perish through misery and various diseases."[49] These figures, however, appear to have been inflated, for an appeal for assistance to the French Duke of Nivernois, dated November 22, 1763, contains the signatures of 383 Acadians. Nevertheless, when one considers that the survivors included children born in exile, the mortality rate certainly exceeded 20 percent.[50]

46. *Ibid.,* 305–306; Ledet, "Acadian Exiles," 124.
47. Ledet, "Acadian Exiles," 124.
48. *Ibid.,* 127.
49. Memorial, quoted in Gipson, *The British Empire,* VI, 314–15.
50. *Ibid.,* 317n. For a list of the Acadian children baptized in Philadelphia, see "List

Only with the cessation of hostilities could the Acadians hope to ameliorate their living conditions. The Treaty of Paris afforded them the opportunity to escape their captivity, and in 1764 comte d'Estaing, governor of the French colony of Saint-Domingue (present-day Haiti) authorized M. Marmon to recruit colonists surreptitiously in Maryland and Pennsylvania. But the Acadians in the Middle Atlantic colonies were generally reluctant to migrate to a tropical climate, and only some of the exiles in Philadelphia accepted Marmon's invitation.[51]

The limited success of the Saint-Domingue colonization belied the exiles' great interest in emigration, but the Pennsylvania Acadians, like their cousins in Maryland, continued to anticipate repatriation or at least resettlement in French Canada. Capitalizing upon the provisions of the Treaty of Paris ending their captivity, they joined with the Maryland Acadians in petitioning Thomas Gage, governor of New York and commander-in-chief of British forces in North America, for permission to relocate in the Gaspé Peninsula.[52]

When Gage failed to approve the Acadian proposal, the exiles were forced to seek a haven elsewhere. Influenced by the Maryland Acadians, who were in contact with their confreres in Louisiana, most Pennsylvania exiles resolved to join in an exodus to the Mississippi Valley. In 1766 and 1767, between 150 to 200 Pennsylvania Acadians "left in a body" for Chesapeake Bay ports, there boarding chartered, Louisiana-bound merchantmen in small groups, as space became available.[53]

Joint departure of the Pennsylvania and Maryland Acadians was fitting, for the two groups had confronted and overcome remarkably similar problems during their long years of exile. Despite significant subregional demographic and economic differences between Maryland and Pennsylvania, the Acadians exiled to both these Middle Atlantic colonies were ostracized socially and denied access to the marketplace, either through lack of necessary skills or the prejudice

of Baptisms at St. Joseph's Church, Philadelphia, from August 29, 1758, to December 31, 1775," *American Catholic Historical Society of Philadelphia Records*, I (1884), 246–75.

51. Voorhies, "The Promised Land?" 81–83.

52. Browne *et al.* (eds.), *Archives of Maryland*, XIV, 211.

53. John F. Watson, *Annals of Philadelphia* (Philadelphia, 1830); Ledet, "Acadian Exiles," 126.

of merchants and consumers alike. In both colonies, the exiles were outcasts, who were feared and reviled by the native anglophones. Responding to public sentiment, the neighboring colonial governments adopted almost identical legislation, both to control and to emasculate the alien culture by depriving the immigrants of their mobility and providing social machinery and assimilation of their children.

The basic similarities of the problems faced by the Pennsylvania and Maryland Acadians had demanded a common response. Both groups had closed ranks to present a common front against the concerted British effort to destroy their ethnic identity. Through group solidarity, they had consistently foiled government efforts to "bind out" their children to proper English households. Cohesiveness had provided the exiles the strength to endure discrimination, malnutrition, disease, and governmental harassment. After a decade of exile and subjugation, Acadian society was battered, but not broken, and its members sought a haven in which to rebuild their shattered world. That refuge was Louisiana.

4

Frontiersmen in Feudal France, 1756–1785

Throughout the long years of exile, the Acadians shared similar problems and later a common solution—emigration to Louisiana. This was true not only of the French Neutrals exiled to the Middle Atlantic colonies but also of their brethren deported to England and later "repatriated" to France.

France's prevailing social and economic systems, like those in the Middle Atlantic colonies, were anathema to the expatriates. As frontiersmen out of step and time with the motherland's feudal society, trapped by their destitution in the slums of the Atlantic ports in which they arrived, the immigrants faced a bleak future. Unable to compete in the urban job market and unwilling to renounce their traditional independence for denigrating employment as peasants in rural areas, the Acadians in France consistently found themselves on the royal dole. The native Frenchmen, already overburdened by taxes, soon resented the apparently indolent exiles they were now compelled to support.

The resulting ethnic friction underscored sociocultural differences between the rival groups. Frenchmen, for their part, usually attempted to treat the exiles as peasants and were dumbfounded when their condescension was greeted with "insolence." Acadians, on the other hand, found little acceptance of their ethnicity and even less appreciation for their insistence upon resettlement in a rural setting, which they believed would restore their sense of personal dignity and independence. Acadian recalcitrance limited cultural interchange between the immigrant and native French populations, thereby hindering rapid assimilation. Acadian insularity also prolonged the interethnic feud.

The lingering confrontation between Acadians and French civilians also characterized the exiles' relations with French administrators charged with their care. This dispute, which frequently eclipsed the less conspicuous cultural warfare, centered upon governmental assurances of economic and cultural rehabilitation, which first attracted many exiles to the motherland.

In the decade following the Grand Dérangement (1755–65), more than three thousand exiled Acadians sought refuge in France. French agents had led them to expect not only a warm reception but also just recompense for the sacrifices that, for obvious political reasons, the expatriates claimed to have made on behalf of Louis XV. Of paramount importance to the exiles was the acquisition of arable lands in sparsely settled areas, as a means of reestablishing their formerly prosperous agrarian society. But His Most Christian Majesty and the ministers of state rewarded their "subjects'" fidelity with empty promises. Neglected by the crown, the Acadians, who steadfastly maintained their claims to compensation, led a miserable existence on a paltry royal dole and refused to become part of France's feudal society. Their misery was compounded by the growing realization that governmental inertia doomed them eventually to assimilation. Increasingly disillusioned and bitter, the exiles ultimately were persuaded by Peyroux de La Coudreniére and his associate, Olivier Terrio (Theriot), to migrate to Spanish Louisiana.

Grievances contributing to the mass exodus stemmed primarily from the conditions under which the Acadians had migrated to France. Between 1758 and 1764, from 3,000 to 3,500 Acadians entered French ports in a variety of ways: First, several hundred Acadians captured at Louisbourg and Quebec were transported to France aboard English cartel ships. Second, 753 exiles in England were transported to St. Malo and Morlaix at French expense in 1763.[1] Though clearly constituting a minority of France's Acadian immi-

---

1. Lauvrière, *Tragédie*, II, 162, 258–59; Winzerling, *Acadian Odyssey*, 43; Dorothy Vinter, "The Acadian Exiles in England," *Les Cahiers de la Société historique acadienne*, 30[ieme] (1971), 388–402; Regis-Sygefroy Brun, "Le Séjour des Acadiens en Angleterre et leurs traces dans les archives britanniques, 1756–1763," *Les Cahiers de la Société historique acadienne*, 32[ieme] (1971), 62–67.

grants, the exiles from England were particularly significant, for they were lured to France by vague promises of compensation and resettlement. For example, through a circular letter to Acadians detained in England, M. de La Rochette, secretary to the Duke of Nivernois, "ambassador extraordinary" to the English court, persuaded the exiles to cooperate with French efforts to secure their release by stating: "Your treatment in France will be still more advantageous than you expect, and you will be under the immediate protection of the king and his minister . . . the Duke of Nivernois." [2] Elated with the French crown's apparent benevolence, the Acadians in England agreed to relocate in France despite repeated British attempts to dissuade them.

France, however, was not the Promised Land; their sojourn in the motherland proved merely the second chapter in a continuing exile. From the outset, living conditions were wretched. Upon debarkation at Morlaix and St. Malo in late May and June, 1763, the Acadians, who had been ferried across the English Channel in overcrowded French vessels, were housed in barracks where smallpox, contracted during the passage, decimated their ranks. The exiles silently endured their uncomfortable and unhealthy surroundings, obviously anticipating prompt assistance from the crown; none was forthcoming. [3]

This virtual abandonment of the exiles at Morlaix and St. Malo was the product of the crown's apathy. First, Louis XV, who had decreed that the exiles must be integrated into the French economy, was obviously unwilling to train Acadian farmers in the various crafts needed in the seaports in which they resided. Antoine-Philippe Lemoine, naval commissary at Rochefort who was entrusted by Etienne-François, duc de Choiseul, minister of foreign affairs, minister of marine, and acting minister of state, with the administration of Acadian affairs, initially requested an operating budget of 100,000 écus; the crown, however, appropriated only 57,900 livres, thus forcing the immigrants to subsist on a per-diem allowance of only 6 sols per adult. The crown also approved but failed to act upon a detailed,

2. La Rochette to Nivernois, March 18, 1763, quoted in Winzerling, *Acadian Odyssey*, 39, 44–45; Voorhies, "The Promised Land?" 81–84; Gipson, *The British Empire*, VI, 286–344.

3. Memoir on Acadian History to 1778 (June, 1778), AE 47:23.

three-point settlement plan, submitted by Nivernois in February, 1763, for the establishment of the Acadians in underdeveloped areas, despite the fact that these proposals generally reflected Acadian aspirations.[4]

Nivernois' plan had failed because the exiles had become a pawn in France's imperial designs. With the end of the Seven Years' War, Choiseul moved quickly to revitalize the defenses of the French Empire's battered remnants. The keystone of this ambitious scheme was the rapid augmentation of the colonies' white population, and Choiseul viewed France's Acadian exiles as a large reservoir of potential colonists. By establishing them in France's Caribbean possessions, he would relieve the crown not only of its financial burden, but also of the unpalatable task of purchasing or expropriating settlement sites within the realm. In late 1763, Choiseul launched a propaganda campaign designed to entice displaced Acadians into the jungles of Cayenne. Although the exiles possessed "a prejudice of repugnance" for the tropics, "several hundreds" were seduced by the glowing descriptions of France's tropical paradise. The choice proved fatal to most of the colonists; so many Acadians succumbed to the oppressive equatorial sun and humidity that the minister was compelled to repatriate the few survivors in 1765.[5]

Following the collapse of the Cayenne colonization project, Choiseul did little more than reject bogus Acadian resettlement schemes put forward by "every [French] land shark and swindler." Among those unsuccessfully attempting to exploit the exiles was Jean Berton, who proposed "sending the Acadians to work in French mines." In August, 1763, Louis Elizabeth de La Vergne, comte de Tressan, futilely proposed the settlement of 120 Acadian families on his barren, war-ravaged Lorraine estates at an initial cost of 8,000 *livres* and subsequent annual installments of 1,600 *livres*.[6]

4. Winzerling, *Acadian Odyssey*, 54–60, 92–93, 176; Ernest Martin, *Les Exilés acadiens en France au XVIIIe siècle et leur établissement en Poitou* (Paris, 1936), 32–33; Memoir on Acadian History to 1778 (June, 1778), AE, 47:23.

5. Lauvrière, *Tragédie*, II, 181–87; Winzerling, *Acadian Odyssey*, 55; Martin, *Les Exilés*, 55.

6. Winzerling, *Acadian Odyssey*, 59; Choiseul to Comptroller-general L'Averdy, June 10, 1764, in Series B (Ordres du roi), Volume 120, folio 195, Archives des Colonies, Archives Nationales, Paris, France, microfilm copy on deposit at Center for Louisiana Studies, University of Southwestern Louisiana; hereinafter cited as AC, B, with volume and folio numbers; Martin, *Les Exilés*, 59–61.

The exploitative settlement projects advanced by unscrupulous French noblemen apparently jolted Choiseul from his temporary complacency. In June, 1765, he advocated placement of 150 to 200 Acadian families on his Chanteloupe estate. The minister was apparently dissuaded by Abbé Louis Joseph Le Loutre, controversial former vicar-general of Acadia, who was fully cognizant of the incongruities of Acadian life amid the feudalistic trappings of Loire Valley society.[7]

Le Loutre personally initiated an Acadian colonization project at Belle-Ile-en-Mer, a windswept island off Brittany that three Acadian representatives had selected in 1763 as an acceptable settlement site. Colonization of Belle-Ile began in early August, 1765, with the establishment of seventy-seven Acadian families from Morlaix and St. Malo. From the outset, the colony was plagued with misfortune: drought, crop failure, destructive livestock epidemics, and inflated tax assessments. Unable to pay their taxes or to secure an extension from uncooperative provincial officials, the Acadians in 1772 were compelled to abandon their new homes and resume their wretched existence in French seaports.[8]

Reduction of the Belle-Ile colonists to poverty intensified the growing dissatisfaction of France's Acadian population. Attracted to France by promises of land grants "equivalent to those which we [the exiles] had lost in Acadia," the government's pledges proved as empty as its coffers. Lacking necessary job skills, the exiles were unable to obtain jobs and thus reduced to pauperism. They reluctantly accepted the government's subsistence allowance of six *sols* per person until the anticipated day of restitution, but it soon became abundantly clear that the crown had neither the means nor the intention of compensating them. The disillusioned Acadians capitalized on every opportunity to leave France for any foreign country or colony that might afford a chance for reunification and restoration of their agrarian, frontier society. Hence, in 1763 an undetermined number of exiles volunteered for Choiseul's colonization project. Similarly, in late 1763 and 1764, additional hundreds sought refuge in the Falk-

7. Martin, *Les Exilés*, 60–61.

8. *Ibid.*; Choiseul to L'Averdy, August 15, 1763, AC, B 117:367; Choiseul to the Bishop of Vannes, February 11, 1765, AC, B 122:110; Praslin to the duc d'Aiguillot, February 11, 1765, AC, B 122:109; Choiseul to Le Loutre, February 11, 1765, AC, B 122:110; Winzerling, *Acadian Odyssey*, 63.

land Islands. The Falklands and Cayenne, however, were not conducive to Acadian colonization, and most of the surviving colonists returned penniless and dejected to France.[9]

Just as their principal avenue of escape—foreign colonization—appeared to be closed, the Acadians were given new hope of deliverance. In September, 1766, one Semer, an Acadian residing at Le Havre, received a letter from his son, Jean-Baptiste, who had recently settled in the Attakapas district in Louisiana. The younger Semer, obviously responding to Governor Antonio de Ulloa's approval of Acadian requests to invite exiled relatives to settle in the colony, lauded the Mississippi Valley's salubrious climate and fertile soil. In addition, he described in glowing terms the "benefits extended by . . . Louisiana's newly installed Spanish administration to him and all of his comrades."[10]

Word of Louisiana's apparently thriving Acadian colony spread rapidly through Le Havre's Acadian community, which notified Sieur Mistral, the provincial intendant, of their "desire to migrate to that colony." In fact, they asked to be transported to the Mississippi Valley at royal expense. Mistral forwarded the petition to Minister of Marine Praslin, who in turn rejected the request on the ground that Louisiana had recently been ceded by France to Spain and that expenses incurred in transporting the Le Havre Acadians would entail a substantial financial loss for the crown.

For the Acadians at Le Havre—indeed for all of the exiles in France—Praslin's actions appeared to have sealed their fate. After a disastrous colonization attempt in 1767 on the French islands of St. Pierre and Miquelon, the exiles, now desperately seeking a means of escaping France's seaport slums, expressed interest in settlement schemes advanced by French noblemen. With proposals similar to those submitted to Choiseul in 1763 and 1764, French landholders sought to induce Acadians to settle upon, clear, and cultivate the dregs of their estates. In 1769, for example, the marquis de Saint-

9. Petition to comte de Vergennes, April 4, 1784, in Papeles Procedentes de Cuba, Legajo 197, folio 954, Archivo General de Indias, Seville, Spain; hereinafter cited as PPC, with legajo and folio numbers; Shelby T. McCloy, "French Charities to the Acadians, 1755–1799," *Louisiana Historical Quarterly,* XXI (1938), 658; Praslin to the duc d'Aiguillot, February 11, 1765, AC, B 122:109; Martin, *Les Exilés,* 90; Lauvrière, *Tragédie,* II, 181–87; Winzerling, *Acadian Odyssey,* 60.

10. Praslin to Mistral, September 13, 1766, AC, B 125:450vo.

Victour offered the exiles a total of 150 arpents (137.9 acres) of his poorest farmland. Ownership of small tracts was contingent upon development of the *landes* as well as twenty annual payments. The Acadian representatives who inspected the settlement site were appalled by the sterility of the soil, the wretched condition of the few French settlers who had preceded them, and, most important, the reduction of the former freeholders to the status of sharecroppers. The delegates rejected such proposals.[11]

The Acadians' repeated refusal to submit to exploitation by the nobility quickly alienated Joseph-Marie Terray, minister of finance, who viewed with exasperation their continued reliance upon the dole. In 1771 he devised a scheme of settling the Acadians in Corsica, thereby ridding the French seaports of their idle population. Acadian leaders sent to inspect the prospective settlement site reported "poor treatment" of settlers, "high rents, sterile lands, and an unhealthy climate." Acting upon the deputies' recommendations, France's Acadian population unanimously rejected Terray's colonization project.[12]

The rejection of the scheme marked a nadir not only in Acadian self-esteem but also in Acadian relations with the French public. Residents of French seaports took no pains to conceal their hostility toward local exiles, whom they considered as idle, parasitic "intruders." The French nobility was clearly disconcerted by the Acadians' fierce independence. Bureaucrats were perplexed by the exiles' unshakable commitment to cultural preservation, an objective incompatible with the government's goal of integrating yeoman farmers into a rigid, feudalistic economy. The resulting dilemma was delineated by a St. Malo Acadian commissioner: "The aim of the state is to incorporate them through their skill into the class of farmers. But they seem to resent being treated as peasants."[13]

The exiles bitterly resented the conditions under which they had been forced to exist by the crown's disinterest, and they also resented the incompetence of the royal bureaucracy. Confined to urban areas by a lack of funds, unable to improve their lot because of a lack of commercial job skills, and thus forced to endure the humiliation of

11. Winzerling, *Acadian Odyssey*, 64–65.
12. *Ibid.*, 65.
13. Memoir on Acadian History to 1778 (June, 1778), AE, 47:24; Winzerling, *Acadian Odyssey*, 92.

subsisting on the French dole, the Acadians by 1772 had come to view themselves as French captives; except for freedom to exercise their religion, their lot was no better in France than it had been in England. In 1772, therefore, the exiles resorted to the expedient of a direct appeal to Louis XVI, who had recently succeeded his grandfather, Louis XV.[14]

Under the pretext of supporting the Spanish government's proposed colonization scheme in Andalusía, an undetermined number of Acadian delegates representing 2,500 of their brethren addressed the French monarch at Compiègne in July, 1772. After vividly describing their circumstances, the representatives asked Louis XVI either to ameliorate their living conditions or provide them with passports to Spain. Much to the Acadians' relief—for they secretly hoped that "the king would not think it suitable to let them go"—Louis XVI, deeply touched by the Acadian petition, lambasted his ministers of finance and state and directed them to establish the exiles in the interior.[15]

Spurred into action by the royal directive, Minister of State Jean Berton feverishly surveyed the realm for settlement sites. Cognizant that France possessed no free arable lands, Berton devised a scheme of establishing the exiles upon the marquis de Perusse des Cars' estate of fifteen thousand arpents. The Perusse manor appeared to be the perfect settlement site, for not only did the property contain nearly ten thousand acres of woodland but the marquis had been unsuccessful in attracting a sufficient number of French and German settlers to place the land under cultivation. Finally, Perusse had recently petitioned the crown for a substantial development loan.[16]

Berton hoped to capitalize upon the marquis' financial dilemma by establishing 1,500 Acadians on the vast, unoccupied expanse of the Perusse manor. This move, it was hoped, would please all of the parties involved. The Acadians would be restored to a rural, agrarian setting, where, through royal subsidies, they would remain technically freeholders. The crown would be freed from the financial burden entailed by the Acadian dole. Finally, the Perusse estate

14. Winzerling, *Acadian Odyssey*, 66.
15. Lauvrière, *Tragédie*, II, 173; Winzerling, *Acadian Odyssey*, 66.
16. Lauvrière, *Tragédie*, II, 173–74; Winzerling, *Acadian Odyssey*, 68–74; Martin, *Les Exilés*, 120–265.

would be theoretically cleared, developed, and worked on shares by the exiles.[17]

The fine points of the resettlement plan were set forth by Berton's subordinate, Acadian Commissioner Antoine-Philippe Lemoine, in 1773. After securing Berton's approval, Lemoine conducted several Acadian representatives to the Perusse estate. The deputies, however, immediately voiced their disapproval of the 2,627-acre settlement site, citing the sterility of the soil, the absence of pasturage, and the scarcity of fresh water.[18]

Most Acadians in France characteristically abided by their delegates' decision. Of the more than 2,000 prospective settlers, only 497 initially volunteered for the Berton-Lemoine project. At least 1,000 additional exiles subsequently relented, joining their confreres in Perusse's Poitou settlement, which had been christened Grand Ligne. The Acadian colony nevertheless was doomed to failure, like its predecessors. The colony began inauspiciously, for the colonists found a total lack of housing at Grand Ligne and were forced to rent rooms in nearby villages, where they were "exploited" by greedy, gouging merchants. The settlers' initial disappointment soon grew into desperation as their agricultural endeavors proved equally frustrating. In 1774 and 1775, the Acadians' crops germinated but, upon breaking the soil, yellowed and died. The crop failures prompted Perusse (who, under the Berton-Lemoine plan, received a portion of the exiles' crops in recognition of his "property rights"), to increase land rental payments drastically. The resulting flames of Acadian discontent were fueled by rumors spread by a mysterious individual known only as the Fleming or "le Flamand." Posing as a horticulturist representing the agricultural minister, the phantom Fleming secretly convinced the Acadians that the lands ceded to them by Perusse were and always would be sterile. Moreover, in clandestine meetings with the colony's leaders, he assured the exiles that he personally would secure for them "the best lands in Normandy."[19]

Though the Acadians were unquestionably skeptical of le Fla-

17. Lauvrière, Tragédie, II, 174–75; McCloy, "French Charities," 660; Winzerling, Acadian Odyssey, 71–74.

18. McCloy, "French Charities," 659; Memoir on Acadian History to 1778 (June, 1778), AE, 47:24.

19. Winzerling, Acadian Odyssey, 74–75, 78–79; Lauvrière, Tragédie, 175–76.

mand's grandiose scheme, they concurred wholeheartedly with his assessment of the lands. In late 1775 the colonists determined by popular vote to abandon the settlement site. By mid-1776, the colony had dwindled to 160 members. The French government, which may well have been le Flamand's employer, made no move to check the Acadian exodus from the Grand Ligne colony, despite its heavy investment in the project, because spiraling inflation in Poitou had raised the projected settlement costs by approximately 300 percent. Berton thus gladly permitted the former colonists to establish themselves at Rouen, Caen, La Rochelle, Bordeaux, and Nantes.[20]

The collapse of the Grand Ligne colony afforded the government—particularly the ministry of finance—only a brief respite. Louis XVI's orders to settle the exiles remained unfulfilled. In 1777 Jacques Necker, the finance minister, seized upon his predecessor's abortive plan of establishing the exiles at Corsica. The project was made all the more attractive by the fact that 2,366 Acadians in France had recently expressed interest in Corsican colonization to M. de Trellier, former cabinet secretary to the Duke of Parma. As Necker and his subordinates refined the settlement proposal, the Acadians wrangled over the merits of participation in a second, government-subsidized colonization scheme.[21]

The debate over Corsica was precipitated by the suggestion, attributed to two French-born husbands of Acadian women, that the American Revolution would liberate Acadia from English domination, thereby permitting the exiles to return to their homeland. Responding to this timely though poorly grounded proposal, several unidentified Acadian elders also voiced their opposition to Necker's scheme, but unlike their French-born confreres, they openly advocated colonization in Spanish Louisiana. An undetermined number of young Acadian leaders rallied around the dissident elders, clamored for the abandonment of the Corsican settlement project and, with the support of approximately eighty families, held a "rump convention" for the purpose of electing two delegates to Versailles.[22]

The Acadian representatives who had been negotiating with

20. Winzerling, Acadian Odyssey, 76–79.
21. Ibid., 26–27; Memoir on Acadian History to 1778 (June, 1778), AE, 47:25.
22. Memoir on Acadian History to 1778 (June, 1778), AE, 47:26–27; Winzerling, Acadian Odyssey, 83, 86.

Necker and De Trellier were remarkably inept in dealing with the devisive tactics of the aggressive pro-Louisiana minority. In an Acadian assembly held in 1777, the neutral majority authorized its delegates to the court to discuss only the back wages owed many exiles by the French government since the collapse of the Grand Ligne colony. No attempt was made to discredit the minority representatives. Necker recognized the rump convention delegates as representatives of all Acadians in France and capitalized upon the schism by browbeating the minority leaders into acceptance of a "compromise" settlement of the myriad problems. The compromise existed in name only, for concessions came only from the Acadians, who not only agreed to the reduction of their per-diem allowance from six to three *sols* after 1779 but also withdrew their claim to back wages. The minority delegates also absolved the French government from responsibility "for debts contracted by individuals of the [Acadian] nation under the authority and quasi-guarantee of the French government's Acadian commissioners" in return for freedom to select a homesite *within the realm.*[23]

Although the minority delegates' actions were theoretically subject to approval or rejection by the 2,542 Acadians in France, Sieur La Bove, intendant of Brittany, rigidly enforced the agreement's provisions—with devastating results. No longer able to pay for lodging with their reduced incomes, many exiles were forced into the streets. The formerly impregnable walls of Acadian group solidarity were leveled by La Bove's actions; factionalism spawned by the "rump convention" intensified as the minority delegates continued to press for popular ratification of the "compromise."[24]

Distrustful of their leaders, unable to subsist on the government dole, and unable to find arable land or a niche in France's feudalistic society, most exiles resolved to leave the mother country—surreptitiously if necessary. In mid-October, 1777, twenty-two Acadians secured permission to migrate to Louisiana through the intercession of the Spanish ambassador, Pedro Pablo Abarca de Bolea, condé de Aranda. An undetermined number of additional exiles from Nantes and St. Malo had secretly returned to Ile St. Jean (Prince Edward Is-

23. Winzerling, *Acadian Odyssey*, 82–86.
24. *Ibid.*, 87.

land), Halifax, and other Nova Scotian ports via the English Island of Guernsey.[25]

Though small-scale, clandestine resettlement operations enjoyed some success, a mass exodus of Acadians from France was initially rendered unfeasible by the French government's opposition to emigration, as well as by the factionalism among the exiles and the resulting leadership vacuum. In 1783, however, Henri Peyroux de La Coudrenière provided the necessary catalyst. Peyroux, a soldier of fortune who had suffered financial reverses during a seven-year sojourn in Louisiana, upon his return to France in 1783, resolved to gain wealth and social position by establishing a new Acadian colony in Spanish Louisiana. From his earliest contacts with condé de Aranda and Ignacio Heredia, the Spanish ambassador's personal secretary, the Frenchman reportedly demanded not only a pension but a commission in Louisiana as well; only when these concessions were secured from Aranda did Peyroux lay the groundwork for the Acadian exodus.[26]

Though Peyroux had married the Acadian Prudence Rodrigue of Louisbourg, he was viewed as a Frenchman—and thus suspect—by the Acadian community in his native Nantes. To gain credibility among the exiles, Peyroux launched his resettlement program by securing an Acadian "intermediary," Olivier Terrio (Theriot), a Nantes cobbler whom he contacted under the pretext of having Mme. Peyroux's shoes repaired. After two interviews Peyroux concluded that Terrio's literacy, familiarity with the Acadian community, and interest in Louisiana colonization rendered him the perfect choice. He was also attracted to Peyroux's project because each successive letter the Acadians received from Louisiana between 1767 and 1783 had rekindled among the exiles an overwhelming desire for familial reunification in the former French colony. Despite his initial hesitancy to cooperate with Peyroux (apparently because of the repeated failures of previous resettlement schemes), Terrio eventually succumbed

25. Minister of Marine to Aranda, October 17, 1777, AC, B 161:429; Notes on Henri Peyroux de La Coudrenière's arrival and sojourn in Louisiana, September 27, 1800, PPC, 217B:112.
26. Lauvrière, *Tragédie*, II, 197–98; List of events regarding the emigration of 1,600 Acadians from France's provinces to the colony of Louisiana, 1792, PPC, 197:951–52; Peyroux to Olivier Terrio, August 8, 1783, PPC, 197:952; Winzerling, *Acadian Odyssey*, 91.

to the Frenchman's promises of "honorable and lucrative" compensation from the Spanish government upon the project's successful conclusion. Terrio voiced interest in Peyroux's schemes because he was intimately acquainted with the misery of his people. Although his trade provided him a larger income than most of his fellow exiles, the cobbler willingly supported numerous relatives who, for various reasons, were "incapable of earning a living."[27]

As evidence that Terrio's motives for participation in the project were not altogether mercenary, his letters from France never mention personal financial matters—even though he received no compensation for his labors—while repeatedly manifesting a desire for Acadian reunification. Terrio leaped enthusiastically to the task of contacting, organizing, and motivating the hundreds of exiles remaining in French ports. During the summer of 1783, he not only exhorted numerous exiles to support the project but also circulated a petition among the Acadian communities at Nantes, Morlaix, Rennes, St. Malo, Caen, and Cherbourg, "imploring His Catholic Majesty [with His Most Christian Majesty's approbation] to grant [the Acadians] permission to go to Louisiana in order to rejoin our relatives from Acadia and to establish ourselves among them." Leery of yet another grandiose settlement scheme, the overwhelming majority of exiles in France rejected the petition, and when Terrio forwarded the document to Peyroux in early August, it contained only five signatures, including that of the cobbler. Peyroux, nevertheless, presented the petition to Aranda, who in turn forwarded it to the Spanish court.[28]

The timing was fortuitous, for Governor Bernardo de Gálvez of Louisiana, who had recently made a triumphant return to Spain, addressed King Carlos III on its behalf. The Spanish monarch postponed judgment on the project until Peyroux had been given security clearance by Minister of the Indies José de Gálvez. Despite the delay, as well as initial misgivings about the Spanish treasury's ability

27. Lauvrière, *Tragédie*, II, 197; Milton P. Rieder and Norma Gaudet Rieder (comps.), *The Crew and Passenger Registration Lists of the Seven Acadian Expeditions of 1785* (Metairie, La., 1965), 25; List of events, 1792, PPC, 197:951–52.

28. List of events, 1792, PPC, 197:951–52; Terrio to Heredia, May 27, 1784, PPC, 197:956; Terrio to comte d'Aranda, 1785, PPC, 197:960; Memoir on the transportation of 1,730 Acadians to Louisiana, 1792, PPC, 197:966.

to fund the project, Carlos III in October, 1783, issued a royal *cedula* authorizing Aranda to transport to Louisiana the Acadian population of France.[29]

News of the *cedula* did not reach Paris until late January 1784, just as Peyroux was on the verge of abandoning the colonization project. Reinvigorated by the victory, Peyroux and Terrio mounted a clandestine campaign to recruit colonists. Acting under Peyroux's orders, the Nantes cobbler secretly disseminated reports of the Spanish *cédula* to France's exile communities, while Terrio personally toured Brittany, urging the Acadian residents to join the anticipated migration.[30]

News of the colonization scheme generated tremendous interest and excitement in France's Acadian communities. But the exiles, having no wish to be disappointed again, disregarded orders to cloak the project with secrecy. Converging upon Nantes from several French seaports, an undetermined number of Acadian delegates appeared before the local subdelegates in March, 1784, and demanded to know whether or not the French government had approved their departure from the realm.[31]

This indiscretion prompted an immediate response from the Spanish embassy. Acting upon Peyroux's advice, chevalier de Heredia, Spanish *chargé d'affaires* in Paris, defused potentially devastating French accusations of subversion by making a full disclosure of the Louisiana colonization project to Charles Gravier, comte de Vergennes, France's finance and foreign affairs minister. Heredia concluded his communiqué with a request, in the name of Carlos III, for permission to remove the exiles from France. To demonstrate Acadian support for the Spanish project, Terrio, acting upon Peyroux's instructions, drafted a petition to Vergennes—ultimately signed by thirty-five exiles—enumerating the Acadians' grievances against the French government and requesting permission to establish themselves in Louisiana, where the Spanish monarch had received previous Acadian immigrants "as though they were his own subjects."[32]

29. Winzerling, *Acadian Odyssey*, 96.

30. Peyroux to Terrio, January 24, 1784, PPC, 197:953; Peyroux to Terrio, July 18, 1784, PPC, 197:958; Peyroux to Terrio, August 1, 1784, PPC, 197:959.

31. Peyroux to Heredia, March 18, 1784, quoted in Winzerling, *Acadian Odyssey*, 98, 99; Lauvrière, *Tragédie*, II, 199–200.

32. Winzerling, *Acadian Odyssey*, 99; Petition to comte de Vergennes, April 4, 1784, PPC, 197:954.

While the French government weighed the merits of Hispano-Acadian proposals, creditors of the Acadians in France attempted to scuttle the project by arranging the arrest of its authors, Peyroux and Terrio, who had failed to resolve the festering problem of the exiles' substantial personal debts. Reacting to mounting pressure from local businessmen, Sieur Balais, *intendant subdélégé* of Nantes, invoked a hitherto ignored governmental directive to arrest all secret agents who were "seeking to spirit the Acadians abroad," and dispatched a detachment of archers to "arrest and incarcerate" Peyroux and his Acadian associate. Although the Spanish agent was arrested and imprisoned, Terrio eluded his pursuers, eventually taking refuge at the home of Criminal Judge Bourgoin.[33]

While in hiding, Terrio issued a desperate appeal for assistance to Heredia. As Peyroux carried several diplomatically sensitive documents on his person at the time of his arrest, the Spanish *chargé d'affaires* responded promptly and effectively. Armed with Vergennes' communiqué of May 11 announcing Louis XVI's willingness to cooperate fully with Spain's Louisiana colonization project, Heredia contacted Intendant La Bove and secured from him not only Peyroux's immediate release but also a permanent injunction against "subsequent prosecution of him or his agent."[34]

Sheltered from bureaucratic harassment, Peyroux and Terrio resumed their activities. In conformity with orders issued in late May by Aranda (who had just received royal orders to formalize the government's verbal agreement with Peyroux and "achieve removal of the Acadians from France" at minimal expense) Spain's agents canvassed Acadian settlements throughout France for potential colonists. As in the past, Terrio took the lead in organizing his countrymen: In mid-July, he publicized the new Franco-Spanish accord for unrestricted Acadian emigration from France as well as his "new status as Spain's official agent." Moreover, in early August, he called for signatures from all Acadian volunteers.[35]

33. Terrio to Aranda (1785), PPC, 197:960; Terrio to Heredia, May 27, 1784, PPC, 197:956; Fernando Solano Costa, "Emigración acadiana a la Luisiana española," *Jerónimo Zurita. Cuadernos de Historia*, II (1954), 99; Terrio to Aranda (1785), PPC, 197:960.

34. Terrio to Heredia, May 27, 1784, PPC, 197:956; Terrio to Aranda (1785), PPC, 197:960.

35. Winzerling, *Acadian Odyssey*, 101; Vergennes to Aranda, July 15, 1784, PPC, 197:955; Peyroux to Terrio, August 1, 1784, PPC, 197:959.

The indefatigable Terrio's labors were crowned with mixed results. A small but vocal minority viewed the colonization project as a ploy to discontinue their meager dole. In Nantes, Terrio was "cursed by one, insulted by another, and threatened with murder by a third." Words were translated into action in other Acadian communities. At an inn located in an unidentified French seaport, he was accosted by three Acadian opponents of emigration. A discussion of the Louisiana colonization project soon deteriorated into a shouting match, and according to Terrio, "the most furious of the three . . . assaulted me like a desperado, struck me several times, and would undoubtedly have killed me if some friendly Acadians, who took his knife away, had not intervened."[36]

Violent opposition to emigration from France was atypical; the vast majority of the Acadians in French seaports were cautiously optimistic—even to the point of notifying relatives in Louisiana of a possible reunion. But the exiles had seen numerous illusory resettlement schemes turn to dross in recent years and thus had no intention of committing themselves until the Spanish crown pledged full financial responsibility for the project. Financial aid was of vital importance to the Acadians; although Louis XVI agreed to pay the Acadians' debts in order to facilitate their departure, he refused to continue the dole beyond July. Deprived of the French subsidy, the exiles feared starvation, particularly as Spanish efforts to organize the colonization expedition were far from complete.[37]

The Spanish government responded to the demands in early September, agreeing not only to transport the exiles to Louisiana at the royal exchequer's expense but also to assume responsibility for their support from July, 1784, until the date of departure. In addition, the crown agreed to provide free transportation for the Acadians' French spouses, provided the latter secured permission from the local intendants to emigrate. The exiles were required to congregate at Nantes and to absorb all traveling expenses "as far as Minden."[38]

36. Memoir on the transportation of 1,730 Acadians to Louisiana, 1792, PPC, 197:959; Terrio to Aranda (1785), PPC, 197:960; Solano Costa, "Emigración acadiana," 98, 100.

37. Louis Judice to Estevan Miró, December 19, 1784, PPC, 197:359–60; Winzerling, *Acadian Odyssey*, 100, 104.

38. Solano Costa, "Emigración acadiana," 104, 108–109; Peyroux to Terrio, October 9, 1784, PPC, 197:962.

News of Spain's generosity was disseminated by Peyroux and Ter-rio, with dramatic results. Over 1,500 volunteers—70 percent of the Acadian population in France—rushed to take the oath of allegiance to Carlos III, thereby committing themselves to the colonization project. At least thirty additional Acadian families—many with French spouses—expressed interest.[39]

Having cast their lot with the Spanish government, the Acadians wished to depart immediately. But the exodus was delayed for several months by lengthy negotiations between Spanish representatives and several French mercantile houses. Peyroux, Heredia, and Aranda had negotiated secretly and unsuccessfully with various shipping companies between April and September, 1784. In late September, Manuel d'Asprès, Spanish consul at St. Malo, was entrusted with the task of securing transportation for the exiles. Asprès' hard bargaining produced results; by early November, the consul had secured the services of six large French merchantmen.[40]

The successful completion of Asprès' negotiations with French mercantile firms coincided with an outburst of Acadian dissatisfaction over what they interpreted as unwarranted Spanish procrastination. The exiles realized that the onset of winter meant closure of Nantes's port facilities and would inevitably delay their departure by several months. As this delay had been unforeseen also by the Spanish government, many Acadians feared termination of the Spanish dole. Other exiles, seduced by unfounded rumors of poor living conditions in Louisiana, had grown suspicious of the Spanish government's motives. Coalescing, the dissident groups demanded a determination by the Spanish crown regarding continuation of the dole beyond January 1, 1785, as well as concerning "their lot and destination in Louisiana," as conditions for their continued participation in the colonization project. The Spanish government's response permanently quelled Acadian misgivings about the expedition. The crown promised not only that the dole would be continued until the exiles' departure but also that upon arrival at New Orleans, the colonists would be given food, arable land, implements, and financial support

---

39. The actual number of volunteers was 1,508. Winzerling, *Acadian Odyssey*, 107–109.

40. *Ibid.*, 106, 109–29, 150–51; Peyroux to Terrio, November 16, 1784, PPC, 197: 963; Solano Costa, "Emigración acadiana," 150–51.

until self-sufficient. Convinced finally of the resettlement project's ultimate validity, the exiles endured another winter of inactivity in silence. Then, between mid-May and mid-October, 1785, a total of 1,596 Acadians turned their backs on France, joined the seven transatlantic "expeditions," and faced the challenge of creating a new life in Louisiana.[41]

41. Winzerling, *Acadian Odyssey*, 124–28; Solano Costa, "Emigración acadiana," 107–108; Richard E. Chandler, "A Shipping Contract: Spain Brings Acadians to Louisiana," *Louisiana Review*, VIII (1979), 73–81.

5

Allons à la Louisiane: Acadian Immigration, 1765–1769

Between 1757 and 1770 approximately one thousand Acadians migrated to Louisiana, an underdeveloped colony in which they hoped to reunite families divided during the dispersal, thereby reestablishing life as they had known it in Acadia. Sustained by this dream, Acadians in Saint-Domingue (present-day Haiti), Maryland, Pennsylvania, New York, and Halifax, Nova Scotia, sold the household articles they had carried into exile, as well as their few subsequent acquisitions, to secure passage aboard Louisiana-bound English merchant vessels. Their hope of reuniting with loved ones, upon landing at New Orleans, was dashed by settlement policies rigidly maintained by Antonio de Ulloa, the colony's first Spanish governor. The Acadians' bitter resentment of Ulloa's intransigence prompted them to participate in the New Orleans rebellion of October 29, 1768, which ousted the Spanish chief executive.[1]

Displeasure with Ulloa stemmed largely from his refusal to adhere to the extremely flexible settlement policies of his French predecessors. Although governors and commissaire-ordonnateurs reserved the right to grant property titles, settlers were traditionally permitted to select home sites from any vacant lands. Under this policy the first Acadian immigrants were settled, thereby giving rise to hopes of eventual reunification of the ethnic community.[2]

1. Gabriel Debien, "Les Acadiens a Saint-Domingue," in Conrad (ed.), *The Cajuns,* 255–71; Gipson, *The British Empire,* VI, 243–344.
2. Jean-Jacques-Blaise d'Abbadie to Étienne-François, duc de Choiseul, January 10, 1764, in Series C 13a (Louisiane, Correspondance générale), Volume 44, folio 22, Archives des Colonies, Archives Nationales, Paris, France, microfilm copy on deposit at

Such expectations were entertained most faithfully by the displaced former members of the Acadian resistance. Led by Joseph Broussard *dit* Beausoleil, 193 Acadians departed the Nova Scotian capital in late November, changed ship at Saint-Domingue, and arrived at New Orleans in late February, 1765. The immigrants' impoverishment elicited genuine compassion among Louisiana's leading officials. Although Choiseul, the French minister of marine, had authorized only essential expenditures by the caretaker government, Commissaire-ordonnateur Denis-Nicolas Foucault, chief administrative officer, provided the immigrants, whose number by April, 1765, would grow to 231, with foodstuffs, tools, muskets, and building materials worth 15,500 livres.[3]

The material assistance seriously depleted the royal warehouses at New Orleans, necessitating prompt settlement of the immigrants. In a letter to Choiseul dated February 25, 1765, acting Governor Charles Philippe Aubry, who first encountered the Acadians while a British prisoner of war in "New England" during the early 1760s, indicated that he would "try to place them on the right bank of the river, and as close to town as possible." Examination of the proposed settlement site revealed that the riverfront was not only subject to inundations but was blanketed by dense, hardwood forests as well. Settlers would be required to "build levees and do considerable clearing, which would result in great expense because it would be necessary to feed them for several years in order to give them time to establish themselves." Because of the impediments to settlement on the initial site, sometime between February 25 and 28 Aubry "allowed them to go to Attakapas," a developing post to which several Creole families had recently migrated from Fort Toulouse and Mobile, trans-Appalachian posts that had been ceded to England. The treeless Attakapas prairies, Aubry noted, could be settled quickly, and their broad grasslands were also quite conducive to cattle production. Development of the cattle industry at Attakapas was vital, the acting

---

Center for Louisiana Studies, University of Southwestern Louisiana; hereinafter cited as AC, C 13a, with volume and folio numbers.

3. Denis-Nicolas Foucault to Choiseul, February 28, 1765, AC, C 13a, 45:108; Aubry to Choiseul, February 25, 1765. AC, C 13a, 45:42; "List of provisions and supplies delivered to the Acadian families who have taken refuge in Louisiana, April 30, 1765," AC, C 13a, 45:30; Aubry and Foucault to Choiseul, April 30, 1765, AC, C 13a, 45:21–24.

governor argued, because "since the cession of Mobile, we are entirely without cattle." Finally, the cattle produced at Attakapas could support New Orleans in times of war, because the post's lines of communication with the capital were not exposed to British raids.[4]

The Acadians' role as ranchers was assured on April 4, when eight leaders agreed to raise cattle on shares for Antoine Bernard Dauterive, a retired French military officer and a large Attakapas landholder. Under terms of the contract, Acadians agreed to tend Dauterive's livestock for six years; in consideration for their labor, they would receive not only half of the herd's increase but also the land grant Dauterive and his partner, Edouard Masse, had acquired in 1760.[5]

The Acadians' actions were clearly endorsed by the French colonial administration. In late April Aubry and Foucault stated, "We were persuaded [to approve the contract] all the more readily, for the fertility of these lands . . . will shortly place them, the majority of whom are very industrious farmers, in a position to . . . furnish the needs of this city [New Orleans]."[6]

Governmental support of the settlement project was also evidenced in material assistance. In a report dated April 30, Foucault indicated that the prospective Attakapas settlers had been given sufficient flour, hardtack, hulled rice, and salt pork and beef to support them for six months. As the exiles were expected to support themselves when their provisions were exhausted, the ordonnateur also provided them with tools to clear their lands, as well as with seed rice and corn.[7]

Having furnished the Acadians the necessities of frontier life, Foucault and Aubry directed Louis Andry, a veteran military engineer, to conduct them to the former Dauterive-Masse concession via Bayou Plaquemine and the network of waterways lacing the Atchafalaya Basin. According to carefully worded instructions, Andry, al-

4. Aubry to Choiseul, April 24, 1765, AC, C 13a, 45:41–42; Aubry to Choiseul, May 14, 1765, AC, C 13a, 45:56–56vo; Aubry to Choiseul, February 25, 1765, AC, C 13a, 45:50–51.

5. Grover Rees (trans.), "The Dauterive Compact: The Foundation of the Acadian Cattle Industry," *Attakapas Gazette*, XI (1976), 91.

6. Aubry and Foucault to Choiseul, April 30, 1765, AC, C 13a, 45:21–24.

7. List of provisions and supplies, April 30, 1765, AC, C 13a, 45:30; Aubry and Foucault to Choiseul, April 30, 1765, AC, C 13a, 45:21–24.

though retaining supreme command over the expedition, was to work very closely with Broussard, leader of the Attakapas-bound Acadians, to lay out a village, establish a commons around the community, and distribute lands beyond the commons to the families—the size of the land grants being contingent upon the number of family members.[8]

Although Aubry and Foucault clearly intended that the Acadians reside in the village and cultivate outlying lands in the European tradition, it is apparent that the settlers prevailed upon the colonial engineer to establish them on widely separated parcels of land between La Manque (near present-day Breaux Bridge) and Fausse Pointe (present-day Loreauville), thereby duplicating the settlement patterns of their native Acadia.[9] The resulting rural communities constituted a noteworthy departure from the expressed intentions of the colonial regime, but the settlement program's administrators exhibited their characteristic laissez-faire attitude toward land occupation. If the Acadians had no intention of settling in a village, why did Louisiana's chief officials devote a remarkable amount of time and attention to the portion of Andry's instructions regarding the anticipated settlement? The answer lies in the directive's opening paragraph: "We have ordered Sr. Andry to leave this city with the Acadian families and to go to the district of the Attakapas, and in agreement with them to choose the most suitable site for the establishment of a village *where these new colonists wish to be reunited*" (emphasis added).[10] It is apparent that the colonists wished to be reunited with the exiled families whose impending arrival they

8. Andry was assisted by Francois Olivier de Vezin, *fils*. Foucault to Choiseul, April 30, 1765, AC, C 13a, 45:112vo; Edward T. Weeks, "Some Facts and Traditions About New Iberia," in Glenn R. Conrad (comp.), *New Iberia: Essays on the Town and Its People* (Lafayette, La., 1979), 17–18; Aubry to Choiseul, April 24, 1765, AC, C 13a, 45:50–50vo; Jacqueline K. Voorhies (trans.), "The Attakapas Post: The First Acadian Settlement," *Louisiana History*, XVII (1976), 91–96; Grover Rees, *A Narrative History of Breaux Bridge, Once Called "La Pointe"* (Lafayette, La., 1976), 13–14.

9. Jacqueline K. Voorhies (comp.), *Some Late Eighteenth-Century Louisianians* (Lafayette, La., 1973), 124–25; Voorhies (trans.), "The Attakapas Post," 92–94; Jean-Baptiste Grevemberg's complaint about the Acadian squatters on his property, July 1, 1763, in Pintado Papers, Book 1, Part 2, Opelousas Office, Attakapas Region, Land Claims in the United States Land Office, Register of State Lands, Baton Rouge, Louisiana, microfilm copy on deposit at Jefferson Caffery Louisiana Room, Dupré Library, University of Southwestern Louisiana.

10. Voorhies (trans.), "The Attakapas Post," 92.

prophesied. Indeed, it is no coincidence that Fr. Jean-François, who accompanied the Halifax Acadians to Attakapas, christened the post "New Acadia."[11]

Hopes for reunification at Attakapas were shattered. Neglected by France since the outset of the Seven Years' War, Louisiana's royal warehouses were almost completely bare by 1765.[12] Moreover the province's depleted storehouses had been practically exhausted by the arrival of the first Acadians. Foucault, who again sympathized with the exiles' plight, was unable to extend his customary generosity to immigrants who followed. In mid-May, the ordonnateur reported that "The 80 [exiles] who were the subject of my letter of May 4 . . . cause me much anxiety. They are overwhelmed by misery and request lands upon which to establish themselves. Nothing would be easier than to give them some [property] at Opelousas or Attakapas, where the others are, but how can I enable them to go there? They require provisions, tools, supplies, boats, and the royal warehouses are completely empty."[13] Lacking alternative solutions, Foucault was compelled to furnish to the immigrants goods purchased from local merchants for 8,890 livres, but the May arrivals were compelled to settle "along the right [bank] of the [Mississippi] River, above the German District."[14]

This precedent of establishing settlements along the lower Mississippi was followed by Governor Antonio de Ulloa. Although he refused to take official possession of Louisiana, after arriving at New Orleans on March 5, 1766, Ulloa focused his attention upon colonial defense. Through the Treaty of Paris (1763), French Louisiana east of the Mississippi River was transferred to Great Britain. France's most powerful Indian allies—the Choctaw, Creek, and Cherokee tribes—

11. Foucault to Choiseul, August 8, 1765, AC, C 13a, 45:152; "Copie d'un vieux registre de St. Martin de Tours," typescript of the oldest St. Martin de Tours Catholic Church registers, in Jefferson Caffery Louisiana Room, Dupré Library, University of Southwestern Louisiana; hereinafter cited as "Copie d'un vieux registre."

12. Carl A. Brasseaux, "L'Officier de Plume: Denis-Nicolas Foucault, commissaire-ordonnateur of French Louisiana, 1762–1769" (M.A. thesis, University of Southwestern Louisiana, 1975), 24–107.

13. Foucault to Choiseul, May 13, 1765, AC, C 13a, 45:118vo-19; Foucault to Choiseul, April 30, 1765, AC, C 13a, 45:112vo; Aubry and Foucault to Choiseul, May 4, 1765, AC, C 13a, 45:115.

14. The actual amount was 8,890 livres, 9 sols, 5 deniers. Foucault to Choiseul, August 8, 1765, AC, C 13a, 45:152; Foucault and Aubry to Choiseul, September 30, 1765, AC, C 13a, 45:31vo-32.

subsequently were subjected to an intensive British propaganda campaign. As Louisiana enjoyed no natural defenses and as British Indian agents labored unceasingly to alter the local balance of power by persuading some tribal bands to migrate to the intercolonial frontier, the colony was—as the Spanish correctly concluded—vulnerable to attack along its extensive eastern border. In mid-June, 1766, Ulloa devised a scheme of thwarting potential English aggression by juxtaposing Spanish forts to newly established British installations at Natchez and Manchac. Complementing the Spanish fortifications were extensive riverside settlements from which the government could draw men and supplies in wartime.[15]

Ulloa's anti-British strategy profoundly influenced his settlement policy. In late June, 1766, he appointed commandants for the predominately Acadian districts of Cabannocé, Attakapas, and Opelousas. Though invested with civil and judicial authority, these local magistrates were fundamentally local military officers and Indian agents. Established colonial defenses were enhanced by the subsequent settlement of Acadian immigrants at strategic locations. In late September, 224 exiles, who had sailed from Maryland to Louisiana aboard a chartered English ship, were settled along the Mississippi River in the region now known as the Acadian Coast (St. James and Ascension parishes). An undetermined number who arrived at Balise in December, 1766, soon joined them. Similarly, 210 Acadians from Maryland who reached Balise aboard the *Jane* on July 12, 1767, were settled by Ulloa at "Fort St. Gabriel." Finally, in compliance with the Spanish governor's policy statement of late July, 149 Acadian exiles who landed at New Orleans on February 4, 1768, were dispatched to Fort San Luis de Natchez in three boats commanded by Pedro Piernas.[16]

15. For a sympathetic account of Ulloa's brief, albeit stormy career in Louisiana, see John Preston Moore, *Revolt in Louisiana: The Spanish Occupation, 1766–1770* (Baton Rouge, 1976). For a view of the Ulloa administration from the French perspective, see Brasseaux, *"L'Officier de Plume"*; Ulloa to Jerónimo Grimaldi, May 19, 1766, in Audiencia de Santo Domingo, and June 19, 1766, both Legajo 2585, nonpaginated, Archivo General de Indias, Seville, Spain; microfilm copy on deposit at Center for Louisiana Studies, University of Southwestern Louisiana; hereinafter cited as ASD, with legajo and folio numbers.

16. Ulloa to Grimaldi, June 25, 1766, ASD, 2585:n.p.; Ulloa to Grimaldi, September 29, 1766, ASD, 2585:n.p.; Aubry to Ulloa, December 16, 1766, PPC, 187A:n.p. Ulloa indicates in his correspondence that there were 211 Acadian immigrants, but the

The dispersal of Louisiana's Acadian population among the province's nascent military posts was unquestionably traumatic. Subordination of the Acadian aspirations to military exigencies, however, cannot be attributed to callousness on Ulloa's part. The Spanish governor genuinely sympathized with the destitute immigrants and greatly admired their industry. In a communiqué to Marqués Jeronimo Grimaldi, Spanish ambassador to France, he praised the exiles. Indeed, Ulloa maintained that two slaves could not "accomplish in a year what one of these indefatigable men can do, so much, in fact, that some [Acadians] have died of exhaustion."[17]

Acadians possessed additional traits that made them even more attractive as colonists. Governor Aubry and other French officers assured Ulloa that the exiles were excellent soldiers, having demonstrated their ability and valor "against the British as well as in the type of warfare conducted against the Indians." Such citizen soldiers, Ulloa noted, were of particular "importance in this colony which must always depend upon the settlers for its defense." With such fighters in the colony's arsenal, the Spanish governor boasted, he could "insure the border" against a 100,000-man invasion force. The military prowess of the Acadians, complemented by their virulent anglophobia and group solidarity, not only fostered tranquillity but obviously hardened them against potential English-inspired sedition.[18]

Antonio de Ulloa's initial high regard for the Acadians was reciprocated. Throughout his first year in office, he enjoyed the immigrants' favor for the material assistance he provided them, which compared favorably with that extended by the French regime. In 1766, Ulloa indicated that for 200 *pesos* he provided each incoming family six hens, one rooster, one cow either with calf or pregnant, 160 to 240

official roll includes only 210 names. Richard E. Chandler (trans. and ed.), "End of an Odyssey: Acadians Arrive in St. Gabriel, Louisiana," *Louisiana History*, XIV (1973), 81–87. Ulloa incorrectly lists their point of origin as Virginia. Ulloa to Grimaldi, July 23, 1767, ASD, 2585:n.p. The *Jane*, commanded by Captain Richard Ryder, took on 150 French Neutrals at Patuxent, Maryland, on March 2, 1767. The *Jane* apparently replaced the Louisiana-bound *Virgin*, commanded by Captain Thomas Gerrald, which was scheduled to take on Acadians at Baltimore and Patuxent in early May, 1767. Passport for the *Jane*, March 2, 1767, PPC, 187A:n.p.; Annapolis *Maryland Gazette*, March 26, 1767; Pedro Piernas to Ulloa, June 5, 1767, PPC, 187A:n.p.

17. Ulloa to Grimaldi, May 19, 1766, ASD, 2585:n.p.
18. *Ibid.*

superficial arpents of land, corn, gunpowder, bullets, and a musket. It should be noted, however, that the French administration, which continued to operate in New Orleans because of the governor's persistent refusal to take official possession of the colony, funded the settlement program throughout 1766 and early 1767.[19]

Although Ulloa failed to provide the Acadians secondary or follow-up assistance, and although each wave of immigrants fell prey to smallpox, dysentery, and endemic fevers, life was far better in Louisiana than it had been during the exile. The Acadians thus were unrestrained in their affinity for the Spanish regime. Ulloa witnessed one such demonstration of loyalty during his tour of Acadian settlements in April, 1766. After presenting each family with small quantities of shot and gunpowder, he was overwhelmed by the show of profound gratitude. When he subsequently extended the full protection of the Spanish crown, the Acadians, "moved by the greatest demonstration of love," fired rounds of musketry in celebration, promised to serve Carlos III with the same fidelity they had shown Louis XV, and secured permission to "write their fellow Acadians in New England in order that the latter may escape . . . [their] captivity."[20]

Acadian loyalty to the Spanish regime was predicated largely upon the governor's apparent willingness to provide a new homeland in which the exiles could gather. This fact is most clearly reflected in the circumstances surrounding the establishment of St. Gabriel in 1767. Acting upon Ulloa's authorization, settlers corresponded with their kinsmen in Maryland, notifying them of the Spanish regime's willingness to accept them. Spurred by this encouragement, Maryland exiles secured passage to Louisiana. Upon arrival they were exasperated to learn they could not be settled at Cabannocé; instead they were to be settled near Fort St. Gabriel, twenty-five miles up-

19. *Ibid.*; Foucault to Choiseul, November 18, 1766, AC, C 13a, 46:73–74; Brasseaux, "*L'Officier de Plume*," 116; Foucault to Dubuq, March 30, 1767, AC, C 13a, 47:34–35vo.

20. Interview with descendants of Catherine Pierre: Carolyn Stemley, "Attakapas Indian Healers," File 181, in Center for Acadian and Creole Folklore, University of Southwestern Louisiana; Aubry to Choiseul, May 14, 1765, AC, C 13a, 45:56–56vo; Delavillebeuvre to Ulloa, September 18, 1768, PPC, 187A:n.p.; Verret to Ulloa, June 10, 1766, PPC, 187A:n.p.; Jacques Le Duc to Ulloa, September 23, 1767, PPC, 187A:n.p.; "Copie d'un vieux registre," 2–11; Ulloa to Grimaldi, May 19, 1766, ASD, 2585:n.p.

stream. They voiced their objections, indicating they had no intention of establishing themselves at this frontier post.[21]

Ulloa bitterly resented the "ingratitude," and he dealt firmly with
them. He recalled the resulting confrontation in his memoirs.

> A group of Acadians arrived [at New Orleans] in the month of July or
> August 1767. We destined them for Fort St. Gabriel, but, as they put
> it into their heads [that we] must permit [some of] them to remain va-
> grants in the city [and allow] the others to occupy lands contiguous to
> those of the other Acadians who were established opposite the Caban-
> nocé coast, we had all of the trouble in the world to subject them to
> our arrangements. It was necessary to tell them that, if they did not
> wish to take themselves there, it would be necessary to expel them
> from the colony, as it [their intransigence] was unprecedented, for His
> Majesty, who satisfied all of the needs of a destitute nation, must be
> allowed to prescribe these conditions [of settlement].[22]

Faced with expulsion from Louisiana, the Acadians reluctantly ac-
quiesced in Ulloa's demands, and, once they were established at St.
Gabriel, ceased grumbling, apparently realizing that the communities at Attakapas and Cabannocé were readily accessible by boat.
They were also preoccupied with an epidemic. Ill will toward the
Spanish regime nevertheless persisted among both the St. Gabriel
and Cabannocé Acadians, surfacing once more when 149 fellow
Marylanders arrived in February, 1768. According to Ulloa, the February arrivals "exhibited no reluctance in going to their destination
which was San Luis de Natchez," but contact with "their compatriots
established at Cabannocé," who obviously recounted the disappoint-
ments of the St. Gabriel settlers, caused the immigrants to become
"quickly disenchanted" with the Spaniard's settlement scheme.[23]

Most vocal in their opposition to Ulloa's plans were Honoré and
Alexis Braud. Natives of Pisiquid, Nova Scotia, the brothers had been
exiled to different Maryland counties in 1755. Now, twelve years

21. Ulloa to Grimaldi, May 19, 1766, ASD, 2585:n.p.; Kinnaird (ed.), *Spain in the
Mississippi Valley*, II, Pt. 1, 35–37.
22. Ulloa, "Observations on the memorial presented by the settlers to the Superior
Council," 1769. AC, C 13a, 47:120.
23. *Ibid.*, 47:120–21vo; Jacques Le Duc to Ulloa, September 23, 1767, PPC,
187A:n.p.; Richard E. Chandler (trans. and ed.), "Odyssey Continued: Acadians Arrive in Natchez," *Louisiana History*, XIX (1978), 447.

later, they led 152 friends and relatives to New Orleans in hope of reuniting the Braud clan. Their dream of joining families now settled at Cabannocé was shattered when Ensign Andrés de Balderrama conveyed Ulloa's intention to settle the new arrivals at San Luis de Natchez. Honoré Braud, whose memoirs are preserved in France's Archives Nationales, clearly interpreted the distribution of Louisiana's Acadian population among widely separated military posts as a diaspora and balked at the prospect of being settled 115 linear miles from Cabannocé.[24] When Governor Aubry's impassioned plea for cooperation from Acadians failed to produce results, Ulloa again acted through Balderrama, attempting to pressure the immigrant leader into submission by "suspending Braud's customary ration." When Honoré Braud refused a second order, several days later, to settle at Natchez, he was instructed by Balderrama to board the *Guinea,* upon which he had sailed to New Orleans. Faced with deportation, Honoré accompanied by his brother Alexis, called upon Ulloa, informing him that despite "substantial [British] inducements" to remain in Maryland, he and his fellow exiles had sailed to Louisiana in order to "exercise freely their religion." Honoré and Alexis Braud "begged Monsieur Ulloa to allow them [the February arrivals] to settle along the German Coast or that of the Acadians, for they had cost the king nothing and had consumed the small amount of money which they possessed."[25]

The Spanish leader rejected the Braud brothers' proposals and persisted in his efforts to deport the Acadian "chiefs." According to Honoré Braud, Ulloa then ordered the February immigrants to join their families and embark upon the *Guinea.* They took their families to the dock and boarded the ship upon which they had come, and in which they would have departed, "if they had not feared . . . that they would be arrested at Balize, for subsequent dispersal and deportation to several areas." These fears compelled the Honoré and

24. Bona Arsenault, *Histoire et généalogie des Acadiens* (6 vols.; 2nd ed.; Quebec, 1978), V, 1347–49; Humble petition of the neutral settlers from Acadia detained in the province of Maryland, July 7, 1763, AE, 450:436; Chandler (trans. and ed.), "Odyssey Continued," 446–47; Procès-verbal of the depositions regarding the vexations caused by Antonio de Ulloa, November 8–15, 1768, AC, C 13a, 48:135.
25. Ulloa, "Observations," 1769, AC, C 13a, 48:134vo–35; Procès-verbal of the depositions, November 8–15, 1768, AC, C 13a, 48:135.

Alexis Braud families to leave the ship before departure and go into hiding at a hut on André Jung's farm.[26]

Abandoned by their leaders, the remaining Acadians also disembarked, but faced with the prospect of deportation and prolonged destitution, they succumbed to Ulloa's demand that they settle at Natchez. They were individually summoned before Balderrama and Pedro de Piernas, the Natchez commandant, who happened to be in New Orleans, and were ordered to declare whether or not they "wished to establish themselves on the land assigned to them." They made one more futile appeal to the Spanish for land grants at Cabannocé, and when Ulloa persisted in his decision to populate San Luis with the Braud-led Acadians, they lodged a formal complaint with French Commissaire-ordonnateur Denis-Nicolas Foucault, then first judge of the Superior Council, Louisiana's chief judicial body. Having abandoned the large warehouse in present-day Algiers, in which they had been housed since their arrival in New Orleans, and having had the last word in the matter, the Acadians boarded three *bateaux* in late February for the arduous upriver trek to their new home.[27]

The departure of their friends and relatives did not break the Braud brothers' will to resist. Shortly, thereafter, Alexis Braud purchased Joseph Ducros' Cabannocé farm—with acting French Governor Aubry's knowledge—and then audaciously settled there with his family. Apparently informed by Aubry of Braud's actions, Ulloa, in late April, 1768, directed Cabannocé commandant Louis Judice to "send for and tie up" the impudent exiles. Judice accordingly summoned Braud, but the latter, feigning illness, sought and secured a three-day delay of sentence, and "cognizant of the poor treatment which Monsieur Ulloa had prepared for him as well as his family," he fled the post with the assistance of fellow Acadian Charles Gaudet. Judice ordered an Acadian militia detachment to arrest the fugitive and conduct him to the quarters of Sieur Durolin, commandant of Fort des Allemands, for ultimate deportation. The militiamen, however, openly rebelled, notifying Judice that "they simply did not

26. Procès-verbal of the depositions, November 8–15, 1768, AC, C 13a, 48:135vo.
27. *Ibid.*, 134vo–35vo; Ulloa, "Observations," 1769, AC, C 13a, 47:122vo–23; Chandler (trans. and ed.), "Odyssey Continued," 457; Piernas to Ulloa, February 29, 1768, PPC, 2357:n.p.

want to arrest their *confrère.*" Insubordination stemming from the Braud incident was so widespread at Cabannocé that Ulloa was compelled to notify the Acadians that "if in the future they refused to obey his [Judice's] orders . . . their belongings would be confiscated and they would be expelled from the colony." Judice was also directed to suspend the exiles' rations.[28]

Civil disobedience was not confined to Cabannocé. At Côte des Allemands, a similar manhunt had been ordered in late April for Honoré Braud, who had sought refuge at the Jacques Enoul Duguay de Livaudais farm, apparently at the same time his brother negotiated for Ducros' Cabannocé *habitation,* but according to Honoré, "Monsieur Livaudais petitioned Monsieur Darensbourg [commandant at the Côte des Allemands post], and he closed his eyes."[29]

Flagrant disregard for Ulloa's authority was also evidenced among the Brauds' Natchez-bound relatives. After departing New Orleans on February 20, 1768, they put ashore at Cabannocé to take on Commandant Nicolas Verret, who had been ordered by Ulloa to act as tour guide for Jacob Walker, an Irishman representing a group of potential Maryland Catholic immigrants. In compliance with Verret's instructions, the convoy stopped whenever possible at the settlements of Cabannocé and at St. Gabriel to make Walker "appreciate the fact that people who arrived as late as July have already cleared and opened up their land; are living in their own houses; are herding a little livestock; and no doubt will do some planting this year." As Walker and Verret inspected the river posts, the Braud immigrants sought and located relatives at Cabannocé and St. Gabriel, where a portion of the clan had established themselves in 1766. It is thus hardly surprising that the travelers—sixty-one of whom were members of the Braud family—quickly rued their decision to settle at San Luis and plotted their return to the existing settlements.[30]

28. Procès-verbal of the depositions, November 8–15, 1768. AC, C 13a, 48:130–30vo, 135vo–36; Judice to Ulloa, April 25, 1768, PPC, 187A:n.p.; Judice to Ulloa, April 29, 1768, PPC, 187A:n.p.; Judice to Ulloa, May 30, 1768, PPC, 187A:n.p.; Ulloa to Judice, June 6, 1768, PPC, 187A:n.p.

29. Procès-verbal of the depositions, November 8–15, 1768, AC, C 13a, 48:136.

30. Since July 31, 1767, when Ulloa sent an unsigned letter to Henry Jerningham, the Spanish governor had been actively recruiting Maryland Catholics as Louisiana colonists. Kinnaird (ed.), *Spain in the Mississippi Valley,* II, Pt. 1, 36–42; Verret to Ulloa, March 26, 1768, PPC, 2357:n.p.; Ulloa to Judice, February, 1768, PPC, 187A:n.p.;

A relocation scheme was implemented upon their arrival at Natchez on March 20, 1768. Animated by what Ulloa termed "insubordination . . . a sense of liberty and independence, and the little regard they show for the advantages which they have just received under the protection of His Majesty," the immigrants adamantly refused to establish their families at San Luis. When the convoy landed at Natchez, Verret inspected the prospective home sites with several Acadian leaders, and although he pronounced them habitable, "none of the Acadians wished to remain there." The exiles, while "conceding that the land is good," maintained—despite Verret's repeated statements to the contrary—that the settlement sites were "remote" and exposed to Indian raids.[31]

In the face of this intransigence, Pedro Piernas assembled the exiles on March 27 and heard their grievances, but despite his remarkable flexibility and willingness to accommodate the settlers as much as he could, the immigrants persisted in their opposition to the proposed San Luis settlement. Piernas soon became so exasperated with his charges—whom he now commonly labeled as "troublesome," "demanding," and "impertinent"—that he cursed his assignment, stating in his official report: "I would rather lead an army than six of these families." As negotiations had clearly broken down, the Acadians appointed three representatives, including Joseph Braud, the most outspoken critic of the Natchez colonization project and cousin of the fugitives Alexis and Honoré; provided the delegates with letters of procuration; and directed them to petition Ulloa personally for permission "to evacuate the post."[32]

The delegates' mission to New Orleans only served to alienate the once sympathetic Ulloa. After hearing arguments for resettlement at Cabannocé, he threatened the deputies with imprisonment aboard the *Volante*, a Spanish frigate moored in the Mississippi River, and

Chandler (trans. and ed.), "Odyssey Continued," 450, 455–56; Piernas to Ulloa, March 8, 1768, PPC, 2357:n.p.

31. "Mandate which will be shown to the Acadians at Natchez in the name of His Majesty," 1768, PPC, 187A:n.p.; Verret to Ulloa, March 26, 1768, PPC, 2357:n.p.; Piernas to Ulloa, March 26, 1768, PPC, 2357:n.p.

32. Piernas to Ulloa, March 26, 1768, PPC, 2357:n.p.; "Mandate," 1768, PPC, 187A:n.p.; Piernas to Ulloa, March 8, 1768, PPC, 2357:n.p.; Piernas to Ulloa, March 27, 1768, PPC, 2357:n.p.; Piernas to Ulloa, March 27, 1768, PPC, 187A:n.p.; Ulloa, "Observations," 1769, AC, C 13a, 47:124vo.

then summarily dismissed them with a threat to deport the entire Natchez contingent. The threats were followed by regulations establishing stringent controls over the Natchez settlers. Acting in conformity with a "mandate" entrusted with the Natchez representatives, Piernas convoked a meeting of the immigrants within his jurisdiction on April 23 and delivered an ultimatum: either accept land to be assigned near Fort San Luis or face deportation as well as financial responsibility for the Spanish expenditures on their behalf. Facing a second diaspora, the exiles, who only three days before had persisted in their "repugnance" toward the settlement site, "readily accepted" the proffered lands.[33]

Having coerced the Acadians into settling at San Luis, Ulloa established means for permanently restricting them to the Natchez district. On April 4 the Spanish governor issued a circular letter requiring the commandants at Attakapas, Opelousas, Allemands, Cabannocé, and Pointe Coupée to "prevent . . . any newly arrived Acadian from residing" at their respective posts. Residents of these regions were also banned from harboring fugitive Acadians under pain of property confiscation.[34]

Acting in conformity with Ulloa's decree, Commandant Duplessis of Pointe Coupée published, in mid-April, an ordinance "conforming perfectly to the import" of the circular letter. Deprived of a vital stopover for a large-scale migration to Cabannocé, the Natchez Acadians were cowed into submission. By late 1768 the Acadians had selected home sites, begun construction of their homes, completed a road from "the first *habitation*" to Fort San Luis, and agreed to organize a militia company. The industriousness persisted throughout the summer, despite an epidemic of dysentery that decimated the children. Though the exiles accepted hard work and illness as an unpleasant fact of everyday life, they could not brook arbitrary treatment. The forced settlement of the exiles at Natchez created a legacy of bitterness among the colony's entire Acadian population, for Ulloa had clearly subordinated their aspirations for familial reunification to strategic considerations.[35]

33. Procès-verbal of the depositions, November 8–15, 1768, AC, C 13a, 48:136vo; "Mandate," 1768, PPC, 2357:n.p.; Ulloa, "Observations," 1769, AC, C 13a, 47:124–26; Piernas to Ulloa, April 30, 1768, PPC, 2357:n.p.

34. Circular letter resulting from the mandate, April 4, 1768, PPC, 187A:n.p.

35. Duplessis to Ulloa, April 4, 1768, PPC, 187A:n.p.; Proclamation by Duplessis

Acadian ill will was gauged by Lieutenant Governor Montfort Browne of British West Florida, who secretly visited the exiles' river settlements during his tour of English Manchac and Natchez in late spring, 1768. According to Browne, the Acadians had become so disenchanted with the Spanish regime that "they wish themselves again in our colonies."[36]

The resentment felt toward Ulloa by Acadians along the lower Mississippi was enhanced by his efforts to separate members of the Joseph Braud family. While en route to Natchez in March, 1768, Joseph, succeeding his cousins as one of two chiefs of the Maryland immigrants, had secured permission to leave his wife—who had recently given birth to a son—and three children at his father-in-law's St. Gabriel farm. Serving as a representative of the disgruntled Natchez Acadians in April, Braud sought gubernatorial permission to settle permanently "next to" his wife's family. Not only was his inopportune request rejected, but he was threatened with deportation unless he returned to Natchez with his family. Although Braud replied impudently that he preferred expulsion to life at Natchez, he soon relented, returning with his fellow representatives to Fort San Luis. Shortly thereafter he dutifully "descended" to St. Gabriel to retrieve his family. Upon arrival at the lower river post, he discovered that his family had been stricken with an undetermined malady. Verret, who feared that the illness was contrived, required Braud to secure a medical certificate and then, realizing that his departure would not take place immediately, ordered Braud in late June to secure a temporary stay of sentence from Ulloa.[37]

Though the outcome of Joseph Braud's subsequent petition to Ulloa is unknown, it is certain that the Spanish administration's persistent efforts to separate the reunited Braud family alienated the lower Mississippi's large Acadian population. The exiles were quite receptive to the anti-Spanish propaganda of a small but powerful

at Pointe Coupée, April 17, 1768, PPC, 187A:n.p.; Piernas to Ulloa, May 29, 1768, PPC, 2357:n.p.; Piernas to Ulloa, May 18, 1768, PPC, 2357:n.p.

36. Montfort Browne to the Earl of Hillsborough, July 6, 1768, in Record Group 585, folios 160–62, Colonial Office, Public Record Office, London, England, microfilm copy on deposit at Center for Louisiana Studies, University of Southwestern Louisiana; hereinafter cited as CO, with record group and folio numbers.

37. Verret to Ulloa, June 30, 1768, PPC, 187A:n.p.; Procès-verbal of the depositions, November 8–15, 1768, AC, C 13a, 48:136vo–37; Ulloa, "Observations," 1769, AC, C 13a, 47:129–30; Verret to Ulloa, June 17, 1768, PPC, 187A:n.p.

clique of French Louisianians, led by Attorney General Nicolas Chauvin de Lafrénière. Certain that they had been drawn to the colony under false pretenses, the Acadians awaited an opportunity to retaliate. The New Orleans rebels provided that chance in late October, 1768. On the night of October 26, three of Lafrénière's lieutenants—Jean-Baptiste de Noyan, Joseph Milhet, and Ensign Bienville de Noyan—persuaded an undetermined number of Cabannocé Acadians who were "disgusted with Ulloa's administration," to take up arms against the Spanish regime. Under the pretext of pressuring Ulloa into redeeming 107,517 livres in Canadian paper currency that the French government had failed to honor, the Acadians marched unarmed to New Orleans. Upon arrival at the Crescent City in early afternoon, October 28, five hundred Acadians and German Coast residents were led by insurrectionist Pierre Caresse to the François Chauvin de Léry residence, where they were supplied muskets and generous drafts of Bordeaux wine. Their fighting spirit bolstered by French liquor, the exiles assisted the rebels in ousting Ulloa, their misguided benefactor.[38]

Although the ousted Spanish regime was temporarily replaced by a more sympathetic revolutionary council, the Natchez Acadians remained on their concessions, apparently fearing the consequences of southward migration in the event of Spanish reoccupation. The Cabannocé families shared their relatives' fear of the return of Spanish rule in Louisiana and subsequent prosecution for high treason. Acadians along the lower river joined their German neighbors in offering token resistance to Spanish Governor Alejandro O'Reilly's two-thousand-man army of occupation in August, 1769. The immi-

---

38. David Ker Texada, *Alejandro O'Reilly and the New Orleans Rebels* (Lafayette, La., 1970), 29, 56, 77, 85, 88, 89; Aubry and Foucault to Choiseul, April 30, 1765, AC, C 13a, 45:21–24; "Recapitulation of the receipts furnished by one [St.] Maxent to the Acadians, (February, 1765)," AC, C 13a, 45:29; "Ledger of the paper currency forwarded by Sr. Maxent to his French correspondent, who is charged with soliciting payment, March 8, 1766," ASD, 2585:n.p.; Ulloa to Grimaldi, March 9, 1766, ASD, 2585:n.p.; Ulloa to Grimaldi, December 4, 1768, quoted in Charles Étienne Arthur Gayarré, *History of Louisiana* (4 vols.; 1854–66; rpr. New Orleans, 1965), II, 236; O'Reilly to Judice, September 6, 1769, PPC, 187A:n.p. On the Spanish perception of the Acadian participation in the Rebellion of 1768, see Moore, *Revolt in Louisiana*, 150–53. The Acadians were apparently housed at the New Orleans residence of a man named Denville (Derneville?) on the night of October 28. See Texada, *Alejandro O'Reilly*, 88–89.

grants' fears were unfounded; the Irish-born chief executive not only granted amnesty to the Cabannocé inhabitants but also lent a sympathetic ear to the grievances of the Natchez settlers. In a petition dated October 18, 1769, the "Acadians established above Fort San Luis de Natchez" notified O'Reilly that they were "continuously exposed to assassination" by local, warlike Indians and requested permission to join their relatives at St. Gabriel. San Luis Commandant Jean Delavillebeuvre and post Engineer Guy Dufossat, in an addendum to the petition, agreed that the Acadians' position was untenable. As the nearest farm was one league distant from the fort, settlers were vulnerable to raids by the two thousand Indians the British had recently amassed near Natchez, and the lands upon which the exiles were established were also acknowledged to be "quite sterile." In early November, Aubry advised O'Reilly that the Acadian requests were "just" and "sound." Acting upon the aforementioned recommendations in late December, 1769, the Spanish governor permitted the Natchez residents to select lands "twenty to thirty leagues . . . above the capital." The Acadian dream was now realized, and the exiles were wedded to the Spanish regime.[39]

39. Texada, *Alejandro O'Reilly*, 56, 61; O'Reilly to Judice, September 6, 1769, PPC, 187A:n.p.; Petition to O'Reilly from the Acadians established at San Luis de Natchez, October 18, 1769, ASD, 2585:n.p.; O'Reilly to Grimaldi, December 29, 1769, ASD, 2585:n.p.

6

Acadian Settlement Patterns

Acadian participation in the Rebellion of 1768 demonstrates the importance of settlement patterns in the collective Louisiana experience. Yet this most significant feature of Acadian life has long suffered from scholarly neglect, primarily because Louisiana historians have generally failed to recognize the significant sociocultural differences existing among the state's various Francophone groups. As a result, French speakers in proximity to the Acadian settlements—even those traditionally hostile to the exiles' descendants—have been lumped together with genuine Acadians under the euphemistic label *Cajun.* With few exceptions, chroniclers of the Pelican State's past, particularly modern-day state historians, have offered either overly broad or extremely narrow views of the area of Acadian occupation, with estimates ranging from the entire southwestern quarter of the state to only the Bayou Teche and Vermilion River valleys. These misconceptions have filtered down to the general public, thereby perpetuating popular and long-enduring false impressions regarding original settlement sites. Dissemination of such misinformation was accelerated in the 1970s and 1980s by the emergence of Louisiana's Cajuns as a phenomenon of international interest that drew tourists, journalists, and scholars from all corners of the globe. Eager to capitalize upon the influx, local government agencies, tourist bureaus, and business groups produced vast quantities of promotional material designed to lure outsiders to their particular corner of "Cajun Country." In the haste to get these brochures to market, public-relations firms entrusted with the task of "selling Acadiana" sacrificed historical detail and accuracy on the altar of marketability, often embellishing or even recasting well-worn settlement sagas to suit their purposes.

The resulting legacy of confusion has given rise to a seeming parody of the "Washington slept here" phenomenon, as every community of consequence in Acadiana began to proclaim itself the world capital of its market share of things Cajun: Tour guides, and clearing houses of information on Francophone Louisiana have routinely directed French-speaking tourists to the Evangeline Parish communities of Mamou and Ville Platte, which have been characterized as distinctly Acadian. Other South Louisiana agencies, prominent citizens, newspapers, and magazines have pointed to St. Martinville as the cradle of Cajun culture on the Gulf Coast. Meanwhile, Ascension and St. James parishes have proudly referred to themselves as the Acadian Coast, while residents of Lafourche and Terrebonne parishes openly cherish their rich Acadian architectural and cultural legacy. Not to be outdone, French-speaking residents of the Pointe Coupée, Avoyelles, and Plaquemines regions have proclaimed their home parishes old Acadian settlements.

The proliferation of ostensibly authentic settlement sites and the corresponding growth of the geographical area supposedly occupied by the 2,600 to 3,000 Acadian immigrants to colonial Louisiana has served only to compound hopeless popular confusion. The situation is paradoxical in that it exists, indeed thrives, in the face of the superabundance of early land and conveyance records that provide a nearly comprehensive view of land acquisition and ownership in the predominately Acadian parishes. These documents reveal a remarkable record of residential stability based on familial cohesiveness. Even in modern Louisiana, it is not uncommon to find Acadian families residing on their ancestral Spanish land grants, and the vast majority of Cajuns currently live within fifty miles of their birthplace. Lack of mobility heightened the impact of South Louisiana's diverse environments upon individual settlements, thus making the question of early Acadian demography of crucial importance to the development of New Acadia. But, in order to unravel this tangled historical mystery, one must examine the arrival of each major Acadian group between 1765 and 1786.

The oldest of the pioneer communities, called first *"le dernier camp d'en bas"* and later Fausse Pointe, was established near present-day Loreauville by late June, 1765. The long-revered St. Martinville myth notwithstanding, the Acadians did not permanently establish themselves as anticipated on the east-bank *vacherie* formerly owned by Dauterive and Masse. Indeed, within days of their arrival at the post, the Acadians were denounced as trespassers by Dauterive's neighbors. Moreover, in 1771 Dauterive, who had recently become sole proprietor of the ranch, donated a large portion of the designated settlement site to St. Martin de Tours Catholic Church. Finally, rather than raise cattle on shares for Dauterive, the exiles purchased an undetermined number of cattle from Jean-Baptiste Grevemberg shortly after their arrival at Fausse Pointe. These early settlers immediately sought patents to the land, thereby invoking the wrath of their neighbor, Jean-Baptiste Grevemberg, who claimed the area between Fausse Pointe and the Vermilion River as his personal fiefdom. In mid-July, Grevemberg addressed a memorial to Governor Aubry and Commissaire-ordonnateur Foucault, asserting his right to the land and requesting a patent to his fourteen-year-old *vacherie*. Despite the cattle baron's tenuous legal claim to the campsite, located on the east bank of Bayou Teche, Aubry and Foucault permitted the Acadians to remain on their new farmsteads; Grevemberg could console himself with a concession of 7.5 square leagues (18.75 square miles).[1]

Although confronting inevitable land disputes in other prime

1. Aubry to Choiseul, April 24, 1765, AC, C 13a, 45:50–50vo. Upon arrival at Fausse Pointe, several Acadian families petitioned the colonial government for land grants; this document, however, has apparently been lost, for unlike related documents, it is not in the state land office. In addition, Louis Andry, who was ordered to keep a journal during the Acadians' voyage to Attakapas, disregarded his instructions, allegedly because an emergency forced the postponement of many assignments. Aubry and Foucault to Choiseul, September 30, 1765, AC, C 13a, 45:32–33; "Memorial of Jean-Baptiste Grevemberg," July 14, 1765, and "Concession to Jean-Baptiste Grevemberg," both in Pintado Papers, Opelousas District, Book I, Part 2, pp. 159–61; Register of State Lands, Baton Rouge; Claim of Bernard Dauterive's heirs, Pintado Papers, Opelousas District, Book I, Part 2, p. 95; Register of State Lands, Claims, Southwest District, Reel 257, T.11S, R.6E, microfilm copy on deposit at Jefferson Caffery Room, Dupré Library, University of Southwestern Louisiana, hereinafter cited as Claims, with reel, township, and range number; Claude Boutte to Bernardo de Galvez, February 22, 1770, PPC, 190:131–33; "Copie d'un vieux registre," 8; Silvain Broussard to Luis de Unzaga, February 4, 1771, in Claims, Southwest District, Reel 255, T.9S, R.6E; 1766 Census of Attakapas, in Voorhies, *Some Late Eighteenth-Century Louisianians*, 124–25.

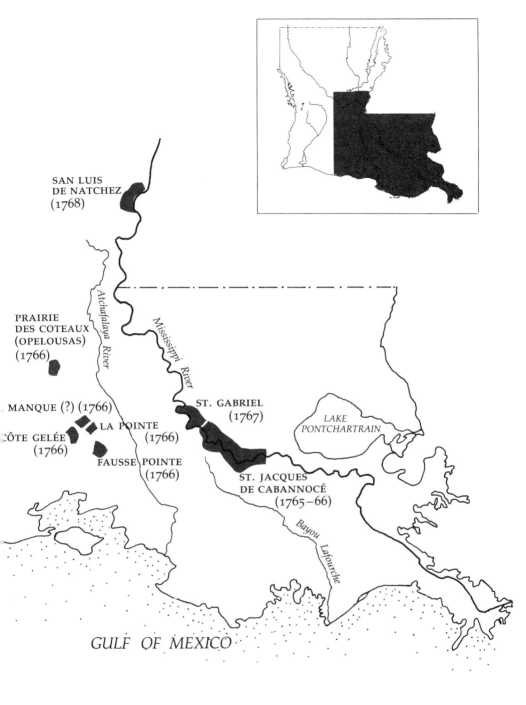

SAN LUIS
DE NATCHEZ
(1768)

PRAIRIE
DES COTEAUX
(OPELOUSAS)
(1766)

MANQUE (?) (1766)

CÔTE GELÉE
(1766)

LA POINTE
(1766)

FAUSSE POINTE
(1766)

ST. GABRIEL
(1767)

ST. JACQUES
DE CABANNOCÉ
(1765–66)

LAKE
PONTCHARTRAIN

Atchafalaya River

Mississippi River

Bayou Lafourche

GULF OF MEXICO

MAP 2: AREAS OF ACADIAN SETTLEMENT, 1760S

settlement areas, the Acadians were determined to select their own homesites, as they had in their homeland. Ascending the Teche to the large westward bend above present-day Parks, these immigrants founded a settlement they christened La Pointe de Repos. Many La Pointe settlers, however, quickly dispersed after the death toll from an epidemic began to mount in June, 1765. By March, 1766, thirty-seven refugees established themselves at Côte Gelée (the area between present-day Pilette and Broussard), on the west bank of Bayou Tortue directly opposite Dauterive's new Prairie Vermilion concession. An additional forty-four Acadians migrated to La Manque, probably the area adjoining the northern border of the La Pointe district and extending to the François LeBeau farm two miles below present-day Breaux Bridge. At least thirty-two other immigrants sought refuge at the Opelousas post, then located along Bayou Teche below present-day Port Barre. Apparently moved by pity for the latter group, militia captain Jacques Guillaume Courtableau personally settled the exiles at Prairie des Coteaux, along the Teche Ridge in an arc contiguous to the eastern and southeastern corporate limits of modern-day Opelousas.[2]

The dispersal of the settlers profoundly shaped the course of settlement in the Opelousas and Attakapas areas. First, the exiles maintained the time-honored Acadian tradition of establishing widely separated communities of family clusters. An examination of the Opelousas colony, for example, indicates that fourteen of the sixteen component families (87.5 percent) boasted immediate family members as neighbors. Family unity remained the top priority in their value system and thus the integrity of the original communities, in most instances, remained intact. Indeed, in southwestern Louisi-

2. The St. Martin de Tours burial register indicates that seventeen Acadians died at the *camp d'en haut* between June and December, 1765. "Copie d'un vieux registre," 1–16; Voorhies, *Some Late Eighteenth-Century Louisianians*, 124–25; Claims, Southwest District, Reel 256, T.10S, R.5E. The location of La Manque, long a matter of speculation, is based on 1771 land grants to Bonaventure Martin, Olivier Thibodeau, Simon LeBlanc, and Joseph Martin—all 1766 residents of the settlement. Voorhies, *Some Late Eighteenth Century Louisianians*, 124–25, 128; Claims, Southwest District, Reel 255, T.9S, R.6E, Reels 249–50, T.6S, R.4E; Gertrude C. Taylor, *Port Barre to St. Martinville*, Part 1 of *Land Grants Along the Teche* (3 maps; Lafayette, La., 1979–80); Silvain Saunier, Michel Comaut, Pierre Richard, Charles Comaut, and Michel Cormier to Unzaga, June 3, 1773, PPC, 189A:55.

ana, it is not unusual to find descendants of the original Acadian settlers presently residing on the family's Spanish land grant.[3]

Not all Acadians were content to remain in the five original settlements. The persistent frontier spirit among many exiles prompted them, like their Scotch-Irish and German counterparts on the Anglo-American frontier, to plunge deeper into the southwestern Louisiana frontier whenever their family settlement became too thickly populated. Fanning out from the five original settlements, most of the Teche Valley Acadians migrated steadily westward. The first wave of emigration broke upon the banks of the Vermilion River. As many as twelve pioneer families from the La Manque, La Pointe, and Côte Gelée settlements congregated sometime before 1777 at Grande Prairie, a large, treeless plain immediately west and north of what is today downtown Lafayette. By 1778, at least eighteen Acadian families, most of whom were former Côte Gelée residents, had established new homes between present-day Lafayette and Abbeville.[4]

Smaller numbers of Acadians sought homes along the upper Vermilion, because the region's low-lying bayou banks were subject to frequent inundations. Yet, the fertility of the soil could not long be ignored, and between 1778 and 1781 six Acadian settlers acquired lands in the Beaubassin area, where the river skirts the Teche Ridge, establishing their homes on the adjoining bluffs.[5]

The exiles demonstrated no such reluctance in occupying the prairies bordering the Vermilion River. Most of the migrants seeking new homes, particularly former La Pointe, Opelousas, and a few San Luis de Natchez residents, bypassed the Beaubassin area for La Grande Prairie de Bayou Carencro. By 1781, this area—between the mouth of Bayou Carencro, present-day Cankton, present-day Sun-

3. Voorhies, *Some Late Eighteenth-Century Louisianians*, 128; Donald J. Hebert (comp.), *Southwest Louisiana Records* (29 vols.; Eunice, La., 1976–81), I, 19–105, 252–85, 539–58; Mario Mamalakis, "Arceneaux Home Dates Back Almost 200 Years," Lafayette *Daily Advertiser*, May 18, 1980, p. 81.

4. Of the twenty-five heads of households at Grande Prairie in 1803, thirteen were either original settlers or their middle-aged children. Census of Grande Prairie, May 26, 1803, PPC, 220B:66; Claims, Southwest District, Reel 253, T.8S, R.5E; Claims of Theodore Thibodeau, Land grant dated January 5, 1777, Pintado Papers, Opelousas District, Book I, Part 2, p. 554; Claim of Olivier Thibodeau, Land grant dated January 5, 1777, Claims, Southwest District, Reel 254, T.9S, R.4E; Claims of André Martin, Land grant dated 1778, Claims, Southwest District, Reel 254, T.9S, R.4E.

5. Claims, Southwest District, Reel 253, T.8S, R.4E.

set, and Bayou Blaise—became thickly settled, boasting fifteen grantees. Settlers along the lower Vermilion also demonstrated a clear preference for prairielands bordering waterways, congregating in large numbers at Grande Prairie de Vermilion, the flat plains west of the river, between Lafayette and Maurice. By the mid-1790s, twenty-eight Acadian families had established their homes in Township 9 South, Range 4 East (the Lafayette area) alone.[6]

As the westward migration to the Vermilion Valley gained momentum, a second and smaller movement of Acadians occurred to the southeast. At least ten Acadian families from the Bayou Tortue, Opelousas, and Cabannocé settlements occupied and acquired Spanish titles to properties in the Jeanerette area. Beginning approximately five miles above present-day Jeanerette and running to the Chicot Noir area immediately below Jeanerette's southeastern corporate boundary, this community, like its counterparts elsewhere in Attakapas, consisted of tightly knit family groups. And like their compatriots in the Central and Upper Teche Valley, these settlers, too, succumbed to pressure from hostile Creoles. On January 25, 1782, five Chicot Noir pioneer families sold their grants to Creole Catherine Toupart and migrated to the central and lower Vermilion valley.[7]

Though the lower Vermilion Valley settlers consciously selected homesites in prairie areas that required little or no clearing, most Acadian migrants exhibited little interest in occupying the uncharted

6. O'Reilly to Grimaldi, December 29, 1769, ASD, 2585:n.p.; Claims, Southwest District, Reel 253, T.8S, R.4E, Reel 254, T.9S, R.4E.

7. Conveyance, Claude Duhon to Catherine Toupart, January 25, 1782, Vol. 3, St. Martin Parish Original Acts, St. Martin Parish Courthouse (hereinafter abbreviated SMOA); Conveyance, François Boudreaux to Catherine Toupart, January 25, 1782, Vol. 3, SMOA; Conveyance, Victor Blanchard to Catherine Toupart, January 25, 1782, Vol. 3, SMOA; Conveyance, Charles Duhon to Catherine Toupart, January 25, 1782, Vol. 3, SMOA; Conveyance, Baptiste Duhon to Catherine Toupart, January 25, 1782, Vol. 3, SMOA; Gertrude C. Taylor, *St. Martinville to Sorrel*, Part 2 of *Land Grants Along the Teche* (3 vols.; Lafayette, La; 1979–80); Voorhies, *Some Late Eighteenth-Century Louisianians*, 117, 125–28, 205, 271–72; Hebert (comp.), *Southwest Louisiana Records*, I, 52; Arsenault, *Histoire*, VI, 2481–82; Jane Cazaudebat, "Grand Prairie, 1803–1853," *Attakapas Gazette*, XIV (1979), 178, 183; Conveyance, Mme. Vincent Barras to Claude Duhon, October 7, 1782, Vol. 3, SMOA; Conveyance, Rene Trahan to Charles Duhon, December 8, 1782, Vol. 3, SMOA; *American State Papers: Documents, Legislative and Executive, of the Congress of the United States*, Class VIII: *Public Lands Series* (Washington, D.C., 1832–73), III, 196.

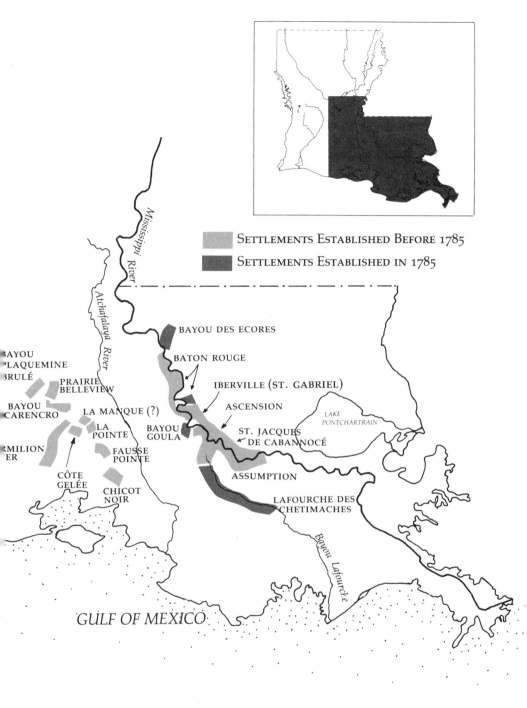

SETTLEMENTS ESTABLISHED BEFORE 1785

SETTLEMENTS ESTABLISHED IN 1785

Mississippi River

Atchafalaya River

BAYOU DES ECORES

BATON ROUGE

BAYOU PLAQUEMINE BRULÉ

PRAIRIE BELLEVIEW

IBERVILLE (ST. GABRIEL)

BAYOU CARENCRO

LA MANQUE (?)

ASCENSION

LAKE PONTCHARTRAIN

LA POINTE

BAYOU GOULA

ST. JACQUES DE CABANNOCÉ

VERMILION RIVER

FAUSSE POINTE

CÔTE GELÉE

ASSUMPTION

CHICOT NOIR

LAFOURCHE DES CHETIMACHES

Bayou Lafourche

GULF OF MEXICO

MAP 3: AREAS OF ACADIAN SETTLEMENT, 1785

lands beyond the alluvial plain. Although the grasslands facilitated pioneer settlement, they lacked firewood and building timber to sustain the settlers. Thus, only one Acadian established himself in the vast area bounded by the modern-day communities of Lafayette, Crowley, Lake Arthur, and Abbeville, and only one secured property in the Cow Island area of Vermilion Parish. Two Acadians occupied Gros Isle, between Abbeville and Erath, venturing into the extreme southern prairie only because the small salt dome contained the area's only dependable spring.[8]

The settlers at the Opelousas post shared their southern cousins' temerity about open prairie settlements. Like the Côte Gelée, La Pointe, and La Manque migrants, they sought isolation along the easternmost waterways in the southwestern prairies, but unlike their southern neighbors, the relocation was not entirely voluntary.

The Opelousas Acadians had been settled in 1765 by Jacques Courtableau, the post's largest landowner, at Prairie des Coteaux, along the west bank of Bayou Del Puent, and in northern Prairie Bellevue, along the west bank of Bayous Sandy and Callahan. The communities were inspected by Ulloa and former governor Aubry in the spring of 1766, and the exiles were given verbal assurance that they "would never be troubled in the possession of their properties." Ostensibly guaranteed a clear title to their lands, the settlers cleared and improved their properties without incident until the early 1770s, despite the fact that Courtableau, who had established himself along Bayou Marie Croquant in 1765, acquired in 1768 the Louis Pellerin grant, whose vague boundaries overlapped those of the Prairie des Coteaux property owners. Peaceful coexistence ended with Courtableau's death, when his widow attempted to invoke a clause in the Pellerin patent stating that the former commandant's concession included the woods bordering the land grant to a depth of one-half league. Mme Courtableau pressed this claim despite the fact that in 1771 Governor Luis de Unzaga had proclaimed the disputed woodlands "a commons for all settlers." Responding to this legal challenge, the Prairie des Coteaux settlers in June, 1773, asked the chief

8. Claims of Michel Leger, *American State Papers: Public Lands Series*, III, 106; Claim of Marin Mouton, Claims, Southwest District, Reel 259, T.13S, R.8E; Claim of Jean-Baptiste LaBauve and Charles Dugas, Claims, Southwest District, Reel 258, T.12S, R.4E; Deposition of Claude Broussard in Claims, Southwest District, Reel 258, T.12S, R.4E.

executive to reaffirm their titles to the properties and to order Mme Courtableau to stop harassing her neighbors.[9]

In an effort to resolve the matter, Commandant Fuselier de La Claire urged Unzaga in 1773 to revoke the Pellerin concession and to issue the widow a new land grant with definite boundaries. Unzaga appears to have closed his eyes to the dispute, and the matter ended abruptly in 1774 when François Marcantel bought the disputed property at the Jacques Courtableau succession sale.[10]

Although retaining their lands, the Prairie des Coteaux Acadians were clearly shaken by the incident, and when they secured Spanish patents after the land surveys of 1776 and 1778, the beleaguered exiles sought new homes elsewhere. Selling to Creole and Anglo-American immigrants, they established themselves in Prairie Belle-vue, between Bayou Silvain to the north and Bayou Bourbeux to the south. As a result of the migration, the Prairie Bellevue district became densely populated; in fact, by 1788, it had become the most thickly settled area of the Opelousas district.[11]

From Prairie Bellevue, second generation Louisiana Acadians migrated, in small numbers, during the late 1780s and 1790s into the

9. Petition to Unzaga, June 3, 1773, PPC, 189A:55; Jacques Courtableau Succession, October 16, 1772, Opelousas Colonial Records, Louisiana State Archives and Records Service, Baton Rouge; Abstract of the Jacques Courtableau Succession Sale, October 14, 1774, Records of the States of the United States, 1754–1789, Louisiana, Film 533, Louisiana Section A, Reel 2, Part 3, Jefferson Caffery Louisiana Room, Dupré Library, University of Southwestern Louisiana; *American State Papers: Public Lands Series*, III, 100–102. Among the Prairie des Coteaux settlers were Michel Comeau, Pierre Cormier, Michel Cormier, and Louis Richard. Claims, Southwest District, Reels 249–50, T.6S, R.4E. Among the Bellevue settlers were Pierre Thibodeau, Silvain Sonnier, Fabien Richard, Pierre Richard, Joseph Cormier, Charles Comeau, Pierre Savoy, Victor Richard, and Joseph Grange. Claims, Southwest District, Reels, 249–50, T.6S, R.4E; Foucault to Choiseul, April 2, 1766, AC, C 13a, 45:212–13; Ulloa to Grimaldi, June 2, 1766, ASD, 2585:n.p; Petition to Ulloa from the Acadians at Opelousas, March 13, 1768, PPC, 187A:n.p.; Inventory of the Jacques Courtableau Estate, October 16, 1772, Opelousas Colonial Records; Gabriel Fuselier de la Claire to Unzaga, June 18, 1773, PPC, 189A:56–57.

10. Fuselier to Unzaga, June 18, 1773, PPC, 189A:56–57; Abstract of the Jacques Courtableau Succession Sale, October 14, 1774, Records of the States of the United States, Louisiana, Film 533, Sec. A, Reel 2, Part 3.

11. Claims, Southwest District, Reels 249–52, T.6S, R.4E; T.7S, R.4E. Among the transplanted Opelousas settlers were Louis Richard, Fabien Richard, Jean-Baptiste Richard, Olivier Richard, and Augustin Comeau. Claims, Southwest District, Reel 251, T.7S, R.3E, T.7S, R.4E; Voorhies, *Some Late Eighteenth-Century Louisianians*, 321–44.

Grand Coteau and Plaquemine Brulée areas. The young pioneers' homesites were not randomly selected, but consisted of earlier land grants to their fathers. Six early Acadian settlers from the Opelousas district, for example, acquired and maintained properties along Bayou Plaquemine Brulée, between Pointe Noire Gully and present-day Lewisburg. As late as 1788, only one of these grantees actually resided upon his then remote *vacherie*. In the 1790s, however, settlers trickled into the area, and by 1796 the district boasted twenty-six second- and third-generation Acadian residents.[12]

Few Acadians sought homes along Bayou Plaquemine Brulée, and fewer still ventured into the wilderness beyond this prominent plains landmark. The hardy souls who, with a handful of Creole and Anglo settlers, did brave the rigors of life on the northwestern prairies, established themselves at the Faquetaique district of the Opelousas post (the area southeast of present-day Eunice) around 1790. Widely scattered along Bayous Blaize LeJeune and Des Cannes, this pioneer settlement comprised only four families totaling twenty-nine individuals. The occupation of Prairie Faquetaique marked the western limit of Acadian expansion in the eighteenth century. At the dawn of the next century, the exiles gained renewed interest in the unoccupied prairies, as six prominent Acadian cattlemen from the upper Vermilion and Carencro valleys acquired—usually through purchase from the Attakapas Indians—lands along the lower Plaquemine Brulée, between the modern-day communities of Estherwood and Crowley, and along the Mermentau River near present-day Mermentau. In addition, at least seven Acadian families from the Opelousas post established themselves along lower Bayou Nezpiqué, near its junction with the Mermentau River, and along Bayous Jonas, Des Cannes, and Mallet by 1803.[13]

The pattern of land occupation in the early nineteenth century differed little from that of the preceding decades. Beginning in the late

12. Voorhies, *Some Late Eighteenth-Century Louisianians,* 302–303, 329, 345–65; Claims, Southwest District, Reel 252, T.7S, R.5E, Reel 251, T.7S, R.3E, Reel 250, T.7S, R.2E, Reel 253, T.7S, R.3E; Pintado Papers, Opelousas District, Book I, Part 2, p. 551.

13. Claims, Southwest District, Reel 250, T.7S, R.2E, T.7S, R.1E; Claim of Joseph LeJeune, Pintado Papers, Opelousas District, Part I, Book 2; Mary Alice Fontenot and Paul B. Freeland, *Acadia Parish, Louisiana: A History to 1900* (Baton Rouge, 1976), 29, 38, 55–60; Voorhies, *Some Late Eighteenth-Century Louisianians,* 359; *American State Papers: Public Lands Series,* III, 93.

1760s and persisting throughout the colonial period, Acadian settlers voluntarily sought the isolation of the prairies not only for cultural preservation but also for familial cohesiveness and economic independence for their children through private ownership of land. In order to secure their socioeconomic objectives, the typical prairie Acadian family relocated at least once between 1765 and 1785, acquiring new and usually larger landholdings from the Spanish government with each move.[14]

The Acadian migrations typically involved family units: reunited relatives or, more commonly, middle-aged adults and their married children. These migrants consistently ventured only as far as the nearest prairie stream, or *coulee*, establishing themselves along the wooded banks where firewood and building materials were plentiful. Having selected homesites, some Acadian pioneers, particularly those along the lower Vermilion, established "villages" consisting of temporary shelters to accommodate the settlers until permanent homesites could be selected and cleared or until more desirable lands were found. Residential propinquity of family members became less common as pioneers pierced the frontier beyond Bayou Plaquemine Brulée, an area in which choice waterfront properties were few and widely separated. Hence, though families, such as the LeJeunes, entered the Faquetaique district as a unit in the early 1790s, individual family residences were separated by as much as five linear miles.[15]

Prairie topography was not the only factor contributing to the late-eighteenth-century Acadian dispersal. Facing an alien environment as well as openly hostile Creole colonists and European-born colonial administrators, the exiles closed ranks and found strength in group solidarity. Many Acadians quickly tired of the escalating intercultural feud and, in the late 1760s, sought the stability afforded by isolation along the Vermilion River, on the banks of Bayou Carencro,

14. Claim of Joseph Duhon, Pintado Papers, Opelousas District, Book I, Part 2, p. 126. The prairie dweller's mobility is best reflected in the Opelousas post's Acadian community, in which 75 percent of the exiles relocated at least once between 1765 and 1780, moving from the original settlements to a frontier area. Voorhies, *Some Late Eighteenth Century Louisianians*, 128, 212, 284–365; Claims, Southwest District, Reels 249–52, T.6S, R.4E, T.7S, R.4E.

15. Claims, Southwest District, Reels 249–58, T.6S, R.4E–T.12S, R.4E; Claim of Joseph Duhon, Pintado Papers, Opelousas District, Book I, Part 2, p. 126.

and in Prairie Bellevue. By the late 1770s and early 1780s, when Bayou Plaquemine Brulée was settled, an entire generation had reached maturity in the tranquillity of the prairies region and hence no longer feared the oppression of the colony's social elite. It is not surprising, therefore, that Acadian land grants, like those in pre-dispersal Acadia, were widely scattered, often separated by at least a mile from their nearest neighbor. The growing independence of the pioneers, as reflected in the western settlement patterns, suggests that the exiles had grown accustomed to the individual freedom and mobility afforded by the open prairie. It is apparent that by the 1780s the western Acadians had found a niche in a physical and cultural environment far different from that of their frozen homeland.[16]

As the western Acadians adapted to the southwestern prairies, the eastern exiles carved a new homeland from the virgin forests bordering the Mississippi River. The first Acadians to settle along that river were twenty exiles from New York who reached New Orleans in April, 1764, and were apparently settled by Governor Jean-Jacques-Blaise d'Abbadie at Cabannocé (present-day St. James Parish). The New York exiles were joined, in May, 1765, by eighty Acadian refugees from Halifax and possibly Saint-Domingue. These refugees were in turn joined in mid-September, 1765, by eighty-two Acadians from the Attakapas post, who, like their pastor, Fr. Jean-François, had fled the Teche region's raging malarial or yellow fever epidemic.[17]

16. Claims, Southwest District, T.6S, R.3E, T.7S, R.3E; Clark, *Acadia*, 94–185.

17. D'Abbadie to Choiseul, April 6, 1764, AC, C 13a, 44:37; Janet Jehn (comp.), *Acadian Exiles in the Colonies* (Covington, Ky., 1977). Charles Mouton was apparently accompanied to Louisiana by his brothers, Acadian resistance leaders Salvador and Louis, who had been imprisoned at Fort Edward (present-day Windsor), Nova Scotia, from 1760 to 1763. Arsenault, *Histoire*, VI, 2560–61; Voorhies, *Some Late Eighteenth-Century Louisianians*, 114–19; Foucault and Aubry to Choiseul, September 30, 1765, AC, C 13a, 45:31–32. Among the eighty Saint-Domingue refugees were several veterans—perhaps as many as six—of the Battle of Restigouche, who sailed for Saint-Domingue around 1761. Arsenault, *Histoire*, I, 294–96; Judice to Gayoso de Lemos, September 26, 1797, PPC, 213:387; Aubry to Choiseul, May 4, 1765, AC, C 13a, 45:56; "Copie d'un vieux registre," 3–11. The register ends abruptly in January, 1766, and according to church historian Roger Baudier, the missionary "probably returned to France." Roger Baudier, *The Catholic Church in Louisiana* (New Orleans, 1939), 190. The number of transplanted Attakapas pioneers has been determined by a comparison of the Halifax prisoner rolls for 1763 with the list of Acadian card money holders in Joseph Broussard's party and the 1766 census of Cabannocé. Jehn (comp.), *Acadian Exiles*, 243–47; Voorhies, *Some Late Eighteenth-Century Louisianians*, 114–19; Recapitu-

Cabannoce's tightly knit immigrant groups formed the nucleus of a rapidly expanding frontier settlement. By early March, 1766, all subsequent Acadian immigrants were required, by gubernatorial decree, to settle along the Mississippi River. Upon arrival at the forts, Acadians were placed upon homesites by military engineers. At St. Gabriel, "farms" were assigned to each of the immigrant heads of households by Commandant Joseph Orieta. All of the concessions were initially confined to the east bank of the Mississippi River, and the forty-seven land grants accorded the immigrants stretched from a point 4,200 yards below Fort St. Gabriel to a spot six to eight miles downstream, near the present boundary between the parishes of Iberville and Ascension. At Fort San Luis de Natchez, the exiles were settled on long, narrow, contiguous riverfront sites, the northern-most of which lay approximately 2.5 miles below modern-day Vidalia, Louisiana.[18]

Selection of the settlement sites often reflected poor judgment on the part of military engineers. At San Luis de Natchez, the homesites were vulnerable to Indian raids, and the area lacked a sanitary source of fresh water. The San Luis settlers consequently suffered from chronic dysentery. While health conditions were better at St. Gabriel, several settlers were given lands subject to rapid erosion, particularly at river bends.[19]

Despite the manifold problems faced by the newly established immigrants, Ulloa refused to permit the San Luis and St. Gabriel Acadians to settle elsewhere. The exiles were enraged by what they considered to be the governor's callous disregard for their health, safety, and, of paramount importance, their desire for reunification with relatives in other posts. It is hardly surprising, then, that a large

---

lation of the receipts furnished by Sr. Maxent to the Acadians, April 1765, AC, C 13a, 45:29.

18. Voorhies, *Some Late Eighteenth-Century Louisianians*, 429; Chandler (trans. and ed.), "End of an Odyssey," 69–88; Chandler, "Odyssey Continued," 451–57; Petition to O'Reilly from the Acadians established at San Luis de Natchez, October 18, 1769, ASD, 2585:n.p.

19. Depositions regarding the vexations caused by Antonio de Ulloa, November 8–15, 1768, AC, C 13a, 48:134vo; Verret to Ulloa, March 26, 1768, PPC, 2357:n.p.; Pedro Piernas to Ulloa, March 27, 1768, PPC, 187A:n.p.; Delavillebeuvre to Ulloa, October 14, 1768, PPC, 187A:n.p.; Delavillebeuvre to Ulloa, September 29, 1768, PPC, 187A:n.p.; Ignace Babin to Unzaga, October 18, 1770, PPC, 188B:175; Dutisné to Unzaga, July, 1770, PPC, 188A:1c/2.

number of Acadians did join with other colonists in ousting Ulloa on October 28, 1768.[20]

Although Spanish hegemony was restored in August, 1769, the Rebellion of 1768 had demographic ramifications for Louisiana's Acadian population. At least six Cabannocé and St. Gabriel families capitalized upon this opportunity to join family members at Opelousas and Attakapas. And, apparently to regain Acadian goodwill, Governor Alejandro O'Reilly permitted the San Luis settlers, in late December, 1769, to abandon their unhealthy homesites for equivalent properties in present-day Ascension and northern Assumption parishes.[21]

The migrations of 1768–1769 marked the last great Acadian demographic movement east of the Atchafalaya River until 1785. Small numbers of settlers, however, continued to trickle into the colony, usually after a long and arduous overland journey. The first and largest of these immigrant groups to reach Louisiana—thirty Acadians from Maryland—boarded the *Britain*, a New Orleans–bound schooner, at "the port of [Port Tobacco,] Maryland" on January 5, 1769. The English vessel reached the mouth of the Mississippi River on February 21, but fog delayed ascent of the river, and strong easterly winds drove the vessel to Matagorda Bay, Texas. Upon reaching the Texas coast, the *Britain* was seized by Spanish authorities and the passengers and crew were arrested as smugglers. For a time the prisoners were confined at hard labor in Presidio de La Bahia (present-day Goliad, Texas), but they were soon released. Arriving at Natchitoches in late October, the Acadians paused before pressing on to New Acadia. Commandant Athanaze Demézières attempted to force them to remain at his Red River post, but he ultimately succumbed to Acadian recalcitrance. In mid-April, 1770, the exiles were given west-bank land grants in present-day Iberville Parish.[22]

20. Circular letter to Fuselier de La Claire *et al.*, April 4, 1768, PPC, 187A:n.p.; "Directive to be read to the Acadians at Fort San Luis in the name of His Majesty," 1768, PPC, 2357:n.p.; Verret to Ulloa, March 26, 1768, PPC, 2357:n.p.
21. The six families were those of Joseph Bourque, Blaize Brasseux, Claude Duhon, Jean Blanchard, L'Ange Bourg, and Jean Jeansonne. Voorhies, *Some Late Eighteenth-Century Louisianians*, 114–19; O'Reilly to Grimaldi, December 29, 1769, ASD, 2585:n.p.
22. Kinnaird (ed.), *Spain in the Mississippi Valley*, II, Pt. 1, pp. 137–38, 140–42; Hebert Eugene Bolton (trans. and ed.), *Athanase de Mézières and the Louisiana-Texas Border, 1768–1770* (2 vols.; Cleveland, 1914), I, 131, 155–56, 173–74. The Acadians

The efforts of other exiles to reach Louisiana are less well documented, but it is certain that the overland odyssey described in Felix Voorhies' *Acadian Reminiscences* has no basis in fact. The vigilance of colonial forces ordered to fire at Acadians approaching the Appalachian frontier, the belligerence of trans-Appalachian Indian tribes both during and after the Seven Years' War, and the exiles' general ignorance of the interior routes to Louisiana militated against a transcontinental trek. It is also certain that few, if any, Acadians reached the lower Mississippi Valley via Quebec. Indeed, Acadian refugees in Quebec appear to have ventured no further south than Detroit, where one couple was married on January 3, 1773. Louisiana's Spanish-period commandants, moreover, make no mention of Acadian arrivals on the upper Mississippi River in hundreds of highly detailed late-eighteenth-century reports. In addition, a comparison of late-eighteenth-century Louisiana census schedules with lists of Acadian refugees in Quebec reveals no evidence of a southward migration. Many Acadians, such as Firmin Breaux, who supposedly came to Louisiana from Quebec, actually sailed to the Mississippi Valley from Saint-Domingue. Indeed, only one Acadian group is known to have migrated to Louisiana from Canada after the first migration (1764–1770). On October 16, 1788, nineteen Acadians boarded the schooner *Brigite* and set sail for Louisiana from St. Pierre Island (St. Pierre and Miquelon); the vessel, commanded by Captain Joseph Gravois, to whom seventeen of the passengers were related, arrived at Pass à L'Outre, the principal entrance to the Mississippi in the eighteenth century, on December 11. Armed with a passport from Ygnacio Balderas, a Spanish official they encountered, they ascended the Mississippi to New Orleans and evidently secured permission to join relatives in present-day Ascension Parish.[23]

---

were given land grants of six arpents frontage by forty arpents depth on the west bank of the Mississippi River below Bayou Plaquemine. Unzaga to Dutisne, April 10, 1770, PPC, 193B:283–84; Unzaga to Dutisne, April 26, 1770, PPC, 193B:290.

23. Jean-Baptiste Pitre and Françoise (*dit* Marianne) Coste, both natives of Port Royal, Acadie, were married at Fort Pontchartrain, Detroit on January 3, 1773. The couple, however, established their home at Detroit and made no effort to reach New Acadia. See Fort Pontchartrain Church Records in Series MG8, Subseries G8, Vol. II, 583, 613, 631, 649, 662, 681, 682, 732, Vol. III, 76, 86, 154, 158, 197, 318, 441, 600, 691, 756, Canadian National Archives, Ottawa, Canada; Jehn, *Acadian Exiles*, 23–131, 159–219; Voorhies, *Some Late Eighteenth-Century Louisianians*, 169–216, 271–345, 421–528; "List of French settlers embarked aboard the schooner *Brigite*, commanded

The absence of significant Acadian immigration between 1769 and 1785, the land surveys of 1771 and 1772, the issuance of formal land grants in 1775 and 1776, and the imposition of increasingly stringent restrictions on intracolonial movement by Governors Luis de Unzaga and Bernardo de Gálvez interacted to confine the overwhelming majority of river and upper Lafourche Acadians to their original homesites until the 1790s. Because the eastern settlement patterns remained remarkably static throughout the Spanish period, the First Acadian Coast's population density increased 226 percent between 1766 and 1777, rising from 241 to 786. The population growth, the resulting occupation of all prime riverfront properties by 1786, and the existence of Spanish Louisiana's forced heirship laws (which divided the original family land grant into progressively small tracts with each successive generation), all created increasing pressure for intracolonial mobility.

The problem faced by the eastern settlers is well illustrated by a few statistics. The typical concession on the Acadian Coast consisted of 4 to 6 arpents frontage by 40 arpents depth (1 arpent = 192 feet). When one of New Acadia's founding fathers died, half of the estate was given to his surviving children, which, in the typical eighteenth-century, river-parish family, numbered three to five persons. The second-generation Louisiana Acadians generally received long, very narrow strips of land, often less than 1.5 arpents wide and 40 arpents long. Indeed, an examination of the *American State Papers, Public Lands Series* reveals that claims for parcels of property measuring ½ to 4 arpents frontage by 40 arpents depth constituted 62 percent of the 251 Acadian river parish land claims filed with American land commissioners. Claims involving less than 2 arpents frontage comprised 24 percent of the total claims. These figures are placed in perspective only when one considers that lands owned by most 1785 immigrants remained undivided.[24]

---

by Capt. Gravois and bound for Louisiana, October 16, 1788," PPC, 14:653a; Ygnacio Balderas to Estevan Miró, December 11, 1788, PPC, 14:653; "List of the passengers aboard the *Brigite*, commanded by Capt. Joseph Gravois, coming from St. Pierre in Newfoundland, December 11, 1788," PPC, 14:652, 652a; Balderas to Miró, December 14, 1788, PPC, 14:656; Diocese of Baton Rouge, *Diocese of Baton Rouge Catholic Church Records*: Vol. II, *1770–1803* (Baton Rouge, 1980), 333–34; *American State Papers: Public Land Series* II, 271.

24. Bellevue to Unzaga, March 3, 1771, PPC, 192:329; Judice to Unzaga, September 7, 1771, PPC, 188B:72; Judice to Unzaga, June 3, 1771, PPC, 188B:94–98; Judice to

The constant reduction of familial landholdings made farming increasingly difficult on the Acadian Coast. The problem was compounded in 1785 by the arrival of 1,598 Acadian immigrants from France. Like their predecessors, these refugees came to Louisiana seeking familial reunification. Since most of their relatives now resided along the Mississippi River, they naturally wished to establish themselves in or near the eastern Acadian settlements. A remarkably flexible colonization program, established by Carlos III and administered by Intendant Martin Navarro, gave them just such an opportunity.

As Governor Ulloa's subordinate in the late 1760s, Navarro had witnessed the disastrous consequences of thwarting the exiles' dream of sociocultural reunification. Rather than dictate settlement policy to the exiles in the manner of the ill-fated chief executive, he resolved to permit the Acadian immigrants to select their own homesites. Drawing upon his twenty years of experience in dealing with the exiles, he sought to secure their full cooperation by establishing and maintaining good rapport with them. Louisiana's chief administrative officer thus became personally involved with his charges, even to the point of volunteering, in December, 1785, to serve as godfather to any Acadian child born during the transatlantic crossing.[25]

Unzaga, January 3, 1772, PPC, 189A:418; *American State Papers: Public Lands Series*, II, 258–300, 394–433; Unzaga to Dutisné, March 4, 1773, PPC, 189A:359; Gálvez to Dutisné, November 10, 1777, PPC, 193B:195–96; Unzaga to Judice, March 25, 1774, PPC, 189B:539. In 1766, a total of 241 Acadians resided on the First Acadian Coast— present-day St. James and Ascension parishes. By 1777, however, Ascension Parish boasted 289 Acadian residents, while 497 exiles made their homes in neighboring St. James Parish—a total of 786 persons. In Iberville Parish, the local Acadian population rose from 220 to 291 individuals, a 32 percent increase. The dramatic population growth experienced by the First Acadian Coast was largely the result of an influx of Maryland refugees in late 1766. Voorhies, *Some Late Eighteenth Century Louisianians*, 210–14, 271–80; Census of St. James Parish, 1777, PPC, 190:192–205; Census of Ascension Parish, 1777, PPC, 190:173–91; Census of Iberville Parish, 1770, PPC, 190: 240–56; Winzerling, *Acadian Odyssey*, 130–53; Thomas B. Lemann, "Forced Heirship in Louisiana: In Defense of Forced Heirship," *Tulane Law Review*, LII (1977), 20–28; Michael P. Porter, "Forced Heirs: The Legitime and Loss of the Legitime in Louisiana," *Tulane Law Review*, XXXVII (1963), 710–64; Hans W. Baade, "Marriage Contracts in French and Spanish Louisiana: A Study in 'Notarial' Jurisprudence," *Tulane Law Review*, LIII (1978), 1–54. According to the 1777 census of Iberville, Ascension, and St. James parishes, the average river Acadian family contained 3.11 children. Census of Ascension Parish, 1777, PPC, 190:173–91; Census of St. James Parish, 1777, PPC, 190:192–205; Census of Iberville Parish, 1777, PPC, 190:240–56.

25. Winzerling, *Acadian Odyssey*, 141. In December, 1785, Navarro informed José de Gálvez that he had made every effort to convince the Acadians of the "humanity

Navarro also gained the immigrants' favor by establishing, in present-day Algiers, Louisiana, dormitories and separate hospitals for male and female patients—a concession to the exiles' "great repugnance for French hospitals," such as Charity Hospital of New Orleans—to accommodate them during the layover at the Crescent City. The hospitals were particularly significant. Although mortality rates during the voyage were surprisingly low, each wave of immigrants, debilitated by the voyage, was stricken by various illnesses, including the Acadian scourge—smallpox. As the ravages of smallpox were particularly severe among young mothers and elderly males, Navarro added wet nurses and orderlies to the clinic staff.[26]

The organizational skills exhibited by Navarro in the quartering of the Acadian immigrants at New Orleans also characterized his efforts to establish the exiles on arable lands. Shortly after the arrival of the first Acadian transport, Le Bon Papa, in late July, 1785, Navarro appointed Anselme Blanchard, a prominent, established Acadian, to supervise settlement of the 156 passengers. He also distributed financial aid to the immigrants, which enabled them to purchase "the necessities of life"; tools and farm implements were distributed directly from the royal warehouse. Having furnished the exiles the means of supporting themselves and having given them a month to recuperate from the transatlantic crossing, Navarro, in accordance with their request, rented a small flotilla of launches and barges to transport his charges upriver.[27]

Preparations complete, the immigrants departed New Orleans for their new homes at Lafourche, Bayogoula, and Manchac on August 28, 1785. These sites had been inspected by Acadian representatives during the layover, and each family had subsequently been permitted to select its future home on the basis of the deputies' reports. Hence, under Blanchard's supervision, one family was settled in the Lafourche district, six families at the Bayogoula post, and the re-

and concern of the Spanish nation." Navarro to Gálvez, December 12, 1785, PPC, 85:574–78.

26. Winzerling, Acadian Odyssey, 140–41; Navarro to Gálvez, December 12, 1785, PPC, 85:574–78; Memoir on Louisiana, 1785, PPC, 633:27.

27. Navarro to Gálvez, August 2, 1785, PPC, 85:516. The subsidy consisted of the following amounts: 10 sols per nuclear family head, 7 sols for each additional adult, and 2.5 sols per child. Winzerling, Acadian Odyssey, 132; Navarro to Gálvez, September 26, 1785, PPC, 85:526–27vo; Navarro to Gálvez, October 4, 1785, PPC, 85:534.

maining twenty-seven families at Manchac. At each settlement, the Acadian "overseer" first secured temporary housing with established settlers for the immigrants and then apportioned land grants of four to five arpents among the exiles. Blanchard remained with the immigrants until they were moved onto their lands.

The establishment of *Le Bon Papa's* passengers best exemplifies Navarro's self-deterministic settlement policy. It was under that policy that the exiles from the six subsequent "expeditions"—in which the vessels *La Bergère, Le Beaumont, St. Rémy, L'Amitié, La Ville de Arcangel,* and *La Caroline,* brought Acadians from France—were established between October 4, 1785, and February 8, 1786. In each instance, the immigrants were furnished funds, supplies, housing, and medical attention at government expense. Each party of settlers was also permitted to remain in New Orleans for approximately one month, during which they elected delegates and, in some cases, Acadian surveyors to reconnoiter vacant properties in the lower Mississippi Valley. Following the inspection tours, which were consistently led by government employees, the immigrants were given absolute freedom to choose a homesite, despite attempts by the Arkansas and Avoyelles commandants to pressure Navarro into settling the Acadians within their respective districts.[28]

The prospective settlers were not restricted to the properties recommended by their representatives; on the contrary, Navarro provided all possible encouragement and assistance to exiles seeking familial reunification. By this means, sixty-seven Acadians from five different expeditions were restored to their families in the Opelousas and Attakapas posts. Familial reunification was infinitely more difficult to achieve in the long-established and now densely populated

28. Jean Landry, Jean LeBlanc, Ignace Hebert, and René Blanchard to Navarro, August, 1785, PPC, 198B:1296; Navarro to Gálvez, December 12, 1785, PPC, 85:574–78; Winzerling, *Acadian Odyssey,* 133, 160; Navarro to Gálvez, September 26, 1785, PPC, 85:526vo-27vo; Blanchard to Navarro, September 1785, PPC, 198B:938–39. The date of the expedition's arrival at Lafourche is unrecorded, but the immigrants reached Bayogoula on September 4 and Manchac on the night of September 6. Blanchard to Miro, October 5, 1785, PPC, 198A:489; Reider and Reider (comps.), *The Crew and Passenger Lists of the Seven Acadian Expeditions of 1785,* 1–84; Navarro to Blanchard, October 4, 1785, PPC, 85:570. The inspection tours were consistently led by either Anselme Blanchard or, in his absence, Jean Cambeau. For his efforts, Blanchard was granted a pension of 500 pesos per annum. Navarro to Gálvez, August 2, 1785, PPC, 85:516; Navarro to Gálvez, October 4, 1785, PPC, 85:534; Jacques Gaignard to Miro, September 15, 1785, PPC, 198A:290–91.

Acadian posts along the lower Mississippi, because the arable lands were generally occupied. Immigrants wishing to settle in these areas were forced to content themselves with vacant properties in newly founded districts near, and frequently adjoining, the older Acadian settlements.[29]

This is not to say that the exiles were dissatisfied with the settlement sites. Although inspectors were occasionally hesitant to recommend one site over its competitors, their constituents invariably endorsed their selection in a remarkable display of group solidarity. Indeed, 84 percent of the 1785 immigrants ultimately established themselves at sites selected by their representatives (see table). Once determination had been made, members of each expedition were settled independently, following the precedent established by *Le Bon Papa*'s passengers, despite the fact that several shiploads of Acadians were in New Orleans concurrently. It is thus most significant that four of the seven 1785 expeditions converged on the Lafourche de Chetimaches post.[30]

The Acadians' marked preference for the Lafourche district was hardly coincidental. Like its major competitors, Manchac, Bayou des Ecores (present-day Thompson's Creek), and Baton Rouge (which three posts attracted 34 percent of the immigrants), Lafourche adjoined existing Acadian settlements. Unlike its rivals, however, it was not uncomfortably near thriving Anglo-American communities. The region was also sparsely populated, since the lower reaches of Bayou Lafourche had been explored only thirteen years earlier. The region's virgin wilderness effectively insulated the exiles from other cultures as well as from governmental interference and thus afforded the settlers a refuge in which to reconstruct their agrarian, frontier society. The determination to resurrect vieille Acadie on the banks of Louisiana's bayous was clearly manifested in nationalistic outpourings at numerous weddings celebrated at New Orleans between November 20 and December 19, 1785. Receptions following the reli-

29. Kinnaird (ed.), *Spain in the Mississippi Valley*, III, Pt. 2, p. 169. Many of the Attakapas-bound Acadians were transported to their new homes aboard the royal sloop *San José*. Winzerling, *Acadian Odyssey*, 137; Judice to Miro, September 22, 1785, PPC, 198A:445; List of the abandoned lands at the Lafourche de Chetimachas post, September 19, 1785, PPC, 198A:446.

30. Winzerling, *Acadian Odyssey*, 130–53; Kinnaird (ed.), *Spain in the Mississippi Valley*, III, Pt. 2, p. 169; Navarro to Gálvez, October 4, 1785, PPC, 85:534–35.

ACADIAN SETTLEMENT PATTERNS, 1785

Ship	Passengers	Post	Settlers	Percentage
Le Bon Papa	155	Manchac	124	80
La Bergère	268	Lafourche	242	90
Le Beaumont	175	Baton Rouge	145	82
St. Rémy	311	Lafourche	303	97
L'Amitié	266	Lafourche	224	84
La Ville d'Arcangel	304	Bayou des Ecores	271	89
La Caroline	77	Lafourche	54	70

gious ceremonies were, as dictated by custom, community celebrations featuring music, food, beer, and cider, but in a significant departure from tradition, the festivities were crowned with lengthy recitations of Acadian "national history."[31]

The rejuvenated spirit of the 1785 immigrants was matched by their eagerness to resume their traditional agricultural pursuits. Within days after the division of the Manchac settlement site into land grants in September, 1785, for example, the Acadians had not only launched a road construction project along the natural levee, but had also begun building crude huts to house their families.[32]

Settlement was followed by the difficulty of adapting to Louisiana's climate, soil, terrain, and agricultural products. This evolutionary process was ameliorated considerably by a continuation of the Spanish dole and by material assistance and advice from established Acadians, who literally rushed to the aid of long-lost friends and relatives. In October, 1785, Ambroise Theriot not only organized a *boucherie* on behalf of the newly established Manchac settlers, but procured Attakapas beef for the occasion, at personal expense. Such philanthropy was commonplace, and largely because of such private

31. While exploring the region in April, 1772, Judice noted that the lands along the Lafourche were "much prettier and higher" than properties fronting the lower Mississippi River. Judice to Unzaga, April 8, 1772, PPC, 189B:423; Winzerling, *Acadian Odyssey*, 145–46.

32. Blanchard to Miro, October 5, 1785, PPC, 198A:491.

assistance, the immigrants were quickly integrated into New Acadia's socioeconomic structure. Despite the detrimental effects of smallpox epidemics in nascent settlements in 1786 and 1787, the typical 1785 immigrant had, by 1788, "cleared a fairly large pasture and field," erected levees on his waterfront property, and "achieved a standard of living equal to that of the earliest settlers."[33]

Thus, the rapid adjustment of the French refugees to their new surroundings in Louisiana resulted in large measure from the material and moral support furnished by established Acadians. Such vital, material assistance from friends and relatives was possible only because the 1785 settlement sites were universally located along the northern and southern peripheries of existing Acadian river settlements. Despite broad geographic distribution, a majority of immigrants demonstrated a clear preference for the Bayou Lafourche, probably because the then isolated area offered minimal contact not only with the provincial government but also with the mainstream of Creole-dominated life in rural Louisiana. The availability of land in the Lafourche area also drew small numbers of young river settlers, who profited from the general relaxation of the stringent colonial settlement regulations after the Spanish occupation of British West Florida during the American Revolution.[34]

Attraction for the Lafourche area was felt even in the northernmost Acadian river settlements. The appeal was most visible in August, 1794, when a hurricane washed away the livestock, crops, and fences of the Bayou des Ecores Acadians. Abandoning their ruined farms, these pioneers "went to establish themselves at Lafourche."[35]

As at the Attakapas and Opelousas posts, Acadian immigrants in the central and lower Lafourche Valley sought progressively more iso-

33. Ibid. Theriot's project was partially subsidized by the Spanish government. Miro to Blanchard, September 20, 1785, PPC, 198A:488; Memoir on Louisiana, 1786, PPC, 633:n.p.; List of persons stricken with smallpox at Nueva Feliciana, 1787, PPC, 219:586; Carl A. Brasseaux, "Acadians, Creoles, and the 1787 Lafourche Smallpox Outbreak," Louisiana Review, VIII (1978), 55–59; Petition to Miro, August, 1788, PPC, 633:96vo-97.

34. The Gálvez Town, West Baton Rouge, and Bayou des Ecores settlements adjoined existing Acadian communities in present-day Iberville Parish, while the newly settled Valenzuela and Bayou Lafourche areas were contiguous to existing settlements in the Lafourche des Chetimachas post. Voorhies, Some Late Eighteenth-Century Louisianians, 114–19, 280–320; Census of the Lafourche, 1788, PPC, 201:668–80.

35. Anselme Blanchard to Carondelet, October 28, 1794, PPC, 209:356.

lated areas. The initial area of occupation in 1767 included only the bayou's confluence with the Mississippi at present-day Donaldsonville, but by the early 1770s, at least seventeen Acadian families—primarily 1767 immigrants from Ascension Parish—had migrated to the upper Lafourche, particularly along the west bank between Donaldsonville and Labadieville. The east bank, which was more susceptible to flooding, remained sparsely settled until 1785, when 274 immigrants established themselves in the Valenzuela district.[36]

An additional 600 immigrants found homes along the central Lafourche between modern-day Labadieville and Lafourche Crossing. The densest concentration of immigrants, however, was in the Napoleonville area, where Acadian refugees from France constituted 85 percent of the local land grantees; though the 1785 immigrants constituted a majority of the settlers on the natural levee between Napoleonville and Raceland, they shared the available lands with a large minority of former Ascension Parish and Cabannocé settlers.[37]

Though the overwhelming majority of Acadian settlers in the Lafourche Valley demonstrated a clear preference for prime lands along the natural levee, a few hardy souls ventured into the wilderness along the bayou's major distributaries. Four Acadians established their homes along the Attakapas Canal sometime between 1793 and 1803, while two more—both 1785 immigrants—settled along Bayou Boeuf. Finally, few Acadians dared to explore, and only seven families actually occupied, lands in the densely forested, natural levee along Bayou Terrebonne.[38]

The exiles' reluctance to inhabit the alluvial lands along Bayou Lafourche's usually unnavigable distributaries profoundly influenced settlement patterns in the predominately Acadian areas east of the Atchafalaya River. As the population density of the First and Second Acadian Coasts grew in the 1770s and early 1780s, at least eighteen Acadian families, the patriarchs of which usually could expect not more than a small, practically uninhabitable slice of their par-

36. Voorhies, *Some Late Eighteenth-Century Louisianians*, 201–14; Petition from the Assumption Parish settlers to Unzaga, October 16, 1773, PPC, 189A:498; Winzerling, *Acadian Odyssey*, 136.

37. Claims, Southeast District, West of the Mississippi River, Reel 177, T.15S, R.17E, T.145, R. 18E, Reel 171, T.13S, R.14E, T.13S, R.15E.

38. *American State Papers: Public Lands Series*, II, 432–33.

ents' estate, capitalized upon the easing of Spanish restrictions on intracolonial movement by migrating to the virtually uncharted central and lower Lafourche Valley. The availability of lands along the Lafourche declined rapidly after 1785, when hundreds of Acadian refugees from France congregated in the Labadieville, Napoleonville, Thibodaux, and Lafourche Crossing areas. Indeed, following the 1785 influx, the upper and central Lafourche Valley became as heavily populated as the Acadian Coasts, with narrow, contiguous farms—usually six arpents by forty arpents—stretching from Donaldsonville to Lafourche Crossing by 1793.[39]

The occupation of the Lafourche Valley paralleled closely the Acadian settlement of the southwestern prairie, despite dissimilarity between the sites. In both instances, the original settlers faced problems often linked to a rapidly expanding population—epidemic disease and the growing scarcity of arable land—as well as the inevitable clashes between the exiles and neighboring sociocultural groups, particularly the long-established and aristocratic Creoles. Intercultural feuds intensified as population density in the original Acadian settlements increased in the 1770s and 1780s, forcing some immigrants to seek a self-imposed exile on the South Louisiana frontier. Other Acadians were driven from the population centers by the rapid decline of familial landholdings through forced heirship laws. Finally, most 1785 immigrants, on both sides of the Atchafalaya River, chose to carve a new life in frontier areas on the periphery of existing settlements.

Regardless of the cause, ever increasing numbers of Acadians sought new homes in the South Louisiana wilderness shortly after their establishment in the colony. With the exception of ten Cabannocé families who had traversed the Atchafalaya Basin and estab-

39. Census of the Lafourche post, 1788, PPC, 201:668–80. The concentration of Acadian settlers on the upper Lafourche is best reflected in the 1810 census, which indicates that Assumption Parish's Acadian population (884 individuals) was second only to that of St. James Parish (Cabannocé) among the predominately Acadian parishes east of the Atchafalaya River. Lafourche Parish, on the other hand, boasted only 299 Acadian residents—the second-lowest total among the eastern Acadian parishes. Third Decennial Census of the United States, 1810, Population Schedules, Louisiana, Assumption and Lafourche parishes, National Archives, Washington, D.C., microfilm copy on deposit at Jefferson Caffery Louisiana Room, Dupré Library, University of Southwestern Louisiana; American State Papers: Public Lands Series, II, 394–433. See also Claims, Southeast District, Reels 171–77, T.13S, R.14E, T.15S, R.17E.

lished themselves at Attakapas and Opelousas by 1783, Acadian pioneers consistently ventured only as far as the nearest unoccupied
waterfront property. In the Attakapas and Opelousas posts, settlers
abandoning their original homes crossed the neighboring prairies
only as far as the nearest stream. The residents of the Acadian
Coasts were hemmed in by swamps, and the surplus population was
forced to migrate into the alluvial lands along Bayou Lafourche and,
after 1795, Bayou Terrebonne.[40]

These large demographic movements in the late eighteenth century would influence profoundly the course of early-nineteenth-cen-
tury Acadian history. By 1803 the exiles and their descendants had
established settlement patterns that have endured to the present; indeed, except for small-scale migrations into the prairies and cheniers
between the Mermentau and Calcasieu rivers, and to the natural
levees along Bayous Black, Blue, Boeuf, and Terrebonne in Lafourche
and Terrebonne parishes, population growth would be largely confined to the colonial areas of population for well over a century.

40. *American State Papers: Public Lands Series*, II, 432.

DEPORTATION OF THE ACADIANS FROM ILE ST. JEAN, 1758
PAINTING BY LEWIS PARKER, REPRODUCED COURTESY OF PARKS CANADA

ACADIANS BUILDING DIKES IN NOVA SCOTIA
PAINTING BY LEWIS PARKER, REPRODUCED COURTESY OF PARKS CANADA

GOVERNOR ANTONIO DE ULLOA
FROM MARC VILLIERS DU TERRAGE, *LES DERNIÈRES ANNÉES DE LA LOUISIANE FRANÇAISE* (1903)

GOVERNOR ALEJANDRO O'REILLY
FROM ALCÉE FORTIER, *HISTORY OF LOUISIANA* (1904)

GOVERNOR ESTEVAN MIRO
FROM ALCÉE FORTIER, *HISTORY OF LOUISIANA* (1904)

ALEXANDRE, CHEVALIER
DECLOUET, COMMANDANT OF
THE ATTAKAPAS DISTRICT,
1774–1789, WHO IN 1782
REFERRED TO "LA NATION
ACADIENNE . . . CETTE
MÉCHANTE NATION."
COURTESY OF THE DECLOUET FAMILY

AN ACADIAN SETTLEMENT ALONG THE MISSISSIPPI RIVER, A PAINTING
BY AN UNKNOWN ARTIST

FROM MARC DE VILLIERS DU TERRAGE, *LES DERNIÈRES ANNÉES DE LA LOUISIANE
FRANÇAISE* (1903)

REPLICA OF AN ACADIAN PIONEER'S HOUSE, LONGFELLOW-EVANGELINE
STATE COMMEMORATIVE AREA, ST. MARTINVILLE

PHOTO BY THE AUTHOR

THE AMAND BROUSSARD HOUSE, REPUTEDLY BUILT AT FAUSSE POINT
BETWEEN 1790 AND 1810. IT WAS RECENTLY MOVED TO NEW IBERIA.
PHOTO BY THE AUTHOR

SUPPORT BEAMS IN THE AMAND BROUSSARD HOUSE, NEW IBERIA. NOTE
THE MUD INFILL (*BOUSILLAGE*) BETWEEN THE BEAMS.
PHOTO BY THE AUTHOR

7

From Barachois to Bayou: The Metamorphosis of Acadian Culture in Spanish Louisiana

The rapid metamorphosis of Acadian society in New Acadia was necessitated by environmental factors. Thrust into the wilderness, these immigrants, like Louisiana's first European settlers, the Creoles, initially sought to impose upon the lower Mississippi Valley's subtropical environment the economic and agricultural regimes of their homeland and, in Opelousas at least, attempted to cultivate wheat. Unlike the Creoles, who for decades attempted unsuccessfully to produce wheat, the Acadians demonstrated far greater flexibility and adaptability. Profiting by the Creoles' mistakes, they quickly adopted time-proven Louisiana crops and agricultural practices. Within ten years most of the exiles attained a standard of living at least equal to that of predispersal Nova Scotia. In 1777, for example, the typical Acadian resident of Ascension Parish owned 14.7 cattle, 11.59 hogs, and 1.03 sheep. These figures compare favorably with corresponding ones—12.7 cattle, 8.95 hogs, and 12.04 sheep—enumerated in the 1701 census of Mines, the area from which most of the immigrants of the late 1760s were drawn. As the void created by the dearth of sheep was filled by large flocks of chickens (22.2 in the average household in 1772), the median livestock holdings in New Acadia were at least on a par with those of vieille Acadie.[1]

1. Petition to Ulloa from the Opelousas Acadians, March 13, 1768, PPC, 187A: n.p.; John G. Clark, *New Orleans, 1718–1812: An Economic History* (Baton Rouge, 1970), 185; Antoine Simon Le Page du Pratz, *The History of Louisiana Translated from the French of M. La Page du Pratz* (1774; rpr. Baton Rouge, 1975), 61, 161–62, 177, 182, 227; Louis Judice, "Report on the Lafourche Valley," January 1, 1786, PPC, 199:247; Ascen-

The exiles achieved a uniform level of prosperity despite the emergence of divergent agricultural pursuits on a subregional basis. This economic diversity reflected their agrarian heritage. Most Attakapas Acadians (77.7 percent), for example, were former residents of the Chignecto area, a sparsely wooded sea marsh and prairie that for half a century before the Grand Dérangement had supported small cattle ranches.[2]

Husbandry was the very foundation of the Chignecto economy, and as early as 1707, the area boasted forty-two ranches. Though chronically neglected, the herds multiplied rapidly, providing the ranchers with large surpluses by the early eighteenth century. In the mid-1740s the provincial government reported that Acadians were smuggling from six hundred to seven hundred cattle—primarily Beaubassin beefs—to the neighboring French settlements on Ile St. Jean and Cape Breton Island.[3]

In view of their background, it is hardly surprising that the 1765 Acadian immigrants, whose leaders were drawn exclusively from the Chignecto Isthmus, selected homesites in South Louisiana's prime grasslands and immediately engaged in ranching. These cattlemen quickly adapted traditional ranching techniques to their new environment, and though their cattle continued to graze unoccupied lands in the royal domain without constant supervision, they nevertheless vigorously protected their livestock from the roving herds of

sion Parish Original Acts (hereinafter abbreviated APOA), Book A, 37–39, Office of the Clerk of Court, Donaldsonville, La., microfilm copy on deposit at Center for Louisiana Studies, University of Southwestern Louisiana; Anne Trahan Succession, January 15, 1775, St. Martin Parish Original Acts (hereinafter abbreviated SMOA), Volume I, Office of the Clerk of Court, St. Martinville, Louisiana, microfilm copy on deposit at Center for Louisiana Studies; List of the goods from the royal warehouse given to the Acadians from St-Domingue, April 30, 1765. AC, C 13a, 45:30; Clark, *Acadia*, 150; Census of Iberville Parish, 1772, PPC, 202:241–46; Census of Ascension Parish, April 15, 1777, PPC, 190:173; Clarence LeBreton, "Civilisation materielle en Acadie," in Jean Daigle (ed.), *Les Acadiens des Maritimes* (Moncton, N.B., 1980), 467–520; Carl A. Brasseaux, "Acadian Life Under the Spanish Regime," *Les Cahiers de la Société historique acadienne*, X (1979), 132–41; Robert Hale, "Journal of a Voyage to Nova Scotia Made in 1731 by Robert Hale of Beverly," *Historical Collections of the Essex Institute*, XLII (1906), 217–41; Anne Saunier Succession, May, 1773, Opelousas Colonial Records, Louisiana State Archives and Records Service, Baton Rouge, Louisiana; Joseph Prejean Estate, July 4, 1772, APOA, Book A, 37–39.

2. Arsenault, *Histoire*, II–VI; Voorhies, *Some Late Eighteenth-Century Louisianians*, 114–28; "Copie d'un vieux registre," 1–8.

3. Rameau de St-Père, *Une Colonie féodale*, I, 172–74; Clark, *Acadia*, 258.

wild cattle that could easily assimilate semidomesticated longhorns. Ranchers also quickly utilized horses, which had been scarce in Nova Scotia and employed primarily as draft animals, to trace the movements of cattle in the broad expanses of the southwestern prairies. Finally, to discourage rustling in their area, the exiles embraced and actively promoted the use of cattle brands.[4]

The Acadians' skill as animal husbandrymen, the fecundity of their cattle, the lushness of verdant grasslands in the Attakapas district, and the region's mild climate (which extended the life span of weak and aged cattle), interacted to produce a remarkable growth rate among the Acadian herds. By 1771, only six years after their arrival as destitute immigrants, the Attakapas ranchers owned an average of 22 cattle and 6 horses—approximately twice the corresponding livestock holdings in the last extant predispersal Chignecto census. This comparison is placed in proper perspective only when one considers that the foregoing Nova Scotian population count reflected over thirty-five years of development in the Beaubassin cattle industry. Median Attakapas livestock holdings rose steadily throughout the late eighteenth century, despite the ranchers' renewed interest in marketing their cattle. In fact, by 1803, Acadian livestock production had increased by at least 500 percent, and in the Quartier de Vermilion alone, the average Acadian *vacherie* included 125 cattle and 23 horses.[5]

Faced with the difficulty of managing large herds with only the family labor pool, the prairie Acadians quickly resumed the practice of driving surplus beef to the nearest outlet. In 1773 Amant and Pierre Broussard, assisted by eight or nine drovers, began moving small herds of cattle to New Orleans. Following the Collet Trail along

4. Rees (trans.), "The Dauterive Compact," 91; Arsenault, *Histoire*, VI; Claude Boutté to Bernardo de Gálvez, February 22, 1777, PPC, 190:131–34; LeDéc to Unzaga, January 27, 1779, PPC, 192:200; LeDée to DeClouet, December 21, 1778, PPC, 198A:176; Dauterive to Unzaga, September 13, 1774, PPC, 189A:101–102; (Unzaga?) to DeClouet, September 13, 1774, PPC, 189A:102–103; Demezières to Unzaga, August 8, 1774, PPC, 198A:92–93; LeDée to Unzaga, April 18, 1774, PPC, 189A:83–83vo, 92–93; Minutes of an assembly regarding the "abandonment" of stray cattle, July 27, 1777, PPC, 190:293; Brasseaux, "Acadian Life," 133; Brand Book for the Opelousas and Attakapas Districts, in the Jefferson Caffery Louisiana Room, Dupré Library, University of Southwestern Louisiana.

5. Census of the Attakapas post, 1771, PPC, 188C:43vo; Clark, *Acadia*, 150; Census of Quartier de Vermilion, 1803, PPC, 220B:68.

Bayou Teche, and the Bayou Black and Bayou Lafourche natural levees, the cowboys initially guided only Creole-owned beef—usually in herds of 100 to 150 head—to the Crescent City slaughterhouse, but following Spain's belated entrance into the American Revolution in 1779, the few surplus beefs on Acadian *vacheries* were also driven to market. By maintaining this crucial supply line to the colonial capital during the war, the Acadian ranchers and drovers not only prevented food shortages in New Orleans but also provided vital logistical support to the Spanish army during Bernardo de Gálvez's Baton Rouge, Mobile, and Pensacola campaigns that ended the British presence along the Gulf Coast.[6]

Trade patterns established during the American Revolution persisted for over half a century. The Acadian percentage of cattle shipped to New Orleans, however, rose sharply as prairie herds proliferated in the 1780s and 1790s. In 1781, for example, the Attakapas post was shipping approximately 150 cattle to New Orleans each month, with Acadians apparently contributing only 10 to 20 percent of these herds. But, in the middle to late 1780s, the Acadian contribution to the New Orleans supply shipments increased substantially as such ranchers as François Pierre Broussard, Olivier Thibodeau, Firmin Breau, and Pierre Dugas were ordered to ship their rapidly expanding beef surpluses to the colonial capital. Despite their changing role in the Louisiana cattle industry, the exiles remained dominant as cattle drovers in the late eighteenth century.[7]

6. Fuselier de La Claire to Unzaga, November 2, 1773, PPC, 189A:66vo–67; Claude Boutté to Gálvez, February 22, 1777, PPC, 190:131–33; Judice to Unzaga, November 15, 1775, PPC, 189B:288; Passport for Pierre Broussard, December 29, 1779, PPC, 192:256; Judice to Gálvez, January 16, 1780, PPC, 193B:324–25vo; DeClouet to Miro, March 31, 1783, PPC, 196:162–63; DeClouet to Unzaga, January 4, 1775, PPC, 187A: n.p.; Judice to (?), October 1, 1796, PPC, 212A:470–75vo; Judice to Miro, May 29, 1787, PPC, 200:530; DeClouet to Pedro Piernas, April 27, 1781, PPC, 194:145vo; Anonymous declaration regarding DeClouet and the New Orleans slaughterhouse, August 27, 1781, PPC, 194:190; Collet to DeClouet, March 24, 1783, PPC, 196:174–75; DeClouet to Gálvez, December 21, 1779, PPC, 193B:43–44; DeClouet to Gálvez, October 3, 1779, PPC, 192:239; DeClouet to Gálvez, December 29, 1779, PPC, 192:254–56; Gálvez to DeClouet, August 16, 1779, PPC, 192:227–28; DeClouet's ordinance, December 29, 1779, PPC, 192:256; DeClouet to Gálvez, April 13, 1781, PPC, 194:138vo–40; DeClouet to Piernas, April 27, 1781, PPC, 194:145vo; Piernas to DeClouet, May 13, 1781, PPC, 194:161vo; Official decree regarding the shipment of beef to New Orleans, August 27, 1781, PPC, 194:190; Piernas to DeClouet, September 21, 1781, PPC, 194:192.

7. DeClouet to Piernas, April 27, 1781, PPC, 194:145vo; Jean Delavillebeuvre to Miro, October 20, 1789, PPC, 212A:371.

The primary economic role of ranching in the Attakapas and Opelousas posts should not obscure the existence of a complementary subsistence farming system. As in Beaubassin, where the rise of the cattle industry had produced a corresponding decline in the region's cultivated acreage, Attakapas ranchers grew progressively smaller quantities of corn, vegetables, and cotton. These commodities, produced solely for home consumption and balanced with the fruits of husbandry, provided the prairie Acadians with all of the resources necessary for life *dans les savannes.*[8]

While agriculture played only a secondary role in the development of the prairie Acadian settlements, it was the very foundation of the Acadian Coast and upper Lafourche Valley economies. Except for the 1765 immigrants established at Cabannocé (who were predominately Cobequid natives), the Acadians settled by the French caretaker and Spanish colonial governments along the Mississippi River were drawn primarily from one Nova Scotian district—Mines and its component villages of Grand Pré and Pisiquid.[9] At St. Gabriel, in present-day Iberville Parish, for example, 83.3 percent of the settlers were natives of Grand Pré and Pisiquid. At San Luis de Natchez, natives of the Mines area resided in 95.8 percent of the local Acadian households. In predispersal Nova Scotia, Mines, lining the southern littoral of the Minas Basin, had been the colonial breadbasket. Renowned for their fine apple orchards, Mines farmers also generally cultivated vegetables, oats, rye, and wheat on five to ten arpents of reclaimed sea marsh. The diminutive fields belied the farms' productivity, and the farmers usually produced grain surpluses for export to New England smugglers at Baie Verte.[10]

The Mines agricultural tradition was perpetuated along the Mississippi River by the immigrants who arrived between 1766 and 1768 from exile in Maryland. In opening the Acadian Coast and upper Lafourche Valley to cultivation, immigrant farmers had to overcome three rather formidable obstacles: First, the most fertile land in the riverbottom farms lay near the waterfront that was invariably blan-

8. Clark, *Acadia*, 145; C. C. Robin, *Voyage to Louisiana*, trans. Stuart O. Landry (New Orleans, 1966), 191; Inventory of Anne Trahan Estate, January 15, 1775, SMOA, Vol. 1; Michel Trahan Estate, January 26, 1784, SMOA, Vol. 2.

9. Voorhies, *Some Late Eighteenth Century Louisianians*, 114–39; Arsenault, *Histoire*, II–VI; Chandler, "Odyssey Continued," 446–65; Chandler (trans. and ed.), "End of an Odyssey," 69–87.

10. Clark, *Acadia*, 150, 176–255; Lauvrière, *Tragédie*, I, 219.

keted by dense thickets of hardwood timber, usually live oak. Clearing the land in Louisiana's debilitatingly warm and humid climate, without the assistance of slaves, oxen, and, in many instances, proper tools, proved to be a painstakingly slow process. The land-clearing problem was compounded by the Acadians' unfamiliarity with "slash and burn" deforestation techniques. In Acadia, particularly in the Mines area, settlers had traditionally shunned woodlands, preferring reclaimed sea marsh that required no clearing. Indeed, by 1750, only five hundred acres of woodland had been cleared by predispersal Acadians, whereas over thirteen thousand acres of sea marsh had been reclaimed from the Bay of Fundy. The exiles nevertheless met this challenge with characteristic industry and determination—frequently working themselves to the point of complete physical exhaustion—and their lands exhibited slow but steady improvement. By the early 1770s the average Acadian farmer in the river settlements had cleared and cultivated at least two arpents—the minimum necessary for Spanish land patents—and had managed to produce at least seventy barrels of corn. In addition, inventories of Acadian estates indicate that an additional six to thirty arpents had been enclosed with cypress *pieux* fences.[11] Although not often subjected to corvées (forced-labor details on public improvements projects), the Maryland immigrants were nevertheless required, upon settlement, to protect their lands from the annual vernal inundations of the Mississippi River and its distributaries by building five- to six-foot levees. Informal settlement regulations of the 1760s acquired force of law through Governor O'Reilly's 1770 land ordinances specifying levee and road construction and maintenance under pain of land-grant revocation.[12]

11. Richard E. Chandler, "The St. Gabriel Acadians: The First Five Months," *Louisiana History*, XXI (1980), 292; Petition of the Opelousas Acadians to Ulloa, March 13, 1768, PPC, 187A:n.p.; Carl A. Brasseaux, "Frontier Tyranny: The Case of Commandant Louis Pellerin, 1764–1767," *McNeese Review*, XXVII (1980–81), 15–24. On the difficulty of clearing hardwood forests, see Carl A. Brasseaux (trans. and ed.), *A Comparative View of French Louisiana, 1699 and 1762: The Journals of Pierre Le Moyne d'Iberville and Jean-Jacques-Blaise d'Abbadie* (Lafayette, La., 1979), 72; Clark, *Acadia*, 237–38; Ulloa to Grimaldi, May 19, 1766, ASD, 2585:n.p.; "List of the St. James farmers who have corn and rice surpluses," November 3, 1770, PPC, 188A:5/16; "List of the Iberville post residents who have corn surpluses," 1770, PPC, 188A:5/13; "List of the Assumption Parish farmers having corn for sale," December 25, 1770, PPC, 188A:5/13; Loyola to Ulloa, August 30, 1767, PPC, 109:158.

12. Chandler, "The St. Gabriel Acadians," 294; Paulette Guilbert Martin (trans.),

Having cleared small sections of land—generally between two and five arpents by the late 1770s—Acadian pioneers faced the task of adapting to Louisiana's long growing season and high annual precipitation levels. Wheat, barley, and oats, for example, which had been the principal crops in the Mines area, were unsuited to South Louisiana's subtropical climate, as the immigrants' initial efforts to cultivate them demonstrated. They were thus compelled to cultivate small quantities of maize—a crop virtually unknown in Acadie— provided to them as seed grain by Louisiana's French and, later, Spanish governments.[13]

Discovery of a substitute grain, which would serve as the staple of the Acadian diet for over a century, was followed by the adoption of a new fiber-producing plant. Grand Pré farmers had consistently produced small quantities of flax for home consumption. Much of the Acadians' summer clothing had traditionally been fashioned from this linen. Flax would not grow well in semitropical Louisiana, and by 1770 the exiles had discarded it. In addition, Acadian winter clothing had been cut from woolen cloth produced by the ubiquitous household spinning wheels and looms. But sheep were scarce in the river settlements in colonial Louisiana, and the immigrants initially lacked the means to purchase them. Only in the late 1770s did significant numbers of Acadians attempt to rebuild their once-large sheep herds, but the number of shepherds and the size of their flocks remained consistently small throughout the late eighteenth century.[14]

"Ordinance Regulating Concessions and Cattle in Spanish Louisiana, 1770," *Attakapas Gazette*, XII (1977), 180–82; Frank H. Tomkins, *Riparian Lands of the Mississippi River . . .* (New Orleans, 1901), 20–22, 35–45; J. P. Kemper, *Floods in the Valley of the Mississippi* (New Orleans, 1928), 21–31.

13. Martin (trans.), "Ordinance Regulating Concessions and Cattle," 180; Ulloa to Grimaldi, May 19, 1766, ASD, 2585:n.d.; Inventory of Charles Babin's Estate, June 3, 1774, PPC, 189B:543–46; Desirée LeBlanc Estate, November 8, 1777, Isabelle LeBlanc Estate, April 18, 1778, and Simon Landry Estate, May 16, 1782, all in APOA, Book A; James Calhoun (ed.), *Louisiana Almanac, 1979–1980* (Gretna, La., 1979), 98; Clark, *Acadia*, 35, 151, 164; Rameau de St-Père, *Une Colonie féodale*, I, 230; Petition to Ulloa from the Opelousas Acadians, March 13, 1768, PPC, 187A:n.p.; Judice, "Report on the Lafourche Valley," January 1, 1786, PPC, 199:247; Michael James Foret, "Aubry, Foucault, and the Attakapas Acadians, 1765," *Attakapas Gazette*, XV (1980), 60–63; Ulloa to Grimaldi, May 19, 1766, ASD, 2585:n.p.

14. Lauvrière, *Tragédie*, I, 183; Paulette Guilbert Martin (trans.), "The Kelly-Nugent Report of the Inhabitants and Livestock in the Attakapas, Natchitoches, Opelousas and Rapides Posts, 1770," *Attakapas Gazette*, XI (1976), 187–93; Clark, *Acadia*, 145, 169, 175; Jeanne Arseneault, *Rapport de recherche sur le costume historique*

Lacking access to traditional fiber producers, the river Acadians, as well as their Teche Valley cousins, soon learned to produce cotton, which was not only more comfortable than wool but also could be used as a year-round fabric. Cotton was easy to wash and fashion into thread and was easily woven into cloth on the looms that re-emerged in the immigrant households by the early 1770s.[15]

Louisiana's new settlers quickly mastered cotton cultivation, harvesting, and processing. As early as 1772, Acadians on both sides of the Atchafalaya (but particularly in the river settlements) were utilizing pre-Whitney cotton gins to remove seeds and facilitate spinning.[16] Cotton threads were woven into broadcloth, and throughout Louisiana, Acadian *cotonnade* (cotton broadcloth) quickly became synonymous with excellence.

Domestic fiber and grain production was supplemented by the fruits of the family gardens. In Acadia, principal garden products had been field peas, turnips, and cabbage. Turnips and cabbage, however, could be produced only in Louisiana's short winter season and hence quickly declined in importance. Peas remained a garden staple and were complemented by various bean varieties. In a 1786 report on agriculture on the First Acadian Coast and in the upper Lafourche Valley, Louis Judice indicated that field peas, kidney beans, "red beans, butter beans, and English peas" were among the most significant local crops.[17]

Despite their significant role in Acadian agriculture, peas and beans were produced exclusively for domestic consumption. Also produced in small quantities for home use were rice, tobacco, squash,

---

acadien (Caraquet, N.B., 1979), 2–4; Census of Ascension Parish, April 15, 1777, PPC, 190:173; Census of Attakapas District, 1771, PPC, 188C:43vo; Voorhies, *Some Late Eighteenth-Century Louisianians*, 201–13.

15. Martin (trans.), "Kelly-Nugent Report," 191–92; Joseph Prejean Estate, July 4, 1772, APOA, Book A; Unzaga to Verret, June 1, 1772, PPC, 189A:137; Joseph Richard Estate, December 24, 1776, and Desirée LeBlanc Estate, November 8, 1777, both in APOA, Book A.

16. Joseph Prejean Estate, July 4, 1772, Joseph Richard Estate, December 24, 1776, and Simon Landry Estate, May 16, 1782, all in APOA, Book A; François Savoy Estate, December 28, 1780, SMOA; Anne Saunier Cormier Estate, May 12, 1773, Opelousas Colonial Records.

17. Clark, *Acadia*, 242; W. F. Ganong (ed.), "The Cadillac Memoir of 1692," *Collections of the New Brunswick Historical Society*, No. 13 (1930), 80; Judice, "Report on the Lafourche Valley," January 1, 1786, PPC, 199:247.

and pumpkins. Although the Acadians had been inveterate pipe smokers from the outset of French colonization in Acadia (a trait they borrowed from their Micmac neighbors), seventeenth- and eighteenth-century travel accounts suggest that they themselves produced little if any tobacco and apparently acquired this commodity by barter from local Indians. Perhaps because of poor Acadian-Indian relations in Louisiana, river Acadians began cultivating small quantities of tobacco by the mid-1770s.[18]

Rice was also cultivated as a secondary crop, particularly by the river Acadians. Sown in lowlands subject to spring flooding, providence rice (so named because of its dependence upon rainfall for irrigation) was used primarily as an insurance crop to provide the farmers with grain in such years as 1785, when the South Louisiana corn crop failed. In the absence of necessary irrigation technology, rice remained a marginal crop, a fact perhaps best demonstrated when in 1788, only 4 of the 276 Acadian households enumerated in the Lafourche census produced the grain in appreciable quantities.[19]

Despite their notable lack of success with rice, the Acadians continued to experiment with subtropical crops throughout the late eighteenth century, and by 1804 small quantities of okra were produced in river settlement farms. This vegetable from West Africa was probably brought in by slaves acquired by river and Lafourche Valley Acadians in the late 1790s.[20]

The remarkable diversity of Acadian agricultural production was not restricted to row crops. The Grand Pré and Port Royal tradition of maintaining small orchards persisted, but the component apple trees were replaced by figs, peaches, and apricots.[21] In addition, by the 1780s, many river and upper Lafourche Acadians tended concord, white, and muscadine grape vines.

18. Judice, "Report on the Lafourche Valley," January 1, 1786, PPC, 199:247; Judice to Unzaga, October 6, 1772, PPC, 189A:448; Piernas to Ulloa, April 6, 1768, PPC, 2357:n.p.; Clark, *Acadia,* 157, 62, 230.

19. Census of the Lafourche post, 1788, PPC, 201:668–80; Miro to (?), March 18, 1785, PPC, 198A:369.

20. Robin, *Voyage to Louisiana,* 115; Wellington (ed.), "The Journal of Dr. John Sibley," 480–81; General Census of the Valenzuela District of the Lafourche post, 1797, PPC, 213:286–311.

21. Clark, *Acadia,* 144, 151, 165–66; Ganong (ed.), "The Cadillac Memoir," 60; Fontaine (ed.), *Voyage du Sieur de Dièreville,* 60; Rameau de St-Père, *Une Colonie féodale,* I, 1:176; Judice, "Report on the Lafourche Valley," January 1, 1786, PPC, 199:247.

Adapting to the plethora of orchard and agricultural products proved no easy task.[22] The evolution of Acadian agriculture was further complicated by the radically different planting techniques demanded by row crops, new insect pests, and longer growing seasons. Finally, Acadian farmers were forced to utilize technology for neutralizing the baneful effects of Louisiana's high precipitation levels.

The most effective weapon in the war against flooding was the plow, a tool with which the Acadian immigrants were not very familiar. Until the early eighteenth century, plows were quite rare in Acadia, and wheat and other cereal crops were sown by broadcasting seed. Even in the mid-eighteenth century, ox-drawn, wooden plows enjoyed only limited use, and furrows were seldom more than two or three inches deep. In Louisiana, such small furrows were incapable of handling the region's torrential rains, and crops were exposed to frequent, extended flooding and the resulting root rot. Hence, river and upper Lafourche Acadians quickly acquired oxen and apparently learned to cut deeper furrows.[23]

The flooding problem was also alleviated by the effective use of ditches. In 1770 Acadian farmers were directed by the colonial government to build and maintain drainage systems on their *habitations*.[24] The immigrants generally complied, with gratifying results. Throughout the decade, production levels increased, and by the mid-1770s the typical Acadian river parish farmer produced annually thirty barrels of surplus corn.

Surpluses soon appeared in other food-producing activities on the exiles' river settlement farms. Upon arrival, the immigrants had been given two cows and seven chickens by the colonial government. Within a few months, they also acquired small numbers of

22. Ulloa to Grimaldi, May 19, 1766, ASD, 2585:n.p.; Ulloa to Grimaldi, September 29, 1766, ASD, 2585:n.p.
23. Ganong (ed.), "The Cadillac Memoir," 80; Fontaine (ed.), *Voyage du Sieur de Dièreville*, 53–54; Clark, *Acadia*, 167, 233; Loyola to Ulloa, August 30, 1767, PPC, 109:158; Anne Trahan Estate, January 15, 1775, and Helène Landry Estate, May 26, 1775, both in SMOA, Vol. 1; Anne Saunier Estate, May 12, 1773, Opelousas Colonial Records; Joseph Richard Estate, December 24, 1776, and Desirée LeBlanc Estate, November 8, 1777, both in APOA, Book A.
24. Martin, "Ordinance Regulating Concessions and Cattle," 180; François-Xavier Martin, *The History of Louisiana from the Earliest Period* (2 vols.; New Orleans, 1827–29), I, 279.

hogs—the principal source of protein in their predispersal settlements—probably from slaves in neighboring settlements. The hogs and hens proliferated quickly, and in 1772 the typical Acadian Coast household owned twenty-four pigs and twenty-two fowl. In addition, though the topography and population density militated against cattle herding, the river and eastern bayou Acadians maintained, by the early 1770s, small numbers of cattle.[25]

Capital for the acquisition of livestock was derived from smuggling. By 1770 immigrants were seeking markets for their surplus grain, and they found eager buyers in the English merchants at Manchac. For half a century prior to the Grand Dérangement, Grand Pré farmers had bartered wheat and barley for manufactured goods and specie with Boston smugglers at Baie Verte. Despite the lingering memories of the expulsion, this economic system was resuscitated by the Acadians themselves on the banks of the Mississippi; the exiles soon realized that English Manchac, an east-bank trading post near present-day Baton Rouge, offered a lucrative market for all types of foodstuffs. High prices fetched by agricultural produce in English territory were made even more attractive by the Spanish government's long-enduring policy of levying artificially low prices on New Orleans-bound, Louisiana-grown goods. The Acadian contribution to this contraband traffic persisted and even expanded, despite increasingly stringent measures taken by the colonial regime to divert all Louisiana produce to the Crescent City. Traveling by night in pirogues and eluding Spanish guards at Fort St. Gabriel by coasting along the west bank, smugglers carried "eggs, milk, pork, and corn" to English Manchac. There the commodities were bartered for manufactured items—particularly cast-iron tools—which were in constant demand in South Louisiana's frontier society. Though the flow of contraband dwindled in the mid-1770s as a result of flood damage to crops, this illicit trade pattern persisted until the American Revolution, when Spanish forces captured British West Florida and annexed the province to Louisiana. River Acadians then, like

25. Ulloa to Grimaldi, May 19, 1766, ASD, 2585:n.p.; Carl A. Brasseaux, "Administration of Slave Regulations in French Louisiana, 1724–1766," *Louisiana History*, XXI (1980), 144–45; General Census of the Iberville post, May 10, 1772, PPC, 202:241–46; Judice to Unzaga, October 29, 1775, PPC, 189B:247; Judice, "Report on the Lafourche Valley," January 1, 1786, PPC, 199:247; Judice to Unzaga, December 4, 1771, PPC, 189A:280; Judice to Carondelet, January 8, 1793, PPC, 208:215–16vo.

their prairie cousins, began shipping to New Orleans their produce—
corn and ever increasing surpluses of corn-fed hogs.[26]

The Acadian eagerness to engage in business with their recent
oppressors bears testimony to their pragmatism and business acu-
men. The contraband trade proved more lucrative than government-
regulated intracolonial commerce, and thus the immigrants simply
pursued their own interests. Similarly, despite chronically poor
Acadian-Creole relations throughout the late eighteenth century,
stemming from boundary disputes and conflicting world views, the
western settlers regularly worked as cattle drovers for the Creole
cattle barons. Cattle drives through Louisiana swamps and mosquito-
infested forests were physically taxing and dangerous, and the drovers were well paid, usually with sufficient funds to stock their own
small *vacheries* with a few cattle. With such monetary incentives, the
Acadians effectively suppressed their burning enmity toward their
present and former oppressors; only during heated civil disputes
and at the time of Spain's declaration of war against England in 1779
did the exiles permit their true feelings to surface.[27]

Pragmatism evidenced in the Acadians' business dealings was also
manifested in the adaptability of Acadian cuisine, costume, and architecture to new materials and climatic conditions. Age-old Acadian
cooking techniques remained fundamentally unaltered throughout
the late eighteenth century, despite radical changes in the immigrants' diet. In Acadia the diet had revolved around the seasonal
fruits of agriculture, fishing and hunting. During the spring and

26. Charles Descoudreaux to Unzaga, (1770), PPC, 188B:182; Rameau de St-Père,
Une Colonie féodale, I, 219; Unzaga to Verret, August 30, 1770, PPC, 188A:1d/42, 44a;
Unzaga to Verret, August 11, 1770, PPC, 188A:1d/42; Descoudreaux to Unzaga,
March 23, 1771, PPC, 188B:211; Margaret Fisher Dalrymple (ed.), *The Merchant of
Manchac: The Letterbooks of John Fitzpatrick, 1768–1790* (Baton Rouge, 1978), 13–20, 87,
95, 102, 104, 196; Judice to Unzaga, January 4, 1776, PPC, 189B:302; Judice to Unzaga,
October 27, 1776, PPC, 189B:343; Judice to Gálvez, February 16, 1780, PPC, 193B:
331–32; Judice to Miro, March 23, 1785, PPC, 197:297; Judice, "Report on the
Lafourche Valley," January 1, 1786, PPC, 199:247; Pierre-Louis Berquin-Duvallon, *Vue
de la colonie espagnole du Mississippi, ou des provinces de Louisiane et Floride occidentale, en
l'année 1802* (Paris, 1803), 51–53.

27. Unzaga to Verret, August 11, 1770, PPC, 188A:1d/42; Contract between Pierre
Dugas, Jean-Baptiste Cavalier, François Grevemberg, and Barthélémy Grevemberg,
October 29, 1777, SMOA, Vol. 1; Rees (trans.), "The Dauterive Compact," 91; Fuselier
to Unzaga, November 2, 1773, PPC, 189A:66vo–67; Judice to Gálvez, September 19,
1779, PPC, 192: 561–63; Judice to Unzaga, February 25, 1774, PPC, 189A:535.

summer months wild game and fish provided settlers a steady source of protein, while the ubiquitous family gardens yielded peas and a large variety of other vegetables.[28]

In autumn, surplus livestock—particularly hogs—was slaughtered, and though some beef and pork were consumed immediately, most of the meat was salted for use during the approaching winter months. Seventeenth- and eighteenth-century observers consistently reported the Acadian affinity for salt pork, noting that the Bay of Fundy area settlers preferred bacon to wild game, including such delicacies as partridges.[29]

The autumnal butchery was merely the first stage of the Acadians' crucial fall food-gathering system. In September farmers harvested wheat, barley, and rye and transported their grain to local mills for grinding. Turnips and cabbages, staples of the winter diet, also matured in autumn, but only the turnips were harvested and stored in cellars. Cabbages were "refrigerated" in snow-covered fields until gathered in small amounts for immediate consumption. Finally, apples and spruce sprouts were stored in cellars for winter consumption, and a portion of the apple crop was diverted into cider production. Cider, however, enjoyed only moderate popularity among the predispersal Acadians, who clearly preferred spruce-sprout beer, a noted Canadian antiscorbutic.[30]

Despite the variety of foods available to them, the Bay of Fundy–area Acadians generally prepared their meals with two basic cooking techniques—boiling and frying. These methods were dictated both by the widespread use of black, cast-iron cauldrons and the heavy consistency of the component foods. Salt pork required extensive boiling, as did most wild game and the shellfish gathered in tidal pools during the spring. Most Acadian vegetables also required cooking in boiling water, particularly turnips and cabbage, which were often cooked together in *soupe de la toussaint*, an extremely popular predispersal delicacy, during the winter months.[31]

28. Clark, *Acadia*, 60–61, 165; Hale, "Journal of a Voyage to Nova Scotia Made in 1731," 233.

29. Fontaine (ed.), *Voyage du Sieur de Dièreville*, 44, 53–54, 56; Rameau de St-Père, *Une Colonie féodale*, I, 176, 219, 224; Clark, *Acadia*, 242; Ganong (ed.), "The Cadillac Memoir," 80.

30. Fontaine (ed.), *Voyage du Sieur de Dièreville*, 45, 60, 85, 116; Clark, *Acadia*, 166.

31. Fontaine (ed.), *Voyage du Sieur de Dièreville*, 58; Hale, "Journal of a Voyage to

Unlike the staples of the Acadian diet, the gaspereau and shad, which served as important secondary sources of protein, required less cooking but higher temperatures. Hence, fish were usually fried in oil, probably bear oil (much to the chagrin of French travelers), because butter was practically unknown in Acadia.[32]

Just as frying was restricted to fish, so was baking restricted to bread. Whole wheat or mixed-grain bread was served at major meals, according to eighteenth-century observers, and the loaves were inevitably consumed with molasses and locally produced maple syrup.[33]

But the major ingredients for this Acadian delicacy were scarce and often unavailable in Louisiana, forcing the immigrants to substitute locally grown products. Corn bread thus quickly replaced whole wheat on Acadian tables, and by the early nineteenth century, the yellow cakes were often eaten with cane syrup.[34]

The flexibility of Acadian cooking techniques was also evidenced in the preparation of other food. Because turnips and cabbage were quite rare in the settlements, cooks quickly incorporated other locally grown vegetables and ingredients into their traditional winter soups. The result was *soupe de maïs* and, later, filé gumbo.

The emergence of gumbo in the Acadian culinary repertoire represented a new departure in Acadian cuisine, for it reflected the melding of cooking techniques developed by Franco-American, Indian, and African cultures. Thrust into a small geographical area with little mobility, the white, red, and black residents of South Louisiana were forced to interact on a daily basis, and although these confrontations were often unpleasant, all of the participating groups were inevitably influenced by their neighbors. This is particularly true of upwardly mobile Acadians and their African slaves.[35]

Nova Scotia Made in 1731," 233; Marielle Boudreau and Melvin Gallant, *La Cuisine traditionelle en Acadie* (Moncton, N.B., 1975), 11–124; Clark, *Acadia*, 166.

32. Hale, "Journal of a Voyage to Nova Scotia Made in 1731," 233; Fontaine (ed.), *Voyage du Sieur de Dièreville*, 58.

33. Fontaine (ed.), *Voyage du Sieur de Dièreville*, 61; Hale, "Journal of a Voyage to Nova Scotia Made in 1731," 233.

34. Clark, *New Orleans*, 179, 258; Brasseaux, "*L'Officier de Plume*," 64–82; Dalrymple (ed.), *The Merchant of Manchac*, 39, 53, 316; Frederick Law Olmsted, *A Journey Through Texas; or, a Saddle Trip on the Southwestern Frontier* (New York, 1857), 405.

35. Patricia Harris, "Cuisine in Acadiana," in Steven L. Del Sesto and Jon L. Gibson (eds.), *The Culture of Acadiana: Tradition and Change in South Louisiana* (Lafayette, La., 1975), 80; Carl A. Brasseaux, "Acadians, Creoles, and the 1787 Lafourche Smallpox Outbreak," *Louisiana Review*, VIII (1978), 55–61.

The vast majority of Louisiana Acadians acquired one to three slaves between 1790 and 1810, and these black laborers imparted elements of their cuisine and diet to their new masters. Okra, for example, is an African vegetable introduced to Louisiana by blacks via the West Indies. By 1804 gumbo featured okra, at least on the Acadian Coast. The black contribution to "Cajun" cooking was not limited to the prolific green vegetable; the ragu sauces now associated with Cajun cuisine bear striking resemblance to those of French West Africa and were perhaps also introduced into South Louisiana by slave cooks.[36]

Such delicacies as gumbo were reserved for weekend social gatherings or special occasions and they broke the monotony of the Acadian pioneers' daily fare all too infrequently. Although no late-eighteenth-century description of Acadian cuisine exists, evidence suggests that the typical meal consisted of salt pork, corn bread, and seasonal vegetables and fruits. Rice was consumed only rarely and then in small quantities, except in years when the corn crop failed. The steady diet of salt pork was often punctuated by eggs and wild game bagged by farmer-hunters on their winter expeditions. These hunting trips probably yielded mostly wild ducks and venison, though scanty archival evidence suggests that, then as now, few species were spared the hunters' onslaught. A less common protein substitute was poultry, because eggs constituted an important link in the Acadian food chain. Hens were slaughtered only when they had grown old and unproductive.[37]

The toughness of the old hens, wild game, and stringy longhorn beef, as well as the necessity of purging salt from the cured pork, dictated the perpetuation of predispersal cooking techniques. As in

36. Third Decennial Census of the United States, 1810, Population Schedules, Louisiana; Interview with Mathé Allain, May 12, 1980, Lafayette, Louisiana; Alexander Mouton Memoirs, in Lucile Meredith Mouton Griffith Papers, Collection 26, Tablet 1, pp. 2–4, Southwestern Archives, University of Southwestern Louisiana; Harris, "Cuisine in Acadiana," 80; Robin, *Voyage to Louisiana*, 115; Wellington (ed.), "The Journal of Dr. John Sibley," 480.

37. Olmsted, *A Journey Through Texas*, 405; Sam Bowers Hilliard, *Hog Meat and Hoecake: Food Supply in the Old South, 1840–1860* (Carbondale, Ill., 1972), 38–39; Berquin-Duvallon, *Vue de la colonie espagnole*, 52; Nicolas Deverbois to Miro, March 18, 1785, PPC, 198A:369; Ulloa to Grimaldi, March 9, 1766, ASD, 2585:n.p.; Judice to Unzaga, October 29, 1775, PPC, 189B:286; Judice, "Report on the Lafourche Valley," January 1, 1786, PPC, 199:247; Petition to kill crows, October 7, 1786, PPC, 199:220–30.

old Acadia, most major meals were prepared primarily by boiling. The typical eighteenth-century Acadian household consequently contained several iron cauldrons, suggesting that meat and green vegetables—primarily beans and peas—were prepared separately.[38]

Spanish-period Acadian households also consistently contained only one frying pan—undoubtedly used to fry eggs, bacon, and freshwater fish. But if late-nineteenth- and early-twentieth-century practice is any indication, the frying pan also doubled as a baking pan for corn bread.[39]

The remarkable adaptability of Acadian cuisine to Louisiana's agricultural products was matched by the capacity to harmonize their costume with Gulf Coast climatic conditions. Faced with bitterly cold winters and very cool weather during most of the spring and autumn months, Acadian men and women had worn woolen garments, often dyed red and black. But in Louisiana, sheep were scarce in the nascent settlements, and woolen garments were impractical in all but the very coldest winter days. Women quickly learned to substitute cotton for wool, and by 1772 cotton had become a major crop in Acadian Coast and Teche Valley settlements.[40]

Production of cotton cloth became the principal cottage industry by 1810. Raw cotton was either cleaned by hand or fed through pre-Whitney cotton gins, which were quite common in late-eighteenth-century Louisiana. The processed fiber was then spun into thread; the spools of thread were mounted on the ubiquitous household looms and woven into *cotonnade*. This rough fabric, which was usually left in its natural state or dyed indigo blue (though other colors were sometimes used), was then fashioned into clothing for the entire family: pants, *garde-soleils* (sun bonnets), shirts, blouses, *carmagnolles* (short, decorated vests), dresses, and floor-length skirts.[41]

38. Census of Iberville District, 1772, PPC, 202:241–46; Descoudreaux to Unzaga, January 14, 1772, PPC, 189A:565–66; Ulloa to Grimaldi, May 19, 1766, ASD, 2585: n.p.; Procès-verbal of the official inventory of Charles Babin's Estate, June 3, 1774, PPC, 189B:543–46; Anne Trahan Estate, January 15, 1775, SMOA, Vol. 1; Joseph Richard Estate, December 24, 1776, APOA.

39. Joseph Richard Estate, December 24, 1776, and Joseph Babin *dit* Dios Estate, December 30, 1783, both in APOA; François Savoy Estate, December 28, 1770, SMOA, Vol. 1; Fontaine (ed.), *Voyage du Sieur de Dièreville*, 58; Olmsted, *A Journey Through Texas*, 405.

40. Arseneault, *Rapport de recherche sur le costume historique acadien*, 4; Martin (trans.), "Kelly-Nugent Report," 192; Unzaga to Verret, June 1, 1772, PPC, 189A:137.

41. Carl A. Brasseaux (comp.), "A Report on Manufacturing and Manufactured

Woolen stockings, an integral part of the male and female costume in predispersal Acadia, were almost completely replaced by their lighter *cotonnade* counterparts. In fact, Acadian cotton stockings were of such fine quality that they formed a part of Governor Luis de Unzaga's wardrobe.[42]

Finally, despite radical environmental changes, Acadian footwear also changed very little in Louisiana. Although the traditional source of shoe leather—moose pelts—was unavailable, both sexes continued to wear moccasins, as they had in their homeland; however, use of moccasins in Louisiana was undoubtedly restricted to the winter months. The less common *sabots*, wooden shoes, made with willow wood and worn by both men and women working in damp environments, particularly on the Acadian dikes or in boats, were impractical in well-drained areas with firm soil. They were quickly abandoned in districts not subject to regular flooding and, by the early nineteenth century, were found only in the flood-prone Lafourche Valley settlements. Like *sabots*, professionally crafted leather shoes and silver buckles were quite uncommon among Louisiana Acadians, appearing in the succession inventories of only the most affluent farmers and drovers and occasionally in the estates of young bachelors. However commonplace the footwear, it was forsaken during Louisiana's hot and humid spring, summer, and fall months.

Articles, 1810," *Attakapas Gazette*, X (1975), 153; Carl A. Brasseaux (ed.), "An 1810 Census Report on the State of Manufacturing in the Northeastern Section of the Attakapas District," *Attakapas Gazette*, X (1975), 102; D. H. Thomas, "Pre-Whitney Cotton Gins in French Louisiana," *Journal of Southern History*, XXXI (1965), 134–48; Pierre Clement de Laussat, *Memoirs of My Life to My Son During the Years 1803 and After*, trans. Agnes-Josephine Pastwa, ed. Robert D. Bush (Baton Rouge, 1978), 64; Anne Saunier Estate, May 12, 1773, Opelousas Colonial Records; Joseph Prejean Estate, July 4, 1772, APOA; François Savoy Estate, December 28, 1780, and Anne Trahan Estate, January 15, 1777, both in SMOA; Martin (trans.), "Kelly-Nugent Report," 192; *Procès-verbal* of the examination and identification of Charles Babin's corpse, June 5, 1774, PPC, 189A:403; Clark, *New Orleans*, 187–88; Berquin-Duvallon, *Vue de la colonie espagnole*, 53–55; Robin, *Voyage to Louisiana*, 115–91; Inventory of Charles Babin's Estate, June 3, 1774, PPC, 189B:543–46; Joseph Richard Estate, December 24, 1776, APOA; François Savoy Estate, December 28, 1780, Anne Trahan Estate, January 5, 1775, and Helène Landry Estate, May 26, 1775, all in SMOA. By the early nineteenth century Acadian weavers used natural dyes to produce blue, white, red, black, yellow and gray cloth. George F. Reinecke (trans. and ed.), "Early Louisiana French Life and Folklore, from the Anonymous Breaux Manuscript as Edited by Professor Jay K. Ditchy," *Louisiana Folklore Miscellany*, II (1966), 21.

42. Joseph Richard Estate, December 24, 1776, Isabelle LeBlanc Estate, April 18, 1778, both in APOA; Martin (trans.), "Kelly-Nugent Report," 192; Robin, *Voyage to Louisiana*, 115.

During these seasons, the exiles—men, women, and children—
went barefoot, even to dances.[43]

Though discarding footwear in summertime afforded some relief
from the incessant heat, abandoning headgear most certainly did
not. Hats had been an integral part of predispersal Acadian costume,
and their design and function changed very little in Louisiana despite radical change in some component materials. In order to gird
themselves against direct sunlight and chilling winds, women had
traditionally draped woolen shawls over their heads and shoulders
when they ventured out of doors, particularly to work in the fields.
In Louisiana the shawl was replaced by the cotton *garde-soleil*, which,
like its woolen predecessor, covered both the shoulders and the head
but was adapted to the climate through the addition of rigid brims
and side panels to pull the neck guard away from the scalp and permit air circulation. Male headgear, on the other hand, required little
alteration. The men continued to wear soft felt hats in winter and for
formal occasions, and straw hats in spring and summer, especially
while laboring in the field. Nineteenth-century engravings, however,
suggest that the shape of the hats changed slightly in the late eighteenth century, with brims becoming flatter, wider, and more rigid,
as folk hatters began utilizing palmetto leaves in place of felt.[44]

By the American Revolution, the Acadian immigrants had completely adapted their Canadian wardrobe to the hot and humid Sun
Belt. Indeed, by 1776 Acadian succession records reveal remarkable
consistency of clothing design throughout South Louisiana, permitting the delineation of the "typical" male and female costumes. Men
commonly wore collarless, loose-fitting cotonnade shirts, usually

43. Fontaine (ed.), *Voyage du Sieur de Dièreville*, 53–54; Procès-verbal of the examination and identification of Charles Babin's corpse, June 5, 1774, PPC, 189A:403;
Robin, *Voyage to Louisiana*, 115; W. W. Pugh, "Bayou Lafourche from 1820–1825: Its
Inhabitants, Customs, and Pursuits," *Louisiana Planter and Sugar Manufacturer* (October 29, 1888), 143. Louisiana Acadians continued to wear moccasins and *cantiers* (moccasins with short leather leggings) until the mid-nineteenth century. Reinecke (trans.
and ed.), "Breaux Manuscript," 22.

44. Lauvrière, *Tragédie*, I, 183; Isabelle LeBlanc Estate, April 18, 1778, APOA;
Jeanne Arseneault and Lynn Losier, "Le Costume traditionel des hommes," in Arse-
neault and Losier, *Confectionnez vos costumes acadiens pour les fetes du 375ᵉ* (Caraquet,
N.B., 1980), 4; Joseph Richard Estate, December 24, 1776, APOA; Michel Meaux Es-
tate, May 10, 1785, SMOA; W. H. Sparks, *The Memories of Fifty Years* . . . (4th ed.;
Macon, Ga., 1882), 374.

undyed or dyed white. Their knee-length breeches were usually dyed indigo blue. Men usually went barefoot, except for formal occasions and during cold winter months, when their feet and calves were sheathed in cotton stockings and leather moccasins or, more rarely, moccasins with leggings. Acadian women generally wore ankle-length, striped cotonnade skirts, cotton corsets, and decorative vests above them. Like their husbands, they wore cotton stockings and moccasins only in inclement winter weather.[45]

The Acadian capacity to resist fundamental change despite the destruction of their insular world was also reflected in the persistence of their frugal and pragmatic values, particularly popular attitudes toward clothing. The numerous stages of clothing production, between the cotton harvest and the fashioning of handwoven cloth, were not only laborious but also extremely tedious. Garments were thus worn until they literally disintegrated, and Robert Hale's 1731 observation that Acadian "clothes were good eno' but they looked as if they were pitched on with pitchforks" was equally applicable to postexpulsion clothing. Many if not most of the garments listed in Spanish-period estates were either *mauvaises* (tattered) or *usées* (threadbare).[46]

The spirit of self-sufficiency and frugality that permeated Acadian clothing manufacture and use also characterized their architectural philosophy. Predispersal Acadian housing had represented a marriage of traditional European design, Nova Scotian building materials, and Indian technology. A handful of very affluent Port Royal residents owned two-story, wood-and-masonry homes, little different from those of western France, and the most wealthy residents of the outposts lived in homes that were three- or four-room structures of *pièce-sur-pièce* construction. But the vast majority of Acadians lived in one- or two-room cottages of *poteaux-en-terre* design.

45. Procès-verbal of the examination and identification of Charles Babin's corpse, June 5, 1774, PPC, 189A:403; Berquin-Duvallon, *Vue de la colonie espagnole*, 52, 251–52; Inventory of Charles Babin's Estate, June 3, 1774, PPC, 189B:543–46; Anne Trahan Estate, January 15, 1775, François Savoy Succession, December 28, 1780, and Basil Landry Estate, September 19, 1785, all in SMOA; Robin, *Voyage to Louisiana*, 115; Estate of "Mr. and Mrs. Landry," March 14, 1778, APOA.

46. Hale, "Journal of a Voyage to Nova Scotia Made in 1731," 234; Berquin-Duvallon, *Vue de la colonie espagnole*, 250–51; Joseph Broussard Estate, December 19, 1788, SMOA.

The focal point of these small, rectangular structures was the multi-purpose dining and living area. In many homes, this unpartitioned area was also a bedroom, though English traveler Robert Hale indicates that some homes contained separate sleeping quarters. These bedrooms were nothing more than cramped cubicles, "made something after the Manner of a Sailor's Cabbin, but boarded all round about the bigness of the bed." Such architectural luxuries, it should be noted, were exceptional, and as it later would in Louisiana, the typical attic contained a *garçonnière* (cockloft). The lack of living area in the predispersal Acadian home, which forced the residents to utilize attics as sleeping quarters for young males, created storage problems, solved in part by small cellars that provided winter storage for agricultural produce. As the ground temperatures remained near or below freezing throughout the winter months, the enclosed apples, turnips, and other vegetables were naturally preserved.[47]

The innovation and pragmatism reflected in the ingenious adaptation to unfavorable weather conditions was but one benefit produced by indigenous Acadian architecture. In the late seventeenth century, Acadians experienced great success in marrying traditional European building methods with Indian home insulation techniques to produce an architectural hybrid for eastern Canada's frigid climate. This amalgam is best reflected in the design of the component *poteaux-en-terre* walls, consisting of posts drawn from the upland woods (traditionally the "backlands" on coastal farms) and bound together by small branches, an Indian architectural innovation that not only strengthened the wall but also created an air pocket for insulation. Once complete, the interior wall was plastered with a mud-and-clay mixture to create a uniform surface and to seal the interior against blasts of arctic air. The soft insulation was itself protected by weather boards.[48]

These multilayer walls were both environmentally sound and quite sturdy; they supported the *garconnière* above in addition to the weight of the main floor, which covered an equally small cellar. To this total was added the weight of a European-style thatch roof of reed and bark.

47. Rameau de St-Père, *Une Colonie féodale*, I, 125–26; Hale, "Journal of a Voyage to Nova Scotia Made in 1731," 233; Clark, *Acadia*, 105, 138, 165–66; LeBreton, "Civilisation materielle," 476.
48. Clark, *Acadia*, 64, 105, 138; Rameau de St-Père, *Une Colonie féodale*, I, 125–26.

The durability of this architectural motif was reflected in its use in chimney construction. Indeed, the chimneys differed from the exterior walls only in the use of an interior and an exterior coating of mud plaster to insulate the component posts from sparks.[49]

The *poteaux-en-terre* house type was brought to Louisiana in the mid-1760s by the New Acadia settlers. Because of its architectural simplicity, it was the first type of home built by immigrants along the banks of the Mississippi River and in the Teche and Lafourche Valley settlements. The post-in-ground construction of homes, however, quickly proved defective in the region's warm, moist climate. Because of South Louisiana's unusually high watertable, the posts rotted quickly, rendering the walls structurally unsound. In addition, Gulf Coast termites quickly attacked and destroyed dry wood at ground level. Houses built flush with the ground were also particularly vulnerable to inundations on the broad Louisiana floodplain. Finally, the traditional Acadian house, with its insulated walls and thick thatch roof, was designed to shield its occupants from Nova Scotia's frigid climate and thus undoubtedly proved unbearably hot in the region's sweltering summer months.[50]

The defective structure was quickly modified to meet the Gulf Coast's environmental demands, and though the *poteaux-en-terre* house persisted in New Acadia until the early nineteenth century, it was rapidly superseded by the house type traditionally associated with Louisiana's Acadian population. The Louisiana Acadian house represented a melding of Maritime Canadian, Norman, and West Indian architecture. The settlers adopted the simple lines of the Norman country home, perhaps because many 1785 immigrants had been trained by Norman carpenters while in France. As in the West Indies, the houses were raised on piers, usually large cypress blocks, to permit increased air circulation in warm months as well as increased flood protection. Large parallel doors and windows were introduced to promote cooling of the central living area. Front galleries were incorporated as a cooling mechanism, cypress shingles replaced straw roofing materials to permit the upward radiation of

49. Hale, "Journal of a Voyage to Nova Scotia Made in 1731," 233; Clark, *Acadia*, 138.

50. Simon Landry Estate, May 16, 1782, APOA; Inventory of the Charles Babin Estate, June 3, 1774, PPC, 189B:543–46; Anne Trahan Estate, January 15, 1775, and Michel Meaux Estate, May 10, 1785, both in SMOA.

heat from the attic at night, and above-ground cellars (usually measuring sixteen by twenty feet) were established as outbuildings to offset the loss of storage space. Finally, though the floor was supported by massive cypress beams, the traditional walls were necessarily lightened by the removal of most vertical beams. Support timbers were braced by large diagonal posts to which they were bound by peg-and-mortise joints. The walls' resulting internal cavities were filled with a mud-and-moss mixture, called *bousillage*, as in traditional Acadian architecture. The Acadian chimney remained unchanged.[51]

The metamorphosis of Acadian housing proceeded slowly but steadily throughout the late eighteenth century. Some West Indian architectural innovations (such as galleries and matched windows for cross ventilation), borrowed from Louisiana's well-established Creole population, were first adopted by the Opelousas Acadians sometime before 1773. The Michel Cormier house, located near present-day Grand Coteau and built prior to 1773, represented the initial stage in this evolutionary process, for it embodied features of both the Acadian and French-Creole building traditions. Erected "on ground level" and of *poteaux-en-terre* construction, it featured *bousillage* walls, an earthen floor, and an encircling gallery. The Cormier house type, however, was clearly not the solution to Acadian housing needs, and the design of the Acadian dwelling continued to change throughout the 1770s and 1780s before emerging in the 1790s as the archetypal Louisiana Acadian house, relics of which can still be found throughout South Louisiana.[52]

While the evolution of the Acadian house made the structure increasingly functional, it did not appreciably augment creature comforts. The Acadians' nonmaterialistic values dictated the persistence of their simple life-style, spartan by modern standards, and as in old Acadia, homes contained only a minimum of furnishings. Visiting an Acadian residence in 1731, Robert Hale found only beds with their storage chests located at the foot, one table, two or three chairs, and a collection of badly worn earthenware plates and saucers; cups

51. Brasseaux, "Acadian Life," 140; R. Warren Robison, "Louisiana Acadian Domestic Architecture," in Del Sesto and Gibson (eds.), *The Culture of Acadiana*, 67–68, 71–72; Martin, *Les Exilés*, 172; Isabelle Richard Estate, April 18, 1778, Mathurin Landry Estate, November 10, 1800, and Felicite Landry Estate, March 6, 1800, all in APOA.

52. Anne Saunier Cormier Estate, May 12, 1773, Opelousas Colonial Records.

and mugs were extremely rare and reflected long and continuous usage.[53]

Hale would have found the same furnishings in New Acadia households. Extant Acadian antiques indicate that the design of the furnishings differed only slightly from their predispersal counterparts but that the Louisiana furniture was constructed of very different materials. Acadian furnishings were usually fashioned from the region's superior cherry wood, while New Acadian furnishings were generally made with softer, more workable cypress lumber. As some exiles gained affluence in the mid- to late Spanish period, however, imported cherry furniture once again found its way into Acadian households. Modestly wealthy immigrants also acquired, after the 1770s, armoires to replace the small wooden chests that stored clothing and small valuables. Hollow ware and flatware were a final barometer of wealth, as earthenware bowls and broken tin cutlery were replaced by porcelain vessels and iron spoons and forks.[54]

Such luxuries were exceptional, and the average eighteenth-century settler sat on a worn-out wooden chair at a hand-carved table and ate from chipped dishes, with damaged cutlery. He slept in the same room, on a feather or straw mattress, in a handmade cypress bed at the foot of which he stored his few threadbare garments in a small cypress chest.

This was indeed an unpretentious existence, a rejection of conspicuous consumption. Anglo-American and European travelers tended to dismiss it as slothfulness.[55] The Acadian ethos was not geared to materialism, but rather to the precepts of land and family. The Acadian attachment to the soil is vividly reflected in their agrarian life-style and in their very deep attachment to the family estate. From the very establishment of their homeland, Acadians had consistently defended their personal property with ferocious tenacity against spurious claims. Even the most minor property disputes were brought before the colonial magistrates, particularly after the

53. Hale, "Journal of a Voyage to Nova Scotia Made in 1731," 233.
54. Anne Trahan Estate, January 15, 1775, SMOA. Photographs of Acadian antiques in the Ira Nelson Collection, Southwestern Archives, University of Southwestern Louisiana; Desirée LeBlanc Estate, November 8, 1777, Joseph Richard Estate, December 24, 1776, and the Armant Gotreau Estate, 1811, all in APOA.
55. Isabelle LeBlanc Estate, April 18, 1778, APOA; Basil Landry Estate, September 19, 1785, SMOA; Berquin-Duvallon, *Vue de la colonie espagnole*, 51–53.

establishment of English rule in 1713. Local court dockets were pe-
rennially cluttered with such complaints, causing Lieutenant Governor Lawrence Armstrong to lament in 1731 that the Acadians were "a
Litigious Sort of people and so ill natur'd to one another, as Daily to
Encroach upon their Neighbours' properties, which occasions Con-
tinual complaints."[56]

Acadian litigiousness lay dormant in the 1760s, as the exiles were
preoccupied with the task of developing frontier settlements. With
the first land surveys of the 1770s, however, Louisiana surveyors and
colonial administrators were bewildered by the flurry of resulting
land disputes. Royal surveyors were sued and extralegally harassed
by landowners whose land grants were reduced by the initial surveys, while Acadians and Creoles alike were quick to feel the wrath
of their neighbors when attempting to expropriate cypress timber
from isolated *cyprières*. The latter disputes were usually settled
peaceably through legal channels, but victims of livestock encroachment and the resulting crop damage frequently resorted to violent
means of redressing their grievances—often indulging in the whole-
sale destruction of the offending animals.[57]

The intensity and spontaneity of the Acadian defense of property
rights is an accurate measure of the prominent position of land in the
Acadian hierarchy of values. The farm was viewed in every respect
as a personal domain, open only to friends and invited guests. Land
boundaries were considered sacrosanct, and intruders were to be re-
pelled at any price. Indeed, the Acadian farm was a sanctuary against
a hostile world.

Acadian ties to the land were also clearly subjugated to family con-

56. Brebner, *New England's Outpost*, 61, 139–40; Lauvrière, *Tragédie*, I, 190.

57. Chevalier de Bellevue to Unzaga, May 27, 1771, PPC, 188C:64; Judice to
Unzaga, January 3, 1772, PPC, 189A:418; Petition to Unzaga from the Opelousas Acadians, June 3, 1773, PPC, 189A:55; Fuselier de la Claire to Unzaga, June 18, 1773,
PPC, 189A:55, 56vo–57; Verret to Unzaga, February 11, 1771, PPC, 188B:72; Verret to
Unzaga, December 9, 1771, PPC, 188B:134; Judice to Unzaga, June 3, 1771, PPC,
188B:94–98; Petition of the Assumption Parish Acadians to Unzaga, October 16,
1773, PPC, 189A:498; Judice to Miro, December 4, 1790, PPC, 202:377–78vo; Nicolas
Verret to Miro, January 3, 1790, PPC, 203:274; Judice to Miro, March 15, 1790, PPC,
203:295–97; Miro to Judice, February 20, 1790, PPC, 203:285; Nicolas Verret to Miro,
April 8, 1790, PPC, 203:302; Verret to Miro, July 19, 1790, PPC, 203:328; Brasseaux,
"Acadian Life," 134–36; Antoine Bernard Dauterive to DeClouet, September 13, 1774,
PPC, 189A:101–102; LeDée to DeClouet, December 21, 1778, PPC, 198A:176.

siderations. Isolated in the Nova Scotian frontier, Acadian pioneers, particularly the 1632 immigrants, who shared a common cultural background, banded together against unfamiliar and hostile elements. This social amalgam constituted the seed of Acadian society, and the durability of its social fabric was subsequently demonstrated by the pioneers' ability to absorb all rival Francophone groups within the colony. In addition, despite the geographic expansion of the Acadian areas of settlement and the resultant subregional clan mentalities in the late seventeenth and early eighteenth centuries, the integrity of the Acadian group identity remained intact largely because of the strength of the extended families. With the absence of an effective colonial government prior to the mid-eighteenth century, familial relationships were the only viable means of tying together Acadia's isolated settlements.[58]

The vitality of the extended families also permitted Acadian society to endure years of exile successfully, despite hostile lands and the demands of resettlement. Though nuclear families were torn from their immediate relatives by the Grand Dérangement, they consistently found themselves surrounded by cousins sharing their values and language. Thus able to interact on a cooperative basis for the group's interests, the Acadians preserved their culture and group identity. These sociological defense mechanisms operated effectively in Spanish Louisiana, where they had been drawn by hope of familial and cultural reunification.[59]

From 1770 to the end of the American Revolution, river Acadians repeatedly petitioned Spanish administrators for permission to join their relatives along Bayou Teche. To mask their real motives, the supplicants based their requests upon "illness, or the poor quality of the land which they inhabited." Such requests were initially judged by the various governors on the merits of individual cases, and a few exiles were allowed to relocate at Attakapas, despite the commandants' vocal opposition. Policy concerning migrants shifted drastically in November, 1777, as Governor Bernardo de Gálvez succumbed to the pressure of river-parish commandants who feared that continued migration, even on the existing miniscule scale,

58. Griffiths, *Creation of a People*, 14–18.
59. Ulloa to Grimaldi, May 19, 1766, ASD, 2585:n.p.

would depopulate their districts. This development, they argued, would have been disastrous for New Orleans, which relied heavily on the river settlements for provisions.[60]

Under the terms of Gálvez's orders, issued on November 10, 1777, all requests to migrate to Attakapas were to be refused unless the petitioner could fill the void created by his departure. As early immigrants usually preferred developing gratuitous land grants to purchasing established farms, securing a replacement was no easy task, especially after Spain's conquest of British West Florida temporarily stemmed the influx of Anglo-American immigrants. Acadian society thus remained geographically fragmented, and the subregional differences that had emerged in the extended families by 1755 were reinforced and perpetuated.[61]

Though Spanish settlement policies effectively discouraged the melding of distinctive Acadian immigrant groups, they paradoxically strengthened social bonds within the subregional groups. Spanish administrators consistently bowed to the Acadian tradition of residential propinquity within nuclear families. In 1770, for example, Alexis Braud had relinquished his developed, eight-arpent concession for an undeveloped, six-arpent land grant adjacent to his son's properties. Custom was reinforced by Spanish laws providing for forced heirship and the consequential division of estates into narrow, adjoining strips of land.[62]

Familial ties permeated all facets of Acadian life; as in vieille Acadie, nuclear family members worked together, played together, and worshiped together. Most household tasks were sexually differentiated, with men cultivating the fields, cutting timber, and building levees, and women taking care of the barnyard, milking cows, spinning and weaving cotton, sewing, and cooking. Such distinctions evaporated at harvest time, when entire families went into the fields to pick corn and cotton. Aged family members incapable of

60. Gálvez to Louis Dutisné, November 10, 1777, PPC, 193B:195–96; Unzaga to Verret, November 14, 1770, PPC, 188A:1d/50a; Gálvez to Dutisné, November 10, 1777, PPC, 193B:195–96; Judice to Unzaga, March 21, 1774, PPC, 188B:540.

61. Gálvez to Dutisné, November 10, 1777, PPC, 193B:195–96; Jack D. L. Holmes, *Gayoso: The Life of a Spanish Governor in the Mississippi Valley, 1789–1799* (1965; rpr. Gloucester, Mass., 1968), 11.

62. Judice to Unzaga, December 3, 1770, PPC, 188A:1d/34.

strenuous physical labor apparently tended their young grand-
children, particularly during the harvest.[63]

Families and friends also gathered at homes of ill neighbors to assist in the household management and, in autumn, to participate in
the harvest. In case of death, they consoled the bereft. Just as they
shared the loss of a loved one, the exiles shared the joy of living,
hosting—probably on a rotating basis, as in the antebellum period—
les bals de maison. These weekly neighborhood dances were an important diversion from the dreadful monotony of frontier life and also
served periodically to renew social bonds.[64]

As in Acadia, where the gatherings featured "*les chansons rustiques
et la danse*," New Acadia *bals* were unostentatious. Documentary and
ethnomusicological evidence suggests that the Acadian immigrants
reached Louisiana without their cherished musical instruments, particularly fiddles. The destitute musicians were thus compelled to
mimic fiddles verbally when presenting the traditional Celtic reels
and jigs that constituted a major part of the early Acadians' musical
repertoire. By the late 1770s most of the fiddlers had achieved a comfortable existence and enjoyed the leisure time to make, or the financial resources to purchase, new instruments. In the mid-1780s *les
bals de maison* once again featured local fiddlers, the best of whom
enjoyed regional prominence.[65] Though the instrumentation reflected the Acadians' improving economic position, the simple fare
shared by the dancers was a reminder of more austere times. As
French traveler C. C. Robin noted in 1804, Acadian Coast residents
"give balls . . . and will go ten to fifteen leagues to attend one.
Everyone dances, even *Grandmère* and *Grandpère*, no matter what the
difficulties they must bear. There may be only a couple of fiddles to
play for the crowd, there may be only four candles for light . . .
wooden benches to sit on, and only exceptionally a few bottles of
tafia diluted with water for refreshment. No matter, everyone dances.

63. Ulloa to Grimaldi, May 19, 1766, ASD, 2585:n.p.; Robin, *Voyage to Louisiana*,
191.
64. Judice to Gálvez, October 16, 1781, PPC, 194:498; Robin, *Voyage to Louisiana*,
115.
65. Barry J. Ancelet and Michael Doucet, "The Evolution of Cajun and Creole Music" (Paper presented at the tenth annual meeting of the French Colonial Historical
Society, Lafayette, Louisiana, 1980).

But always everyone has a helping of *gumbo*, the Creole dish *par excellence*: then 'Good night,' . . . 'See you next week.'"[66]

While the *bals de maison* remained generally unaffected by the rising Acadian standard of living, other forms of entertainment did not. In the late 1770s, for instance, Acadian Coast men began to congregate in local cabarets—many of which were Acadian owned and operated—to gamble at billiards.[67] But the most notable change in Acadian leisure-time was the growing interest in horses and, concomitantly, horse racing. Horses had been quite scarce in Acadia until the mid-eighteenth century and even then had failed to supplant oxen as the principal draft animals. In the broad southwestern Louisiana prairies, however, horses were indispensable in the cattle industry and for transportation. Because of their importance, herds of Creole ponies were carefully developed in prairie *vacheries*. In the Acadian settlements along the Mississippi River and Bayou Lafourche, farmers relied principally upon waterborne transportation, and because of the local topography and growing congestion along the streams, cattle herds were necessarily confined to small, fenced pastures where they could be controlled easily. Horses were thus a luxury in the eastern Acadian districts and would remain so until the 1790s, when improved roads made overland transportation feasible. Horses also became a status symbol to young, Louisiana-born Acadians, who in the 1790s rushed to acquire riding and sulky horses.[68]

The growing interest in horses spawned, in the 1790s, the great Acadian pastime of horse racing. Beginning at the La Pointe settlement in present-day St. Martin Parish, the fad spread throughout the prairies and later to the river parishes as well. Early South Louisiana horse races were consistently held on straight courses, usually

66. Robin, *Voyage to Louisiana*, 115.
67. Judice to Carondelet, March 29, 1796, PPC, 213:336; Unzaga to Judice, November 22, 1771, PPC, 188C:95; Piernas to Cantrelle, April 9, 1781, PPC, 194:296; Procès-verbal of an investigation into the death of Joseph Hebert, August 21, 1787, PPC, 200:468–70vo.
68. Clark, *Acadia*, 167; Census of the Attakapas post, 1771, PPC, 188C:43vo; Census of the Quartier de Vermilion, 1803, PPC, 220B:68; Judice to Gálvez, July 27, 1777, PPC, 190:290–91; Minutes of an assembly regarding the "abandonment" of stray cattle, July 27, 1777, PPC, 190:293; Robin, *Voyage to Louisiana*, 100; Judice to Carondelet, August 22, 1796, PPC, 212A:460–61vo.

four arpents to a mile in length. Although the featured races generally included pedigreed horseflesh owned by Anglo-Americans and
Creole planters, the bulk of the racing schedule was filled with
match races between Acadian riding ponies and draft animals.[69]
    As exemplified by the rural races, the adaptability of Acadian
sociocultural institutions and economic pursuits to Louisiana's frontier environment ensured survival in the forthcoming decades when
non-Acadian immigration and the rise of the plantation system
would again challenge the traditional Acadian way of life. The pragmatism and flexibility that had long characterized Acadian society
enabled the destitute immigrants immediately to discard obsolete
and impractical agricultural productions, architectural technology,
and culinary skills for their Louisiana counterparts. Acadian society
thereby acquired its distinctly Louisiana or "Cajun" flavor. Despite
the magnitude of this cultural metamorphosis, most changes were
merely superficial, and the core elements of Acadian culture remained unchanged. The continuing uniformity of culture reinforced
group boundaries and underscored diffferences between Cajuns
and other local ethnic groups. Thus, like an old building with a new
façade, the Acadian culture retained its inner strength but showed
the world a new face.

69. Interrogation of Nicolas Roussel, November 23, 1797, PPC, 214:248–49; Deposition by J. C. Dugas, October 9, 1797, PPC, 214:239; Deposition by Olivier Thibodeau, October 9, 1797, PPC, 214:240; Deposition by Firmin Brau, November 29, 1797,
PPC, 214:245; Opelousas *Courier*, February 12, 18, 1853; New Iberia *Louisiana Sugar
Bowl*, May 1, 1873; Baton Rouge *Gazette*, October 4, 1828.

8

Acadian Anticlericalism

From the outset of Acadian settlement in Louisiana, Cajuns have been recognized—both by their detractors and their apologists—as a devoutly religious people. Indeed, their devotion to the Catholic church has been unflagging despite the community's sudden immersion in an increasingly Protestant, American environment. Yet, Acadian piety has been matched by equally intense anticlericalism. This religious paradox is the legacy of the Catholic church's role in the early development of Acadian society.

The first Acadian settlers were not only adventurers but also refugees from a nation torn by religious strife. Because of the intensity of the struggle born of the Counter-Reformation and the holy crusades that it spawned, the Catholic church in France was particularly militant at the dawn of the seventeenth century. Compelled by necessity to abide by the Edict of Nantes granting Huguenots religious freedom and civil rights, Catholic zealots nevertheless longed for the opportunity to eradicate heresy wherever it was found.[1]

Exclusion, therefore, of the most militant Catholic orders, particularly the Jesuits, from early Acadia was hardly coincidental; the colony was founded and initially administered by Huguenots who refused to make religion a political issue in the colony. Intracolonial harmony was absolutely essential to the nascent settlement's economic well-being and ultimate survival, and consequently religious

---

1. W. J. Stankiewicz, *Politics and Religion in Seventeenth Century France* (Berkeley, 1960), 7–64, 67, 196; G. R. R. Treasure, *Seventeenth Century France* (London, 1966), 11–15, 85–89.

factionalization was to be avoided at any cost. Yet, the colony's proprieters could not readily ignore Henry IV's insistence that conversion of Indians to Catholicism be one of the colony's principal objectives. A Catholic missionary, one Father Aubry, was therefore on the first colonizing expedition, but following his untimely death shortly after reaching the New World, the colony's directors made no effort to procure a replacement. This sin of omission provided ample grist for the propaganda mills of the colony's opponents—primarily rival French merchants jealous of the colonial proprietors' exclusive trading privileges—who persuaded the French government to revoke Acadia's colonial charter in 1607. The fledgling settlement was abandoned shortly thereafter.[2]

In 1610, interest in Acadian colonization was rekindled when Jean de Biencourt de Poutrincourt secured a concession to Port Royal. The issuance of Poutrincourt's commercial privileges roughly coincides with the assassination of the religiously tolerant Henry IV and the growing predominance of Catholic power and influence at the French court. Hence, though Poutrincourt was a Protestant who enjoyed financial backing from Dieppe Huguenots, he recruited the services of Jesse Fleché, a secular priest. Moreover, upon arrival at Port Royal, Acadia, Fleché was afforded every opportunity to labor in the colony's fertile ecclesiastical vineyard, and within weeks of the mission's establishment, Poutrincourt's son, Charles de Biencourt de Saint-Just, departed for France with lists of Fleché's Indian converts.[3]

While thus avoiding the pitfalls of his predecessor, Poutrincourt nevertheless alienated his Protestant backers, who refused to extend his credit. In desperate need of funds to outfit a relief expedition to Port Royal, and driven to desperation by the underwriters' intransigence, Biencourt was compelled to seek assistance from the marquise de Guercheville, a friend of the regent and a champion of the Counter-Reformation. Mme. de Guercheville agreed to provide the

2. Stankiewicz, *Politics and Religion*, 75–77; Treasure, *Seventeenth Century France*, 85; Griffiths, *Creation of a People*, 7–8; Rameau de St-Père, *Une Colonie féodale*, I, 47.

3. Lauvrière, *Tragédie*, I, 26–28; Treasure, *Seventeenth Century France*, 85–89; Griffiths, *Creation of a People*, 8; Rameau de St-Père, *Une Colonie féodale*, I, 47; Reuben Gold Thwaites (ed.), *The Jesuit Relations and Allied Documents: Travels and Explorations of the Jesuit Missionaries in New France, 1610–1791* (73 vols.; 1896–1901; rpr. New York, 1959), IV, 87.

necessary assistance, on the condition that the colony accept Jesuit missionaries, and when Poutrincourt's original backers refused to admit Catholicism's most militant clerics, the colony's new benefactor purchased the Huguenot-controlled stocks and transferred them to Jesuits Pierre Biard and Ennemond Massé.[4]

Biard and Massé, arriving at Port Royal in late 1610, caused an immediate disruption of the colony's internal stability by attempting to transform Port Royal from a trading post into a mission. The resultant feud between the colony's religious and secular leaders was resolved only in 1613 when the missionaries, with the financial assistance of Mme. de Guercheville, left and established a religious community on Ile Mont-Desert.[5]

The Jesuits' departure ended the Catholic church's tenuous presence in Acadia, and the colony would be without a priest until 1632. Six Recollet friars migrated to the region between 1619 and 1624, but they worked exclusively with the local Indians, coming into contact with the colony's European settlers only rarely. In fact, contemporary accounts indicate that Acadia's small white population—eighteen to twenty bachelors between 1620 and 1632—had little use for the asceticism and self-mortification of seventeenth-century Christianity, preferring instead the more "casual" morality of their Indian neighbors. As one obviously bitter Catholic commentator indicated, the Acadian Huguenots "lived in the woods . . . mixing with the Indians and pursuing a dissolute and sordid existence, without ever practicing their faith."[6]

The colony's moral climate changed significantly in 1632 with the resumption of French immigration. Three hundred French Catholics—most of whom were natives of the Loudun area—were settled by Isaac de Razilly, with royal support, at Port Royal. Unlike the Huguenot adventurers, whom they immediately displaced as the colony's dominant European cultural group, many of these immigrants were accompanied by their families, and thus the seed of a permanent Acadian colony was finally planted.[7]

4. Rameau de St-Père, Une Colonie féodale, I, 48.
5. Ibid., 52–55, 59; Griffiths, Creation of a People, 8.
6. Clark, Acadia, 69; Pacifique de Valigny, Chroniques des plus anciennes églises de l'Acadie: Bathurst, Pabos et Ristigouche, Rivière St. John, Memramcook (Montreal, 1944), 1–2; Rameau de St-Père, Une Colonie féodale, I, 75.
7. Griffiths, Creation of a People, 12–14; Bujold and Caillebeau, Les Origines, 11–14.

Though they provided a stabilizing influence on the colony and though they were consistently Catholic, popular attitudes toward the Catholic missionaries appear to have changed surprisingly little. Indeed, as historian Naomi Griffiths has suggested, the early Acadian Catholics "looked upon ecclesiastical authority with as critical an eye as they viewed the secular." This phenomenon can be traced to the fact that the exodus of French settlers from Loudun—a town boasting a large Protestant minority and a center of Catholic militance—probably resulted from the trauma of a recently concluded and highly publicized witch-hunt. Once again, the Acadian wilderness provided pioneers with a refuge from the repression and social disruption that the French churches had come to represent. These pioneers came to Acadia as *engagés,* bound to their employers as fur trappers for five years, and encounters between the new male settlers and the newly arrived French clergymen were infrequent.[8]

In the isolation of the frontier, the Catholic Acadian became as independent as his Huguenot predecessor, but unlike the Protestant *coureurs de bois,* he did not completely reject organized religion. Civil warfare between Catholic and Protestant fur-trading operations, moreover, helped to reinforce the Catholics' religious identity.

Maintenance of one's religious identity in a frontier area effectively devoid of resident priests, however, remained a matter of personal faith. The 1632 immigrants had retained a deep and abiding love of God and respect for the Catholic sacramentals, which were universally deemed the key to spiritual salvation. Thus, as extant early Acadian church registers attest, the colony's Catholic settlers made every effort to baptize their children, bless their marriages, and bury their dead in the church. Acadian devotion to the sacramentals was also manifested in attendance at Sunday mass, or *la messe blanche,* a weekly service officiated by local laymen, usually elders, in frontier communities visited only infrequently by Catholic missionaries to the Indians.[9]

8. Lauvrière, *Tragédie,* I, 55–65, 186–93; Eccles, *France in America,* 29; Phileas F. Bourgeois, *Les Anciens Missionnaires de l'Acadie devant l'histoire* (Shediac, N.B., n.d.), 11; Griffiths, *Creation of a People,* 22; *Mandements, lettres pastorales et circulaires des évêques de Québec* (6 vols.; Quebec, 1887–90), I, 184–86, 278–81; Aldous Huxley, *The Devils of Loudun* (New York, 1952); Fontaine (ed.), *Voyage du Sieur de Dièreville,* 53–54; Clark, *Acadia,* 94–98.
9. Diocese of Baton Rouge, *Diocese of Baton Rouge Catholic Church Records* I, 1–135; Rameau de St-Père, *Une Colonie féodale,* I, 241.

Dry masses and baptisms for mortally ill infants were the only basic ecclesiastical services the laymen could provide themselves. Chronic need for the full range of Catholic sacramentals on the frontier became increasingly severe as the population of isolated Acadian settlements grew geometrically in the seventeenth century, prompting the laymen to request a resident priest.[10]

The increasing demand for basic church services was matched by a growing demand for a records-keeping agency among the largely illiterate Acadian Catholics. Indeed, the acquisition of land by former *engagés* in the late seventeenth century necessitated the presence of an archival apparatus that, because of the dearth of colonial administrators, only the church could provide. Acadian Catholics thus assisted in building churches in their principal settlements and provided them with minimal financial support.[11]

The settlers' demand for minimal church services, and concomitantly minimal church interference in their daily lives, complemented the church's own objectives in the colony. From the outset of Catholic evangelical activity in the Bay of Fundy area, French missionaries had clearly preferred converting heathen natives to the more mundane duties of village pastor. As a consequence, throughout the seventeenth century, the bulk of the church's resources were allocated to missionary activity. In 1701, for instance, when the Acadian population had grown to a position of near parity with that of the local Micmac tribe, the colony's white Catholics were served by three full-time priests, while at least eight missionaries followed the wandering tribesmen they had chosen to serve.[12]

The church's limited commitment to the Acadians was formalized in the early eighteenth century, as the English, who legally acquired Acadia in 1713, began to limit the number of clergymen in the Catholic villages and to restrict the priests' activities. Though Acadians

10. *Mandements*, I, 181–83.
11. Clark, *Acadia*, 109–58, 190–91; Brebner, *New England's Outpost*, 57–103, 148–54; Griffiths, *Creation of a People*, 13; Lauvrière, *Tragédie*, I, 189; *Mandements*, I, 181–83.
12. Thwaites (ed.), *Jesuit Relations*, XLV, 58–73; Griffiths, *Creation of a People*, 33; Henri-Raymond Casgrain, "Coup d'oeil sur l'Acadie avant la dispersion de la colonie française," *Le Canada Française*, I (1888), 117; Rameau de St-Père, *Une Colonie féodale*, I, 110; Clark, *Acadia*, 58; Lauvrière, *Tragédie*, I, 189; De Valigny, *Chroniques*, 6–10, 45–54, 77–80.

demanded the right to remain Catholic, they failed to protest the increasingly stringent religious regulations. The parishioners were content so long as their pastors performed their perfunctory, albeit essential religious duties. Clerical nonfeasance, usually resulting from unauthorized evangelical work among the local Indians, however, immediately prompted litanies of complaints to the bishop of Quebec, prelate of the Catholic church in North America.[13]

Acadians had come to view the Catholic church in the same light as the colonial government—that is, as an agency established solely to provide essential services. Such services were to be provided without disruption of the parishioners' routine secular activities and without undue financial burden. Any deviation from this conceptual framework precipitated spontaneous outbursts. Relations between pastor and parishioner consequently varied among the Acadian parishes. The most harmonious church communities, of course, were inevitably those with the most docile clergymen. From the outset of European colonization in Acadia, zealous and militant Catholic priests had consistently been anathema to the colony's white population. The pro-French activities of such warrior-priests as Père Simon and Abbé Le Loutre forced the Acadians to live in the shadow of possible Indian raids throughout the early and middle eighteenth century.[14]

For many if not most late seventeenth- and eighteenth-century Acadians, Catholic missionaries were shadowy figures who provided the settlers minimal contact with the church hierarchy. Forced to fend for themselves, even to the point of conducting paraliturgical services, the immigrants ultimately came to divorce religion from the area's traditionally dominant religious institution. Priests consequently became little more than petty religious administrators, stripped of their cloak of religious invincibility and vulnerable to personal criticism.[15]

It was with this mental framework that the Acadians faced exile in

13. Clark, *Acadia*, 190–91; Casgrain, "Coup d'oeil," 115; Griffiths, *Creation of a People*, 22.

14. Clark, *Acadia*, 376; Casgrain, "Coup d'oeil," 115, 126–27; Brebner, *New England's Outpost*, 156–65; De Valigny, *Chroniques*, 51.

15. Clark, *Acadia*, 376; Griffiths, *Creation of a People*, 22; Brebner, *New England's Outpost*, 158.

the English seaboard colonies after the Grand Dérangement. As in the frontier settlements, contacts between the exiles and Catholic priests were infrequent at best, even in colonies with large Catholic minorities, such as Maryland.[16] Prevailing predispersal attitudes toward the church remained unchanged at the time of the Acadians' arrival in Louisiana.

These attitudes would soon place the exiles in direct confrontation with the rapid expansion of the church's power and influence in Spanish Louisiana. But during the turbulent years of the late 1760s, when the first wave of Acadian immigration broke on the banks of the Mississippi River, Louisiana's transitional government and the local Catholic hierarchy lacked the financial resources necessary to underwrite establishment and initial maintenance of missions. The vicar-general assigned Father Jean-François de Civray, a habitual gambler only recently returned from exile at Mobile, to the new arrivals, but the errant missionary abandoned his post only a few months after his appointment, perhaps because of the epidemic then raging among his parishioners. He failed to return, and the chronically understaffed Capuchin order, the only missionary society remaining active in Louisiana during the late 1760s, failed to secure a replacement.[17]

New Acadia settlements, nevertheless, were visited occasionally by Catholic circuit riders from the neighboring and well established Pointe Coupée, Natchitoches, and Des Allemands posts. On their brief sojourns in the back country, missionaries administered communal baptisms and blessed unions that had been contracted in the absence of a priest. During long intervals between the missionaries' visits, Acadian elders maintained their traditional role of presiding over weekly "dry masses," and at Cabannocé the exiles even erected a shed for this purpose. In the final analysis, Acadian religious life in early New Acadia differed little from that of late predispersal Nova Scotia.[18]

16. Sollers, "The Acadians," 18–19; "List of Baptisms at St. Joseph's Church, Philadelphia," 246–350.

17. Brasseaux, "L'Officier de Plume," 47–83; Moore, Revolt in Louisiana, 42–142; Baudier, Catholic Church, 168–74, 180, 190; Marc deVilliers du Terrage, Les Dernières Annees de la Louisiane française (Paris, 1904), 52–53; "Copie d'un vieux registre," 45; Brasseaux (trans. and ed.), A Comparative View of French Louisiana, 94–95; Jean Delanglez, The French Jesuits in Lower Louisiana (New Orleans, 1935), 491–537.

18. Judice to Ulloa, April 25, 1768, PPC, 187A:n.p.; Judice to Ulloa, May 30, 1768,

Louisiana's Acadian immigrants, however, soon encountered a religious atmosphere radically different from that of their homeland. Beginning in the early 1770s, the newly installed Spanish government demanded and stringently enforced Catholic orthodoxy. To this end, in 1770, Governor Alejandro O'Reilly ordered the construction of chapels and presbyteries in each Acadian settlement and, upon learning of the manpower deficiencies in the province's religious communities, appealed to the diocese of Havana for missionaries to staff the new parishes.[19]

Meanwhile, a few French Capuchins were ordered into the field. These priests were poorly suited to the arduous task that lay before them. According to their Spanish successors, the French Capuchins had forsaken their vow of poverty and, being part of the educated elite in an overwhelmingly illiterate society, had gravitated toward the colony's emerging social aristocracy. Their growing sense of social superiority was undergirded by their traditional leadership position in the local church. It is hardly surprising that the missionaries shared the aristocratic Creoles' view of the exiles as ignorant peasants, definitely socially inferior to men of the cloth.[20]

The Acadians refused to extend to their new pastors the reverence the latter demanded in recognition of their social and religious positions. Moreover, the exiles, who had awaited the priests' arrival with anticipation, soon chafed under the new theocratic local regime. Indeed, many Acadian families were subjected to close scrutiny by Catholic clergymen for the first time in generations and bitterly resented the intrusion into their daily lives.[21]

The incongruity of Acadian independence and equalitarian principles and the cleric's elitism and propensity for meddling in their

PPC, 187A:n.p.; Judice to Ulloa, March 15, 1768, PPC, 187A:n.p.; Judice to Ulloa, November 18, 1767, PPC, 187A:n.p.; Judice to Ulloa, July 2, 1767, PPC, 187A:n.p. Dry masses continued to be a regular weekly ritual for some isolated prairie Cajuns until the 1920s. Interview with Father James Geraghty, archivist and official historian of the Diocese of Lafayette, June 10, 1981.

19. Baudier, *Catholic Church*, 160, 180, 183; Gayarré, *History of Louisiana*, III, 20–21; Unzaga to Dutisné, June 27, 1775, PPC, 193B:220–21; List of the number of religious necessary for Louisiana, February 1, 1770, PPC, 2357:n.p.

20. Father Valentin to Unzaga, March 13, 1771, PPC, 188C:62–63; Baudier, *Catholic Church*, 185–86, 188; Official report of the affixing of seals to the Jesuit properties at New Orleans and the inventory and sale of said goods, July 9–16, 1763. AC, C 13a, 43:315–54.

21. Official report of the affixing of seals, July 9–16, 1763, AC, C 13a, 43:315–54.

parishioners' secular affairs inevitably spawned bitter disputes between the frontiersmen and their pastors. The first such confrontation occurred at St. Jacques de Cabannocé shortly after the installation of the first pastor. In early March, 1771, three Acadians called upon Father Valentin at the post's newly constructed presbytery. Walking into the kitchen with "lighted pipes," and exchanging jokes, the exiles were immediately confronted by their irate pastor, who, interpreting their actions as a gross breach of respect, expelled them. Angered by what they considered an unjustified assault, the parishioners withdrew immediately, but not before cursing their tormentor. The aggrieved Acadians then went directly to the commandant's office to notarize depositions justifying their actions. Exasperated by the exiles' audacity, Father Valentin applied for a transfer and abandoned his ecclesiastical post soon thereafter, leaving the parish without a resident priest for several months.[22]

Confrontations between priests and their parishioners, such as the initial clash at Cabannocé, appeared with alarming regularity following the establishment of permanent frontier missions in New Acadia. Moreover, the level of violence in these disputes escalated with each passing year.[23]

The most violent confrontations involved Spanish missionaries, who consistently initiated them. At Assumption Parish, for example, in early February, 1789, Father Francisco Notario "arrested" Mathurin Landry's slave, apparently for breaking the Sabbath, and impounded the Acadian's oxcart. The priest then conducted the Negro, who had been engaged in a duly authorized personal errand, to the local presbytery at gunpoint. Learning of the arrest, Landry went immediately to the rectory, where he retrieved his property in the face of the priest's heated protests. Enraged by Landry's insolence, Notario ordered his own slave to fetch a gun, yelled to his pa-

22. Judice to Unzaga, October 6, 1772, PPC, 189A:448; Baudier, *Catholic Church*, 149, 151, 156, 172, 173, 182, 189, 190–93; Father Valentin to Unzaga, March 13, 1771, PPC, 188C:62–63.

23. See, for example, Judice to Unzaga, October 6, 1772, PPC, 198A:448; Unzaga to Father Angel de Revillagodos, March 13, 1773, PPC, 189A:156; Judice to Unzaga, January 2, 1774, PPC, 189A:513; Judice to Unzaga, January 15, 1776, PPC, 189B:303; DeClouet to Unzaga, October 26, 1779, PPC, 192:240; Michel Meaux to DeClouet, October 24, 1779, PPC, 192:243; Jean Doucet, Jean Richard, Pierre Arceneaux, Philippe Lachaussaye, and Joseph Bourgeois to Miró, October 29, 1784, PPC, 197:271–72; Judice to Miró, July 2, 1788, PPC, 201:616–17vo.

rishioner that he would kill him, and, when the musket was not in-
stantly forthcoming, beat his black domestic unmercifully.[24]

Violent confrontations were initially confined to the Acadian settlements along the Mississippi River and Bayou Lafourche. Restricted to the natural levees along these waterways by the region's
swampy backlands and shackled by the government regulation of intracolonial movement, the eastern Acadians enjoyed little mobility
and were constantly in the eye of meddlesome local religious authorities. The juxtaposition of authoritarian religious figures and
fiercely independent frontiersmen, who chafed under any form of
control, made conflicts inevitable.[25]

Such antagonisms were less intense in Attakapas and Opelousas,
where the early clerics had little interest in, and little control over,
the widely scattered Acadian population. From the beginnings of
Acadian settlement in these isolated posts, the exiles had enjoyed
considerable mobility, and by the early 1770s, most of the prairie
dwellers resided in areas far removed from the two local churches,
located in the modern commununities of St. Martinville and Washington. The great distances separating most prairie Acadians from
their chapels matched the cultural and ideological gaps dividing
these parishioners from their priests.

The first pastors in New Acadia were often *esprits forts* who had
been removed from previous posts for malfeasance. Obviously con-
sidering their new assignment a form of exile, these frontier missionaries were generally apathetic about their pastoral duties. Extant
civil and ecclesiastical records also indicate that they were far more
concerned with their custodial duties, specifically the maintenance
and gradual improvement of the chapel and presbytery, than with
their spiritual responsibilities. Commandants' reports of the 1770s
and 1780s make frequent reference to demands by Attakapas and
Opelousas priests for the collection of church levies, but as historian
Charles L. Souvay notes, the first documented pastoral visit to the
prairie settlements occurred in 1795, fully thirty years after the establishment of the mother parish. Only fourteen such visitations
were recorded between 1795 and 1803, and in each instance the mis-

24. Judice to Miró, February 16, 1789, PPC, 202:269–70; Baudier, *Catholic Church*,
221, 236; Judice to Miró, February 16, 1789, PPC, 202:269–70.
25. Brasseaux, "Acadian Life," 136.

sionary ventured only as far as the Vermilion River, on the eastern periphery of the southwestern prairies.[26]

Beyond the effective control of their local missionaries, the Acadians of the Attakapas and Opelousas posts were free to deal with the church on their own terms. Church registers reveal that the western Acadians, drawing on their collective religious experience in Nova Scotia, continued to turn to the church exclusively for basic services, particularly the sacraments that marked the milestones of life. The dictates of religion, however, were clearly subordinated to the demands of frontier life and the Acadians' value system. Baptism, for example, constitutes the foundation of Christian religious life. Yet, though the Attakapas and Opelousas church registers record 822 Acadian births between 1765 and 1803, only 311 of these children (37.8 percent) were baptized by a priest. While it is true that the region's primitive road system and the seasonal demands of the agricultural routine would necessarily have delayed many baptisms, these inconveniences would never have absolved the frontiersmen of their religious obligation. Moreover, the infant death rate, while high, does not account for the incredibly large number of officially unbaptized children, suggesting that, as in predispersal Nova Scotia, the sacramental was administered by the Acadian elders. Similarly, only 109 Acadian deaths were recorded during the same period, nearly one-half of which were infants, indicating that many, if not most, burials were also performed by laymen.[27]

The pervasiveness of lay-administered ceremonies is also reflected in the church hierarchy's grudging recognition of the common frontier practice of having marriages solemnized by circuit riders. Correspondence by contemporary clerics suggests that an undetermined

26. Baudier, *Catholic Church*, 159, 190, 291; Brasseaux (trans. and ed.), *A Comparative View of French Louisiana*, 129n; Villiers du Terrage, *Les Dernières Années*, 52–53; DeClouet to Gálvez, October 26, 1779, PPC, 192:240; DeClouet to Unzaga, August 25, 1776, PPC, 189B:110vo-11vo; DeClouet to Unzaga, June 7, 1776, PPC, 189B:333vo; DeClouet to Gálvez, June 5, 1779, PPC, 205:496–98; Francisco Caso y Luengo to Carondelet, August 6, 1792, PPC, 25:1025–26; Jean Delavillebeuvre to Baptiste Boutté, *père*, church warden, November 10, 1790, PPC, 203:180–81; Michel Meaux to DeClouet, October 24, 1779, PPC, 192:243; Grumeau to DeClouet, October 17, 1779, PPC, 192:244; Charles L. Souvay, "Rummaging Through Old Parish Records: An Historical Sketch of the Church of Lafayette, La.," *St. Louis Catholic Historical Review*, III (1921), 243, 245–46.

27. Hebert (comp.), *Southwest Louisiana Records*, I; Baudier, *Catholic Church*, 230–31.

but significant portion of the 497 late-eighteenth-century Acadian marriages performed at Attakapas and Opelousas solemnized earlier parareligious ceremonies.[28]

The large number of officially sanctioned marriages reflects the importance of the sacrament to Acadian society. Family and land were the foundations of Acadian society, and marriages constituted a social-bonding agent and a medium for the orderly transfer of property. The Spanish theocracy in Louisiana recognized the legitimacy only of unions solemnized by the Catholic church; hence the inordinate number of church ceremonies.[29]

Even in the case of marriages, however, religious requirements were subordinated to the demands of the Acadian life-style. Marriages were scheduled during seasonal lulls in agricultural cycles. For example, 76 percent of all Acadian marriages between 1765 and 1803 were celebrated either in January or February or between the end of spring plowing (late April) and the beginning of the fall harvest (late August). During these periods of relative leisure, clans could gather, and the host parents could prepare the sumptuous receptions that inevitably followed the ceremonies.[30]

The seasonal demands of Acadian life also dictated the frequency with which the Acadians attended mass. Although canon law required the frontiersmen to attend Sunday services, it is apparent from all available evidence that most Acadians, especially in the prairie region, undertook the arduous journey to church only on the major Catholic feast days and for sacraments involving a member of their immediate family. Less frequently, parishioners traveled to church to "buy" masses (memorial services) for deceased relatives.[31]

The traditional Acadian ambivalence toward the church thus persisted: in the frontier tradition, they remained largely self-sufficient in religious matters but were nevertheless forced to rely upon the church for many essential services. The church's role in their lives, however, had to be entirely passive. Any effort by clerics to become

28. Hebert (comp.), *Southwest Louisiana Records*, I; Baudier, *Catholic Church*, 230–31.

29. Baudier, *Catholic Church*, 231.

30. Hebert (comp.), *Southwest Louisiana Records*, I.

31. Baudier, *Catholic Church*, 229–30; Delavillebeuvre to the governor, April 26, 1791, PPC, 206:256–58; Receipt issued to Mme. Savoie by Father Grumeau, December 24, 1782, SMOA, Vol. I.

more than a peripheral influence was viewed as a move toward church domination, and any perceived encroachment upon Acadian independence elicited a hostile if not belligerent reaction.

This pattern of response is seen most clearly in the efforts of the Acadians along the upper Vermilion to establish a chapel during the early 1790s. Braving stubborn ecclesiastical and political resistance— and ultimately the threat of incarceration—these frontiersmen carried their case to the governor and eventually prevailed. Yet, when missionaries periodically called on local homes prior to the construction of a church, the very proponents of the chapel refused to attend mass. While their wives and children attended services, they brazenly congregated and exchanged jokes in full view of the altar.[32]

The attitude of prairie Acadians toward the church typified Acadian-church relations throughout South Louisiana in the late eighteenth century. The refusal of the Acadians to stand in awe of their priests and their narrow vision of the clerics' role in secular society were anathema to the colonial Catholic church. Early missionaries to the Acadian parishes were consistently Europeans drawn from cultures in which the church was the pivotal force in everyday life. They viewed themselves as the arbiters of morality, duty bound to impose upon parishioners their own standards of behavior. For example, immigrant priests, particularly Spanish missionaries, were accustomed to the religious austerity and asceticism of their homeland and thus were appalled by the relative laxity of their French-speaking parishioners. These missionaries resolved to correct this problem by enforcing church regulations "to the limit."[33]

The clerics' efforts to rehabilitate wayward parishioners were channeled into three programs: institution of a tithe and church maintenance taxes, imposition of European morality, and the requirement of proper decorum on church grounds. The latter objective was especially dear to the late-eighteenth-century priests, who were mortified by the Acadians' lack of regard for the sanctity of religious facilities. Equally disturbing to the local clergy was the propensity of

---

32. Remonstrance of the Vermilion area residents, April 10, 1792, PPC, 206:244; Delavillebeuvre to Miró, October 20, 1791, PPC, 204:148–49; Interrogation of Jean-Baptiste Broussard et al., (1791), PPC, 204:220–39; Carondelet to Delavillebeuvre, June 2, 1792, PPC, 206:278–79; Robin, Voyage to Louisiana, 216.

33. Baudier, Catholic Church, 183–88.

Cajun men to enter chapels with lighted pipes and without remov-
ing their hats. To curb these practices, the priests persuaded civil authorities to ban public assemblies and cursing in the churchyard
under pain of criminal prosecution. In a futile effort to eradicate dis-
respectful acts, Lafourche Commandant Louis Judice stationed an
armed guard at the front door of the Church of the Assumption before Sunday mass. In addition, local pastors publicly humiliated the
ubiquitous pipe smokers by expelling them from church services.[34]

The missionaries' crusade to alter Acadian standards of religious
conduct produced only mixed results. Cajun behavior in church
gradually conformed to European standards, but at a price. Males
offended by the priests simply stopped attending Sunday services,
thereby disrupting the deep-seated tradition of family participation
at mass.[35]

Efforts to impose European morality on the Acadian frontier
proved equally unrewarding. Especially galling to the missionaries
was the practice among Cajun women of riding astride their horses,
which the Europeans considered immoral. Ecclesiastical efforts to
eradicate this practice apparently proved as unsuccessful as the
efforts of some Spanish missionaries to end the widespread use of
midwives in isolated Cajun communities. The rantings of pastors
only irritated their female parishioners, who responded with vicious
rumors about the priests' sexual exploits. Cajun women, however,
continued to attend church in large numbers. Acadian men generally
disregarded the progressively ascetic mood of the local church by
continuing to frequent cabarets and gamble at billiards and, by the
early nineteenth century, at cards and horses as well. While not commonplace, extramarital affairs as well as sexual liaisons between
Acadian bachelors and Creole and Negro women became increasingly numerous in the late eighteenth century. Finally, men, women,
and children alike boldly circumvented the church's traditional ban

34. *Ibid.*; Gayarré, *History of Louisiana*, III, 21; Baudier, *Catholic Church*, 183–87;
Father Valentin to Unzaga, March 13, 1771, PPC, 188C:62–63; Judice to Unzaga, October 6, 1772, PPC, 189A:448; Judice to Miró, July 2, 1788, PPC, 201:616–17vo; Judice
to Unzaga, February 5, 1775, PPC, 189B:266; Miró to Judice, May 16, 1788, PPC,
201:600–603.

35. Judice to Unzaga, May 5, 1773, PPC, 189A:474; Robin, *Voyage to Louisiana*, 216;
Verret to Unzaga, June 14, 1773, PPC, 189A:160; Magdelaine Trahan and Marguerite
Bergeron to Verret, May 20, 1773, PPC, 189A:165.

on "dancing to instrumental music" during Lent by holding dances, featuring vocal music only. Until the mid-1930s, Louisiana Cajuns customarily gathered "for the 'danses rondes' on Sunday morning after church at the home of the family who extended the invitation." There, as many as a hundred persons "would dance until midnight."[36]

The spirit of independence that characterized the Acadian response to the cultural imperialism of the immigrant priests also characterized their reaction to the church's efforts to tax its members. In 1770–1771, most Acadians enthusiastically agreed to assist in the construction of their local chapels, and some exiles even offered to donate their farms as church sites. The exiles also reluctantly bowed to governmental pressure to subsidize construction of their respective churches through property taxes, and despite the community's rapidly deteriorating relations with the local clergy, the Acadians agreed to support their pastors through annual pew rentals. They consistently balked, however, when the pastors later attempted to raise funds for the periodic renovation of the churches' physical plants. Such levies were seen as unjustifiable; the allocation of funds for improving the clergy's creature comforts or for conspicuous consumption by the church, rather than the improvement of essential services, was anathema to the Acadian credo. Parishioners quickly appealed all church levies to civil authorities and thus, although

36. Judice to Unzaga, October 6, 1772, PPC, 189A:448; Judice to Unzaga, January 15, 1776, PPC, 189B:303; Father Angel de Revillagodos to Unzaga, September 27, 1774, PPC, 189A:205; Unzaga to Angel de Revillagodos, October 10, 1774, PPC, 189A:204; Unzaga to Verret, March 13, 1773, PPC, 189A:156; Robin, *Voyage to Louisiana*, 216; Verret to Unzaga, June 14, 1773, PPC, 189A:160; Magdelaine Trahan and Marguerite Bergeron to Verret, May 20, 1773, PPC, 189A:165; Deposition of Pierre Part, May 20, 1773, PPC, 189A:169; Judice to Unzaga, January 6, 1775, PPC, 189B:264; Carondelet to Verret, July 13, 1794, PPC, 200:254; Interrogation of Nicolas Roussel, November 23, 1797, PPC, 214:248–49; Declaration of Jean-Charles Dugas, October 9, 1797, PPC, 214:239; Declaration regarding the Joseph Landry *dit* Chinoux estate, April 10, 1797, PPC, 213:352; Louis DeBlanc to Gayoso de Lemos, October 20, 1798, PPC, 215A:307–309; Race contract, October 23, 1783, SMOA; Judice to Unzaga, July 27, 1773, PPC, 189A:482; Judice to Unzaga, June 7, 1774, PPC, 189B:541; Louis Dutisné to Unzaga, June 8, 1774, PPC, 189A:401; Judice to Miró, July 2, 1788, PPC, 201:629; Judice to Miró, October 26, 1789, PPC, 202:372; Miró to Judice, November 2, 1789, PPC, 202:373; Joseph Castille to DeClouet, June 12, 1780, SMOA; Deposition of Jean Doucet, 1780, SMOA; Marie del Norte Theriot and Catherine Brookshire Blanchet, *Les Danses rondes: Louisiana French Folk Dances* (Abbeville, La., 1955), 4.

governmental decisions were usually unfavorable, often avoided full payment through procrastination.[37]

The Acadian concept of the Catholic church changed little despite the sudden and drastic expansion of the church's presence in the exile community. Throughout the late eighteenth century, the Acadians and their children consistently demanded only the minimal, essential services offered by the church. These services consisted of the sacramentals, which not only marked the milestones of life but, in the eyes of the religious, milestones on the road to salvation as well. The sacramentals, however, remained their sole contact with the church, and to prevent unwanted and unwarranted enlargement of the church's role in their daily lives, the exiles insisted that their pastors confine their interests and activities to their normal ecclesiastical duties.

In seeking only minimal services and tolerating only minimal interference in return, the Acadians viewed the church in the same light as their civil government, and any action that deviated from their mental image of these institutions elicited a prompt negative response. As the missionaries frequently attempted to impose the morality of their European homeland on their frontier parishioners, deviation from the Acadian ethos was frequent, producing a correspondingly large number of clashes between clergymen and laymen. Disputes over nonecclesiastical matters usually deteriorated into violence, often precipitated by the rash acts of the missionaries, who were personally insulted by what they considered a lack of proper respect among the Acadians. In disagreements involving religious matters, on the other hand, Cajuns generally exercised greater dis-

37. Judice to Unzaga, April 22, 1771, PPC, 188B:80; Judice to Ulloa, November 18, 1767, PPC, 187A:n.p.; Fuselier de La Clair to Unzaga, June 18, 1773, PC, 189A:56–57; Judice to Unzaga, March 2, 1773, PPC, 189A:472vo; Fuselier de La Claire to Unzaga, March 31, 1773, PPC, 189A:46; Judice to Unzaga, January 2, 1774, PPC, 189A:513; Judice to Unzaga, January 6, 1775, PPC, 189B:264; Mme. Firmin Landry to Miró, 1791, PPC, 202:382; Miró to Judice, May 16, 1788, PPC, 201:600–603vo; Verret to Unzaga, June 23, 1776, PPC, 189B:334; Judice to Unzaga, June 2, 1776, PPC, 189B:332–32vo; Father Grumeau to Gálvez, October 17, 1779, PPC, 192:244; Father P. Geffrotin to Miró, January 29, 1783, PPC, 196:161; Jean Doucet, Jean Richard, Pierre Arseneaux, Philippe Lachaussaye, and Joseph Bourgeois to Miró, October 29, 1784, PPC, 197:271–72; Carondelet to Judice, December 7, 1796, PPC, 212A:489–90; Father Grumeau to Gálvez, October 17, 1779, PPC, 192:224.

cretion, manifesting their displeasure in petitions and protests to civil authorities, thereby avoiding a direct confrontation with the priests and probable excommunication.

The lengths to which the Acadians went to avoid direct confrontations with the local clergy over religious questions vividly reflects the exiles' genuine attachment to their Catholic faith. But among the Acadians, religion and the church were not necessarily synonymous.

9

Cultures in Conflict: Acadian-Creole Relations

In early 1770 Governor Alejandro O'Reilly enhanced Louisiana's colonial authority by dramatically expanding the local governmental system. He selected local representatives—men who would possess civil and military authority—exclusively from the ranks of Creole planters and former French military officers, self-styled aristocrats. These appointments reinforced the colonial elite's sense of social and cultural superiority over the newly arrived Acadians, whom they considered peasants. This attitude, coupled with Acadian refusal to exhibit the deference traditionally extended to aristocracy, inflamed relations that had been strained since 1765, when Opelousas Commandant Louis Pellerin absconded with goods the colonial government had intended for the destitute Acadians.

Intercultural friction promoted cohesiveness within each of the feuding parties. French clerics and retired military officers were driven into the aristocratic Creole camp. Absorption of these groups by the Creole elite convinced the latter of their innate superiority and strengthened their resolve to put the upstart Acadians in their place. The exiles, however, were singularly unimpressed by Creole pretensions and were equally determined to retain their dignity, newly restored after a decade of degradation in British captivity. When Creole pride encountered Acadian "impudence," conflict inevitably ensued.[1]

The first recorded Acadian-Creole clash occurred at Cabannocé

---

1. Petition from the Attakapas Acadians to Aubry, August 28, 1767, PPC, 198: 170–71.

during the summer of 1770. The Acadian exiles, impoverished and momentarily preoccupied with the trauma of adapting to an alien land, vociferously objected when Commandant Nicolas Verret tried to compel them to contribute funds (2 livres, 10 sols) for the local "cemetery, yard, and garden" in excess of the amount previously established by Governor O'Reilly. The Acadians balked at the levy and succumbed only when faced with an ultimatum from the chief executive.[2]

This confrontation was followed in rapid succession by two major disputes: the Bellevue and Valentin affairs. In each instance, exiles bitterly resented what they saw as the arrogance and unwarranted meddling of petty civil and religious officials in their private lives. Even such seemingly inoffensive governmental services as surveys were potentially disruptive, for the Acadians had always seen such projects as attempts by the ruling class to deprive them of their lands. The first Spanish surveys only confirmed their suspicions.

In September, 1770, responding to pressure from the Acadians for land patents, Governor Luis de Unzaga directed chevalier Le Grand de Bellevue to survey property holdings along the Mississippi River. In conformity with traditional Louisiana land-measurement practices, Bellevue established property lines perpendicular to the stream's center. By this means, the surface area of farms at many points, especially the interior banks of oxbows, was drastically reduced, and many Acadian landowners were infuriated. In fact, on June 3, 1771, Louis Judice, commandant at Cabannocé and later Lafourche des Chetimachas, reported that "of all the residents of my district, only thirty are satisfied. The remainder are vexatious and quarrelsome." By early December, irate Acadian landholders had refused to pay for what they considered an extremely poor land survey, though they later agreed to pay Bellevue on the condition that the governor permit Louis Andry, the military engineer who had supervised settlement of the first wave of Acadians along Bayou Teche in 1765, to measure their property.[3]

2. Nicolas Verret to Unzaga, August 27, 1770, PPC, 188A:1d/44.
3. Louis Dutisné to Unzaga, July 1770, PPC, 188A:1c/2; Verret to Unzaga, September 25, 1770, PPC, 188A:1d/46; Le Grand de Bellevue to Unzaga, March 3, 1771, PPC, 192:329; Judice to Unzaga, 1771, PPC, 188C:90; Judice to Unzaga, June 3, 1771, PPC, 188B:94–98; Judice to Unzaga, December 4, 1771, PPC, 189A:278; Judice to Unzaga, January 3, 1772, PPC, 189A:418.

Tensions created by this land dispute were heightened by the Valentin incident. Father Valentin, a former priest at Natchitoches and missionary to the Rapides, Opelousas, and Attakapas posts, assumed the duties of curé at St. Jacques de Cabannocé in early 1771. In mid-March, the priest complained bitterly about four Acadian men who not only had the audacity to smoke their pipes in the presbytery but also harassed and cursed Valentin's Negro cook in the churchman's presence. Adding insult to injury, the exiles answered the priest's ensuing reprimand with an oath. Though the troublemakers eventually apologized, Valentin conducted a personal vendetta against the "godless" Acadians, unsuccessfully seeking legal redress first from Nicolas Verret, the cocommandant, then from Father Dagobert, Louisiana's vicar-general, and ultimately from Governor Luis de Unzaga.[4]

The Valentin and Bellevue incidents were merely manifestations of rapidly deteriorating relations between Louisiana's Acadian and Creole populations. Each successive clash underscored ethnic divisions and fostered group solidarity within the respective belligerent factions. The resulting polarization of the colony's French-speaking populations made additional clashes inevitable.[5]

The intensity of the Acadian-Creole feud can be partially attributed to amorous affairs between Acadian men and Creole women. The interest of Creole men in slave women is indicated by the emergence of a significant mulatto population along the Mississippi River during the Spanish Period (1769–1803). Neglected by their husbands, some Creole women formed liaisons with young Acadian bachelors; such illicit unions, however, were usually detected by the cuckold husbands, frequently with violent results.[6] One such incident involved Sieur Bertonville, a French-born surgeon, who returned home in July, 1773, to find his wife and young Jean-Baptiste Braud in bed. According to Judice, "when Sieur Bertonville entered his home and witnessed this ugly spectacle, he became enraged. He got his musket, placed the gunbarrel against his wife's body, and

4. Baudier, *Catholic Church*, 182; Father Valentin to Unzaga, March 13, 1771, PPC, 188C:62–63; Judice to Unzaga, October 6, 1772, PPC, 188A:448.
5. Claude Boutté to Gálvez, February 22, 1777, PPC, 190:131.
6. Unzaga to Judice, May 29, 1772, PPC, 189A:485; Judice to Unzaga, June 17, 1772, PPC, 189A:428; Judice to Unzaga, July 27, 1773, PPC, 189A:482; Dutisné to Unzaga, June 8, 1774, PPC, 189A:401.

would have killed her, as well as the boy, if the gun had fired, but fortunately it misfired. The boy and the worthless woman saved themselves, each running in opposite directions, one holding his pants in his hands, and the other her skirt."[7]

The Creoles and Frenchmen residing along the Mississippi River were placed on the defensive by the Bertonville and Valentin incidents, which clearly demonstrated that the Acadians would not respect the seignorial trappings of the colonial "aristocracy." These bluebloods thus struck instinctively against the rising tide of social democratization. In November, 1771, Louis Judice, commandant at St. Jacques de Cabannocé during the Valentin affair and self-styled protector of Creole privileges, relocated at the predominantly Acadian Lafourche de Chetimachas post and, soon thereafter, supervised construction of the district's first Catholic church, the Church of the Assumption. Once the structure was dedicated, Judice, who retained his commission as commandant, was appalled by the Acadian parishioners' failure to maintain what he considered proper decorum before and during mass.[8] According to the commandant, the exiles "sometimes seat themselves on the steps at the church door, and smoke pipes, and engage in charades, each fighting for his turn. They occasionally fly into a passion and swear."

As Judice thought "it best not to permit this licentiousness," he prohibited the traditional Sunday morning gatherings and warned the exiles that anyone "caught in the act of swearing" in the churchyard would be fined. "Blasphemers against God, our Savior, or His Blessed Mother, the Very Blessed Virgin" would also be sent to the capital to account for their actions. In his crusade to force the Acadians to conform to his standards of conduct, Judice left no stone unturned. Because the church could not seat all of the parishioners, many Acadians stood in the sanctuary during mass, and according to Judice, some of them had the "audacity" to touch the altar. As this undoubtedly interrupted the priest, parishioners were banned from the area around the altar. Finally, "in order to prevent the reverend father from being insulted in his own house, as the Reverend Father

---

7. Judice to Unzaga, July 27, 1773, PPC, 189A:482.
8. Judice to Unzaga, November, 1771, PPC, 188C:90; Judice to Unzaga, October 6, 1772, PPC, 189A:448; Charles Edwards O'Neill, *Church and State in French Colonial Louisiana: Policy and Politics to 1732* (New Haven, 1966), 239–46.

Valentin had been at St. James Parish," the commandant forbade, under financial penalty, cursing and swearing in the presbytery.[9]

The Acadians immediately complained to the governor and thereby compelled the commandant to explain his actions. Judice was apparently intimidated by the inquiry, for, despite subsequent violations of his ordinance, no one was ever penalized.[10]

When not arguing over the issue of church decorum, Acadians and Creoles clashed over property rights. Feuding was especially intense in the Attakapas district, where "four or five" French-born and Creole cattle barons, the original settlers, considered the exiles trespassers, though they had been settled in the area by virtue of a gubernatorial decree. The matter reached a climax in the spring of 1773, with the Courtableau land conflict (see Chapter 6). The Courtableau case seems to have obviated additional land disputes in Attakapas and Opelousas—extant Spanish records fail to mention similar, subsequent disputes—but such was not the case in the predominantly Acadian districts along the Mississippi River and Bayou Lafourche. There, French and Creole planters, especially the Mollère brothers, impudently stole cypress timber from Acadian land grants, thus fanning the flames of ethnic animosity. In fact, commenting upon the situation in late November, 1789, Judice noted, "the Acadians dislike the Mollères, as well as the French who are established in their vicinity."[11]

Acadian ill will toward the Creoles occasionally manifested itself in violence. Fights involving Acadians and Creoles broke out at local cabarets and, in at least one instance, resulted in death. Moreover, in the early 1770s the exiles resorted to violence to defend their herds. At Attakapas, Creole cattle barons initially allowed their immense herds to roam the prairies unattended, and the livestock quickly became wild. Following the settling of the Acadians, the Creoles began to absorb the exiles' domesticated cattle. Resulting public outcry prompted Governor O'Reilly to require construction of fences, restriction of herd movement, and the periodic slaughtering of stray cattle. When the wealthy Flamand brothers, owners of many Atta-

9. Judice to Unzaga, October 6, 1772, PPC, 188A:448.
10. *Ibid.*; Judice to Miró, July 2, 1788, PPC, 201:616–17vo; Judice to Unzaga, June 6, 1773, PPC, 189A:478.
11. Judice to Miró, November 29, 1788, PPC, 201:652–53vo; Marguerite Landry (Veuve Babin) to Miró, July 28, 1787, PPC, 200:436.

kapas strays, repeatedly pressured Commandant Gabriel Fuselier de La Claire into postponing destruction of their stray cattle, the Acadians took matters into their own hands. Led by Jean Berard, a former St. Louis merchant whose wife was Acadian, and Claude Boutté, a Frenchman whose herds had also been victimized by the wild cattle, they slaughtered a significant number of the offending livestock. Outraged by the "brigands'" impudence, the Flamands urged Alexandre DeClouet, Fuselier's replacement, to imprison the ringleaders.[12]

The Flamand incident formed a watershed in Acadian-Creole relations in the Attakapas, crystallizing latent ethnic animosity stemming from previous confrontations. Deteriorating relations were evidenced in the Creoles' heightened fears about the security of their property and a corresponding attempt by the aristocracy's government agent—the Attakapas commandant—to tighten controls over the Acadian population. In the mid-1770s, Joseph Landry lost three of four head of cattle that he was driving to the New Orleans stockyards. When he requested DeClouet's permission to retrieve his wayward livestock, he was told that they were strays belonging to the crown and would be confiscated by a militia detachment. Exasperated by the constant petty harassment from the French elite, many Acadians migrated to the more isolated unoccupied prairies before the end of the eighteenth century.[13]

Unlike their Attakapas cousins, the river Acadians were confined by the local topography to riverfronts and thus tied to their Creole and French-born neighbors. The embers of ethnic animosity continued to glow brightly. In May, 1773, a group of Acadian women failed to close a gate on Sieur Croizet's property as they returned from Sunday mass. Croizet, watching from his nearby gallery, berated them for their negligence and called them "sacré Rosse d'Acadiens, Canailles, toupies, garses, et en un mot mille invectives." Enraged by his abuse, the women, led by Mmes. Alexis Braud and Bonaventure Godin, lodged a formal complaint with Governor Un-

---

12. Minutes of the investigation into Joseph Hebert's death, August 21, 1787, PPC, 200:468–79vo; Martin (trans.), "Ordinance Regulating Concessions and Cattle," 180; Interrogation of Jean Berard, June 19, 1774, PPC, 189A:84; DeClouet to Unzaga, July 26, 1774, PPC, 189A:92; Boutté to Unzaga, February 22, 1777, PPC, 190:131.

13. Boutté to Unzaga, February 22, 1777, PPC, 190:131–33.

zaga and apparently secured a public apology, over the Creole commandant's objections.[14]

The flames of animosity leaped forth again in late February, 1774, when Basile Préjean, an Acadian leader at Cabannocé, who had previously quarreled with Commandant Nicolas Verret, burst into Commandant Judice's quarters and attacked a local Creole who was pressing charges against Préjean for a previous assault. Outraged by Préjean's "audacity," Judice filed a complaint against him, "more as an example than for any other motive, in order to demonstrate to the Acadians that they must not strike anyone, least of all their betters." Préjean was duly sentenced by the governor to three days' imprisonment.[15]

Judice and local Acadian leaders clashed again during a smallpox outbreak. In August, 1787, under pressure from the Lafourche aristocracy, Governor Miró banned smallpox inoculations because the vaccinating of slaves might disrupt the harvest. In October, one of Judice's female slaves contracted the disease. The news spread quickly throughout the post, and on Sunday, October 7, nine Acadian representatives called upon the commandant to determine the reports' veracity. After examining the smallpox victim, "whose fever had broken," Joseph Melancon, speaking on behalf of his fellow representatives, offered to purchase the black woman, reportedly for the purpose of "burning her." Recoiling from the cruelty of the local "barbarians," Judice adamantly refused to relinquish his slave.[16]

Determined to eradicate the threat to their families, however, ten Acadians, led by Joseph Melancon and Isaac LeBlanc, returned to Judice's quarters on October 13. The meeting quickly deteriorated into a shouting match. The Acadians indicated that they would drive smallpox victims from the district and would flog any slave traversing the area. Melancon then "audaciously" denied the charge that he had offered to purchase the woman for the purpose of burning her; he actually intended to drown her.[17]

14. Verret to Unzaga, June 14, 1773, PPC, 189A:160.

15. Judice to Unzaga, December 4, 1771, PPC, 189A:278; Judice to Unzaga, February 25, 1774, PPC, 189A:535; Unzaga to Judice, March 2, 1774, PPC, 189A:536.

16. Miró to Judice, n.d., PPC, 200:570; Judice to Miró, October 13, 1787, PPC, 200:575–76.

17. Judice to Miró, October 13, 1787, PPC, 200:575–76; Judice to Miró, November 13, 1787, PPC, 200:586–87.

LeBlanc then heaped verbal abuse upon the commandant, threatening to isolate all future smallpox victims. In addition, he not only cursed repeatedly but also remained poised, ready to strike his superior officer should Judice contradict him.[18]

Acadian belligerency toward the Creoles and their slaves contrasted markedly with their reaction to smallpox outbreaks among their own people. When Ephrème Babin was stricken with the dreaded disease sometime prior to October 10, no effort was made to remove him from the district. As Judice noted in a subsequent dispatch to Governor Miró, "if that man had been of any nationality but Acadian, all of the Acadians would have demanded that he be expelled from the parish, but, as he is a member of their society, they will endure his illness with patience, persuaded that the contagion will not spread."[19]

The epidemic ran its course by mid-December, 1787, apparently causing no loss of life. Judice's authority, however, had been damaged, for the Acadians had demonstrated they could effectively check his orders, and Miró was compelled to restore order. When LeBlanc and Melancon voluntarily presented themselves before the governor in November, the chief executive was bound to punish them for insubordination, but succumbing to pressure from numerous other Acadians, he imposed the remarkably light sentence of twenty-four hours in chains and a public apology. The sentence was executed in December, but defiant to the end, LeBlanc concluded his public apology with threats against "that bastard of a churchwarden," Judice's staunch supporter, who had been openly critical of the Acadians during the October crisis.[20]

LeBlanc's concluding remarks accurately reflected the growing antagonism between Acadians and Creoles; nor were these relations to improve. In fact, by 1792 the colonial "aristocracy" and the exiles had been involved in two major confrontations. The first, at Lafourche des Chetimachas, sprang from a long-standing dispute over levee maintenance. Although Governor O'Reilly had ordered landholders to build and maintain levees along their waterfront proper-

18. Judice to Miró, November 13, 1787, PPC, 200:586–87.
19. Judice to Miró, October 13, 1787, PPC, 200:575–76.
20. Miró to Judice, December 1, 1787, PPC, 200:592; Judice to Miró, December 10, 1787, PPC, 200:593–95; Judice to Miró, November 13, 1787, PPC, 200:586–87.

ties in order to receive patents to their lands, many large, absentee Creole landowners did not comply. Because of this negligence, many Acadian settlers who scrupulously complied with O'Reilly's demand were subjected to severe spring floods. The problem was especially severe along Bayou Lafourche, where Commandant Judice himself violated the decree. The matter reached a climax in June, 1788, when Claude and Jérôme LeBlanc charged that Judice's negligence had resulted in the inundation of their farmland. Responding to public outcry, Governor Miró commissioned an official inquiry that subsequently confirmed the allegations. Judice was therefore ordered to repair the flood control structure.[21]

Feuding now shifted to the Attakapas, where the Acadians, who had been migrating to the southwestern prairies since the 1770s, requested the establishment of a more conveniently located church along the Vermilion River. The Creoles adamantly opposed creation of a new parish that would force them to increase support of the deteriorating mother church—St. Martin de Tours. The problem festered for approximately one year, until Governor Miró decided the matter in the Acadians' favor, despite the vocal opposition of Commandant Jean Delavillebeuvre, a retired French military officer. During the interim, ethnic factionalism had become so severe the colony's chief executive warned residents that the "authors" of further divisions would be deported.[22]

The absence of major clashes during the remaining years of Spanish rule disguises the feud's persistence; for ethnic animosity endured as long as conflicting life-styles confronted each other. C. C. Robin, a Frenchman touring Louisiana in 1804, one year after the end of Spanish rule, succinctly described this phenomenon: "The Acadians work the land themselves. The women and children go into the fields to pick corn and cotton. . . . The families descended from French officers or merchants live quite differently. They live in indolent ease, even those with little money. They use a portion of their slaves as indoor servants, in an attempt to recapture a sense of the easy and sumptuous life. Several have fallen into this deca-

21. Miró to Judice, June 17, 1788, PPC, 201:610; Procès-verbal of the inspection of Judice's levees, June 29, 1788, PPC, 201:613.

22. Delavillebeuvre to Miró, May 9, 1791, PPC, 204:129–32; Carondelet to Delavillebeuvre, June 2, 1792, PPC, 205:278.

dence. The Acadians, simpler, and more economical, are prosper-
ing. . . . The Acadians like to live to themselves and they had little to
do with the families who are pretentious."[23]

As indicated by Robin, the haughty Creoles, like their counterparts in the Antilles, were descendents of French soldiers of fortune
who had come to the New World to attain high social status and
wealth, neither of which was attainable in France. They jealously
guarded their position as an emerging colonial aristocracy. Their
dream of establishing a feudal system in the Mississippi Valley,
based on slavery and with themselves as the sole beneficiaries, was
shared by the French clerics and retired military officers remaining
in the colony after 1766. Thus, when confronted by frontier yeomen,
the Frenchmen aligned themselves with (and were quickly absorbed
by) the Creoles in a futile attempt to cast the exiles into an image of a
colonial peasantry.

Acadians, too, sought a comfortable existence, but unlike the
Frenchmen and Creoles, they bore the stamp of Acadia's isolated
frontier and had developed an egalitarian outlook. Creole-Acadian
tensions were compounded also by the aristocracy's growing convic-
tion that its less affluent and less ambitious neighbors were a crass
and uncultured people, whose standards of conduct must be altered
to meet Creole standards of behavior. Acadians naturally resented
this interference in their daily lives and eagerly anticipated opportunities to strike back at their tormenters. Continued conflict between the groups was inevitable.

23. Robin, *Voyage to Louisiana*, 191.

10

Red Men and Refugees: Acadian-Indian Relations

Students of Acadian history recognize the significance of assistance provided the first settlers by the Micmac Indians. In the words of geographer Andrew Hill Clark, the success of the nascent colony hinged upon "the existence of a native hunting people who could supply furs, the most desired trading goods from the land, in some quantity." The Micmacs thus provided the *raison d'être* for Acadian colonization, as well as the means for the colonists to weather successfully their first years in the New World. Moreover, Micmac participation in the French fur trade not only attracted colonists to the Bay of Fundy's shores but also provided the settlers' most important cash income for the following century.[1]

Despite the tribe's early beneficence and continuing contribution to the Acadian economy, relations between the colony's major cultural groups were strained by 1755. The gradual deterioration of Acadian-Indian relations can be traced—as can so many other pre-dispersal Acadian problems—to European politics.

Like the Acadians, tribes in the Bay of Fundy area were victims of the seemingly endless European wars and the territorial changes

---

1. Clark, *Acadia*, 68–70, 88–89, 128, 361, 377; Rameau de St-Père, *Une Colonie féodale*, I, 24–45, 153; II, 5; Griffiths, *Creation of a People*, 4–5, 10; Lauvrière, *Tragédie*, I, 1–179; J. A. Hutton, "The Micmac Indians of Nova Scotia to 1834" (M.A. thesis, Dalhousie University, 1961); W. D. Wallis, "Historical Background of the Micmac Indians of Canada," *National Museum of Canada Bulletin No. 173: Contributions to Anthropology, 1959* (Ottawa, 1961), 42–63; W. D. Wallis and R. S. Wallis, *The Micmac Indians of Eastern Canada* (Minneapolis, 1955); Fontaine (ed.), *Voyage du Sieur du Dièreville*, 45; Thwaites (ed.), *The Jesuit Relations*, III, 69.

they inevitably entailed. Thus, when Acadia became a bargaining chip in the Treaty of Utrecht negotiations, the Micmac found that their ancestral lands, intially claimed by the French, were now the *de jure* possessions of the British. With the ratification of the treaty in 1713, the colony's original inhabitants—like their Acadian neighbors—were compelled to choose between fealty to Britain or continued service to France in the French-held territory beyond the Isthmus of Chignecto; many of the tribesmen opted for the second choice.[2]

Their decision was based largely on two considerations. First, the tribe had traditionally been nomadic, residing in present-day New Brunswick most of the year and venturing east of the Isthmus of Chignecto only in summer. As many of the favorite summer campsites were now settled and developed by Europeans, the Nova Scotian peninsula had obviously lost much of its appeal. Second, the Micmacs were among the earliest converts to Catholicism in French North America, and the impact of French missionaries on the tribe during the turbulent years of the early and middle eighteenth century cannot be overestimated.[3]

The Micmacs' decision to remain in the French camp caused little change in tribal relations with the Acadians. Although it is true that between 1713 and 1730 the Acadians used fear of Franco-Indian reprisals as the basis for consistently refusing a routine oath of allegiance to England, the actual probability of such attacks was slight. Indeed, while raiding English positions in Nova Scotia after the cession, French-allied Micmacs consistently marched through major settlements without disturbing the residents or the countryside. Despite the change of domination, the Acadian-Micmac economic partnership persisted and flourished. As they had done for a century, Acadians continued to accompany Micmac hunting parties into the frozen New Brunswick wilderness and to barter Acadian linen and European manufactured goods for pelts. Finally, the economic ties were undergirded by blood relationships, for though many settlers

2. Griffiths, *Creation of a People*, 21; D. C. Harvey, *The French Regime in Prince Edward Island* (New Haven, 1926), 28, 30–33, 71, 78, 118, 119, 126, 212–32; Clark, *Acadia*, 58–64, 361.

3. Clark, *Acadia*, 58–64, 361; Jean Daigle, "L'Acadie, 1604–1763. Synthèse historique," in Daigle (ed.), *Les Acadiens des Maritimes*, 33, 42–43.

had discarded their Indian concubines after the arrival of European women, a few relationships endured and were blessed by the church.[4]

This harmonious intercultural relationship, however, deteriorated rapidly, a result, once again, of European power politics. During the War of the Austrian Succession (1740–1748), vital French shipping lanes to Canada had been severed by the British capture of Louisbourg, a major French military installation on Cape Breton Island. The fall of the seemingly indestructible fortress demonstrated to France the vulnerability of its North American empire, and of New France in particular. Therefore, although Louisbourg was restored to France by subsequent peace negotiations, the French government resolved to drive the British from neighboring Nova Scotia without direct military intervention, thus depriving the British of a base of future operations against Louisbourg.[5]

Major actors in this diplomatic scenario were the francophile Micmacs and the traditionally and officially neutral Acadians. Agitated by militant French missionaries acting under the direction of the French government, the Micmacs declared war on England in September, 1749, and quickly launched a series of raids against English settlements and small military detachments. The Acadians were not spared the horrors of war; indeed, they became a bone of contention between the feuding European powers. As English officials attempted to browbeat the Acadians into taking an oath of allegiance, the French Canadian military forces, now firmly entrenched in new outposts along the Nova Scotian border, launched a campaign to force the Acadians into the French camp, if not French territory, thereby jeopardizing British control over the colony.[6]

The instrument of French coercion was the Micmac tribe. In the spring of 1750 the Indians, under the direction of Abbé Le Loutre, razed Beaubassin, terrorizing the residents along the Bay of Fundy's northern littoral. The result was a small-scale Acadian migration into

4. Rameau de St-Père, *Une Colonie féodale*, I, 41–44, 153; Griffiths, *Creation of a People*, 23, 43; Clark, *Acadia*, 68–70, 361.

5. Eccles, *France in America*, 175; Lionel Groulx, *Histoire du Canada français depuis la découverte* (4th ed.; 2 vols.; Montreal, 1960), I, 338; Brebner, *New England's Outpost*, 107, 110–14.

6. Eccles, *France in America*, 180; Griffiths, *Creation of a People*, 42–45.

French military installations along the western extremity of the Isthmus of Chignecto. As Nova Scotian Governor Edward Cornwallis noted, the refugees made "no scruple to declare this proceeding is entirely against their inclination but that LaCorne and LeLoutre threatened them with a general massacre by savages if they remain in the Province."[7]

The perceived threat became increasingly real as tensions heightened along the intercolonial border in succeeding years, and thus the Acadians in English territory lived in constant fear of Franco-Indian reprisals until the Grand Dérangement. In fact, the perceived potential for success by the Franco-Indian terrorism campaign was sufficient motivation for the English colonial government to deport the potential political apostates.

During the long years of exile following the Acadian diaspora, the displaced French Neutrals received consistently poor treatment in the English seaboard colonies—despite their nominal English citizenship—largely because of hysteria generated by francophile Indian raids along the Appalachian Mountains during the Seven Years War. Thus, although the French-speaking Acadians had remained loyal to England during the last major intercolonial war, they were viewed and treated as French spies and potential collaborators with the Indian raiders who were allied with the French.

The exiles were unable to escape the Indian problems spawned by the last great European struggle for North American supremacy despite their effort to do so by migrating to Louisiana. On the contrary, the Indian problem was far more severe in the lower Mississippi Valley. During the decade following the Seven Years' War (1763–1773), the Mississippi River served as the international boundary between the English and Spanish North American empires. Lacking natural defenses, the border was indefensible, particularly in view of the meager military resources available to colonial administrators in these remote areas. Rival colonial governments frantically attempted to build powerful Indian alliances among the riverfront tribes while simultaneously sabotaging their neighbor's Indian diplomacy. As a consequence, the lower Mississippi Valley Indians were in a constant state of agitation, and settlers on both sides of the river lived in constant fear of attack.[8]

7. Griffiths, *Creation of a People*, 42–44.
8. Ulloa to Grimaldi, May 19, 1766, ASD, 2585:n.p.; Brasseaux (trans. and ed.), *A*

Given the political climate of the Hispano-English borderlands when the first Acadians immigrated to Louisiana (1765–1770), as well as the misfortunes exiles suffered (either directly or indirectly) at the hands of red men, it is hardly surprising that Acadian-Indian relations in the river settlements were chronically poor. Indeed, from the outset, relations between the immigrants and their Native American neighbors—even with those Indians residing in Spanish territory—were tainted with mutual fears and suspicions. On one hand, the Indians allied with Spain feared displacement by the exiles. Even the normally docile Tensas tribe carried its protest to the governor upon hearing rumors of possible Acadian settlement on tribal lands. Acadians thus feared reprisals from fellow Spanish subjects while simultaneously anticipating unprovoked raids by neighboring English-allied tribes.[9]

The exiles were understandably reluctant to settle in such a turbulent area, where, it seemed, they would once again be caught in a crossfire. Upon arrival at San Luis de Natchez, a large group demanded immediate relocation downstream because the isolated Spanish post was quite vulnerable to Indian raids. Particularly susceptible to attack were the lands designated for Acadian settlement—riverfront properties at least one league (2.5 miles) from the small Spanish fortress. Even the fort offered little security, particularly in view of reports that the English were gaining increasing control over the ten thousand Choctaw and Chickasaw warriors near Fort Panmure on the opposite riverbank. Such reports, as well as knowledge of detailed contingency plans for possible Indian assaults, did little to allay the Acadians' fears. The local commandant's reports to the contrary notwithstanding, the Acadians' concern for their own security was genuine, and their demands to join relatives on the less-exposed Acadian Coast were inevitable.[10]

Comparative View of French Louisiana, 84–136; Moore, _Revolt in Louisiana,_ 84–110; Aubry to Ulloa, February 14, 1767, PPC, 187A:n.p.; Verret to Ulloa, March 26, 1768, PPC, 2357:n.p.; Pedro Piernas to Ulloa, March 27, 1768, PPC, 188B:218; Unzaga to Judice, September 12, 1772, PPC, 189A:438.

9. Ulloa to Judice, November 18, 1767, PPC, 187A:n.p.; Judice to Ulloa, November 1767, PPC, 187A:n.p.; Ulloa to Grimaldi, June 19, 1766, ASD, 2585:n.p.; Petition to O'Reilly from the Acadians settled at Natchez, October 18, 1769, ASD, 2585:n.p.; Dutisné to Unzaga, 1771, PPC, 188B:218; Verret to Ulloa, March 26, 1768, PPC, 2357:n.p.; Unzaga to Judice, September 12, 1772, PPC, 189A:438.

10. Piernas to Ulloa, March 27, 1768, PPC, 187A:n.p.; Verret to Ulloa, March 26, 1768, PPC, 2357:n.p.; Depositions by Guy Dufossat, and Jean Delavillebeuvre, No-

To the San Luis settlers, the Acadian Coast appeared to be a haven
of peace and security, but to the residents of Cabannocé, Iberville,
and St. Gabriel, it was as insecure as the new homesites of their
northern cousins. As in the Natchez area, British authorities at Manchac were massing east-bank Indians across the river from areas
of concentrated Acadian settlement. Figuring prominently in this
demographic movement was the Talapousa (Creek) tribe, whose
reputation for ferocity and frequent movements spawned many unfounded rumors of impending attack. The west-bank settlements
were often on military alert, but according to Iberville Commandant
Charles Dutisné, the Acadians lived in a perpetual state of fear.[11]

Acadian worry about Indian attacks was not restricted to the
threat from without. Indeed, as the external threat subsided in the
early 1770s, internal security problems posed by west-bank tribes
loomed increasingly large. Principal culprits were the Houmas of the
upper Lafourche Valley. By the early 1770s, Acadian relations with
the ostensibly friendly tribe had deteriorated to the point that, when
the Houmas erected a weak palisade around their village as a safe-
guard against Talapousa raids, nine Acadian families sought refuge
at St. James and Iberville parishes.[12]

The small number of refugees belied the extent of Acadian reaction to the tribe's seemingly hostile gesture. Construction of the palisade apparently constituted the breaking point for the increasingly
distraught exiles. In mid-March, 1772, Lafourche Commandant
Louis Judice reported that approximately two hundred exiles had resolved to leave Louisiana and had sent delegates to New Orleans,
where they attempted to charter a merchant vessel. The disgruntled

---

vember 5, 1769, ASD, 2585:n.p.; Montfort Browne to the Earl of Hillsborough, July 6,
1768, CO 5, Vol. 285, pp. 154vo–67; Cecil Johnson, *British West Florida* (New Haven,
1942), 36, 42; Piernas to Ulloa, May 29, 1768, PPC, 2357:n.p.; Petition to Ulloa from
the San Luis Acadians, October 18, 1769, ASD, 2585:n.p.; Reasons given by the Acadians for not settling at San Luis de Natchez, March 27, 1768, PPC, 187A:n.p.

11. Piernas to Ulloa, March 27, 1768, PPC, 2357:n.p.; Ulloa to Grimaldi, June 19,
1766, ASD, 2585:n.p.; Dutisné to Unzaga, 1771, PPC, 188B:218; Unzaga to Judice,
September 12, 1772, PPC, 189A:438; Delavillebeuvre to Gálvez, July 13, 1778, PPC,
201:683.

12. Unzaga to Judice, September 12, 1772, PPC, 189A:438; Census of the Indians at
the Cabannocé post, September 5, 1768, PPC, 187A:n.p.; Unzaga to Judice, September 12, 1772, PPC, 189A:438; List of the Assumption settlers who went from Assumption Parish to St. James and Iberville parishes, 1772, PPC, 189A:445.

Lafourche Valley settlers ultimately reconsidered their rash decision, and the anticipated Acadian exodus never materialized.[13]

The exiles soon had cause to regret their decision, for relations between the region's small farmers and the Houmas continued to deteriorate in the following years. In March, 1778, Judice lamented, "I have the honor of informing Your Grace that the Houma Indians cause considerable harm to the settlers, stealing their rice and corn from their fields, and rustling and killing their hogs which they subsequently sell to the English." Acting on the complaints of several aggrieved farmers including Joseph Landry, who lost more than sixty barrels of corn to the thieves, Judice confronted the Houma chief, warning him that unless the thefts ceased immediately, the village would be razed by the local militia.[14]

Judice's warning went unheeded, but the commandant himself conveniently forgot his stern fulminations. The problem festered, and interpreting inaction as a sign of weakness, the Houmas became increasingly bold. Their insolence was reinforced by rum readily available from Jean-Baptiste Chauvin, a local merchant who concealed his cache of liquor in the woods behind the Assumption Parish church. By the 1780s, tribal elders complained the warriors were squandering all of their belongings, bartering them for liquor from white renegade rum runners. Emboldened by alcohol, Houma Indians raided Acadians by day and, when their victims resisted, fired into their homes.[15]

Once again, despite the severity of the Indian problem, Judice confined his public response to a litany of complaints to the governor. In this instance, forbearance paid dividends, for in the fall of 1785 the upper Lafourche Valley was threatened by servile insurrection, and when the local militia proved ineffective, Judice was compelled to call upon the Houmas for assistance. Needing funds to feed their alcohol addiction, twelve Houma warriors readily accepted the proferred one-hundred piastre reward for each of the principal insurrectionaries and immediately initiated their pursuit.[16]

13. Judice to Unzaga, September 20, 1772, PPC, 189A:430.
14. Judice to Gálvez, March 18, 1778, PPC, 193A:466–67.
15. Judice to Miró, May 26, 1785, PPC, 198A:411–12.
16. Judice to Miró, November 15, 1785, PPC, 198A:459–62; Judice to Miró, November 19, 1785, PPC, 198A:463–67.

Though the Houmas succeeded in killing only one of the black rebels, their ready, albeit mercenary, participation in the ultimately successful manhunt earned the red men a short-lived rapprochement with their white neighbors, but following the dispersal of the black rebels, the intercultural feud resumed. Poor Acadian-Houma relations apparently persisted until 1788, when a smallpox epidemic forced the tribe to migrate to the lower Lafourche Valley.[17]

The continuing feud and the unwillingness of local officials to discipline unruly tribesmen heightened the frustrations of Lafourche Valley Acadians. Intimidated by the violent tendencies exhibited by inebriated Houma tribesmen, many settlers had watched helplessly as their hogs—an important source of income to Acadians east of the Atchafalaya River in the late eighteenth century—were destroyed and a portion of their crops was removed. Seething with anger, the Acadians awaited an opportunity to vent their frustrations.[18]

Such an opportunity appeared in 1789, when a small band of Choctaw raiders, who had resided with the Houmas for several months, went to the farm of Commandant Judice's son and threatened to kill him. Notified of the raid by local Acadians, the elder Judice sped toward the trouble, calling to arms the militiamen residing en route. Arriving after nightfall, Judice positioned an undetermined number of Acadians around the farm, then approached the Choctaws alone. When the raiders gathered to confront Judice, the commandant signaled his men, and the trap was sprung. The Choctaws immediately dispersed, and in the resulting melee the militiamen disregarded Judice's orders to hold their fire and shot indiscriminately at the fugitives. Though none of the raiders was killed (because of poor visibility), five were captured and escorted to New Orleans for trial by Acadian militiamen.[19]

17. Jacques Theriot to Miró, January 2, 1789, PPC, 202:232; Judice to Miró, February 7, 1786, PPC, 199:256; Judice to Miró, May 4, 1788, PPC, 201:599vo; Clarence Carter (ed.), *Territorial Papers of the United States* (28 vols.; Washington, D. C., 1927–75), IX, 62; John Sibley, "Historical Sketches of the Several Indian Tribes in Louisiana, South of the Arkansas River, and Between the Mississippi and River Grand," *Annals of Congress*, 9th Cong., 2nd Sess. (1852), 1088. On the Houma withdrawal from the upper Lafourche Valley, see John R. Swanton, *Indian Tribes of the Lower Mississippi Valley and Adjacent Coast of the Gulf of Mexico* (Washington, D.C., 1911), 11.

18. Passport of Amand Hebert, Joseph Melancon, and Ignace Hebert, July 7, 1781, PPC, 194:380; Judice to Gálvez, October 26, 1778, PPC, 193A:466–67.

19. Judice to Miró, February 18, 1789, PPC, 202:266–68.

The cold reception extended to the Choctaw raiders demonstrated renewed resolve on the part of the Lafourche settlers, and the lesson so painfully learned by the Choctaws was not soon forgotten by the local tribes. A rehabilitated image of the Acadians among Indians east of the Atchafalaya River, following closely the Houma migration from the primary areas of Acadian settlement, resulted in an immediate and radical lessening—if not an effective severance—of Acadian-Indian contact in the Lafourche Valley and the river settlements. Indeed, after 1789, matters concerning Indians appear only rarely in the official correspondence of the aforementioned posts.

Indian problems confronted by the eastern Acadians were not shared by their cousins across the Atchafalaya River. Relations between the Attakapas and Chitimacha tribes on one hand and the western Acadians on the other were harmonious throughout the colonial period. The friendship shared by these groups can be attributed to three factors: First, most of the exiles who settled in the Teche Valley—unlike their eastern cousins—had resided in French territory prior to the Grand Dérangement and had maintained good relations with the Micmac Indians. As many of these settlers were former fur traders by profession, maintenance of good Indian relations was an absolute necessity. Moreover, during the Seven Years' War, many Acadians had engaged in guerrilla warfare with the Micmacs against the English. The western Acadians thus shared none of their cousins' apprehensions about red men.[20]

Second, the Indians themselves were sufficiently removed from the Mississippi River to be geographically insulated from the turmoil plaguing Euro-Indian relations along the intercolonial border. In fact, oral tradition in a southwest Louisiana family of Afro-Indian descent maintains that the Attakapas treated Acadians with herbal remedies when smallpox and fever decimated the exiles shortly after their arrival.[21]

Finally, initial good relations were undergirded by economic ties. Unlike the river and Lafourche settlements, where only one resident engaged in fur trading—but only in distant Arkansas—western Acadians resumed their predispersal professions as soon as the eco-

20. Rameau de St-Père, *Une Colonie féodale*, I, 167, 238–41, 247–49.
21. Interview with descendants of Catherine Pierre: Carolyn Stemley, "Attakapas Indian Healers."

nomic situation permitted. By the early 1770s, the Teche Valley Acadians were bartering liquor for furs and horses stolen in New Spain. By the mid-1770s, this contraband trade was expanded to include strays—and occasionally domesticated beefs as well—slaughtered and skinned on the open prairies. Indian rustlers found a lucrative market for fresh beef and apparently for cowhides in the western Acadian settlements. The Attakapas also found the Acadians most eager to buy their lands, and as the tribe migrated westward to the Mermentau and Calcasieu rivers in the late eighteenth century, they sold their tribal property for handsome sums to ranchers and land speculators.[22]

Such mutually beneficial business arrangements were the hallmark of Acadian-Indian relations in western Acadian settlements; hence, it is worthy of note that there is not a single recorded instance of Acadian-Indian confrontation in the civil records and official correspondence of the Teche Valley posts.

Because of the changing demographic and economic face of the Teche Valley at the dawn of the nineteenth century, however, such close intercultural ties could not endure. Westward migrations of the Attakapas, and the confinement of the Chitimacha tribe to an isolated land grant at present-day Charenton, severely curtailed Acadian-Indian contacts. Except for arrangements involving purchase of Attakapas lands in the western prairies, Acadian relations with the local tribes were almost completely severed by 1803.

By the early nineteenth century, therefore, the Acadians had succeeded the Indians as the predominant cultural group in their original settlement sites. Ironically, because of the immigration and the cultural and technological change a new age would bring, the Acadians now faced the same challenges to cultural survival so recently confronted by their Native American neighbors. The exiles, however, were girded for such an eventuality. The bitter struggle for cultural supremacy had underscored the Acadian sense of group identity in the river and Lafourche Valley settlements, regenerating the

22. Marriage contract between Amant Sirre (Cyr) and Marie Rose Bourg, July 2, 1785, in St. James Parish Original Acts (hereinafter abbreviated SJOA), Office of the Clerk of Court, Convent, Louisiana; DeClouet to Unzaga, August 9, 1774, PPC, 189A:95–95vo; Demézières to Unzaga, August 8, 1774, PPC, 189A:92–93; Land sale, Chief Bernard to Anselme Thibaudaut, November 16, 1780, SMOA.

cohesiveness, insularity, and mental toughness necessary for survival in a changing world. But the gains of the eastern Acadians were not without cost, for they altered, if ever so slightly, Louisiana's emerging Cajun culture. By fostering different regional attitudes toward the Indians, who would remain a small, isolated, but culturally significant local minority, the Acadian-Indian feud accelerated the divergent cultural evolution of the eastern and western Acadians.

11

The Rise of Slavery in New Acadia

Louisiana's Acadians have often been noted for their equalitarian principles. In fact, throughout the seventeenth and eighteenth centuries, local administrators charged with Acadian supervision consistently bemoaned their "insubordination," their "republicanism" (or, more correctly, anarchism), and their lack of "proper respect." The parameters of their socially democratic ideals, however, clearly coincided with Acadian group boundaries, as demonstrated in the adoption, by many Acadian exiles, of Louisiana's emerging slave economy. Indeed, by 1810, one of Louisiana's largest slaveholders was an Acadian born shortly before the Grand Dérangement. The roots of this psychological double standard can be traced to sociocultural interaction between the major racial groups in predispersal Acadia.[1]

Forged by the eastern Canadian frontier and tempered by 150 years of isolation, Acadian society had become fiercely independent and equalitarian by the middle of the eighteenth century. These cultural characteristics fostered peaceful coexistence with Acadia's indigenous inhabitants, and an economically symbiotic relationship with the region's red men. Group boundaries, however, were rigidly

1. Akins (ed.), *Acadia and Nova Scotia*, 102; Rameau de St-Père, *Une Colonie féodale*, I, 232; Pedro Piernas to Ulloa, March 27, 1768, PPC, 2357:n.p.; Judice to Unzaga, January 2, 1774, PPC, 189A:513; Deposition of Jacques Faustin, March 9, 1792, SMOA; Third Decennial Census of the United States, 1810, Population Schedules, Louisiana; J. Edgar Bruns, "Joseph Landry (1750–1814): Acadien exilé, senateur de la Louisiane, homme politique à ses heures," *Les Cahiers de la Société historique acadienne*, 43[ieme] (1974), 104–107.

maintained by thinly veiled racism in the red and white camps, and offspring of mixed blood were generally exiled to the isolated Atlantic coast community of La Heve.[2]

Divisions had been reinforced, after the colony's transfer to Britain in 1713, by France's increasing use of the local Micmac and Abnaki tribes as pawns on its imperial chessboard. From 1713 to 1755, French Canadian officials had frequently attempted to lure the neutral Acadians into the French camp with repeated threats of Indian raids. This mental framework, in which Indians were viewed paradoxically as economic partners but also as potential military rivals, was carried to Louisiana as part of the exiles' cultural baggage.[3]

New Acadians on the river found the situation little different in their adopted homeland. Spurred by the activities of English and Spanish Indian agents, the Mississippi Valley tribes were constantly agitated, and rumors of impending Indian attacks usually received immediate public credence and wide circulation. As a consequence, Acadian militia units were frequently maintained on alert, and settlers often lived in fear of attack.[4] Acadian attitudes toward the unstable local tribes were projected to blacks as the Indian threat subsided and then evaporated in the 1770s and as Negro bondsmen were perceived as an emerging threat to public tranquillity. Indeed, in times of crisis, Acadians looked upon local tribes as allies against black insurgency. This psychological transformation resulted partially from the proximity of large slaveholding areas in the neighboring, well established downstream settlements from which runaways preyed on Acadian farms, and partially from the growing Acadian involvement in the "peculiar institution."[5]

2. Clark, *Acadia*, 68–361; Rameau de St-Père, *Une Colonie féodale*, I, 24, 45, 153.

3. A. Doughty, *The Acadian Exiles* (Toronto, 1920), 28–40; Clark, *Acadia*, 191–94; Griffiths, *Creation of a People*, 21, 28.

4. Judice to Unzaga, June 3, 1771, PPC, 188B:94–98; Dutisné to Unzaga, 1771, PPC, 188B:218; Piernas to Ulloa, March 27, 1768, PPC, 2357:n.p.; Judice to Miró, May 26, 1785, PPC, 198A:411–12.

5. Moore, *Revolt in Louisiana*, 84–102; Judice to Miró, November 13, 1785, PPC, 198A:455–59; Judice to Miró, November 15, 1785, PPC, 198A:459–62; Judice to Miró, November 19, 1785, PPC, 198A:463–67; Census of slaves and slaveholders in St. Charles Parish, December 10, 1775, PPC, 189B:242; Note on slaves who became fugitives during the previous year, May 27, 1783, PPC, 196:304; Judice to Miró, January 30, 1786, PPC, 199:253; Deposition by Baptiste Breaux, December 26, 1787, PPC, 191:364; Michel Cantrelle to Piernas, February 12, 1781, PPC, 194:284; Gilbert C. Din,

Upon arrival in Louisiana, only the exiles from Maryland had an intimate acquaintance with slavery. Detained in the tobacco plantation areas of that English colony, Acadians had come into contact with the local slave population, and "able-bodied" exiles worked side by side with them in the tobacco fields. Contact between exiles and bondsmen was of sufficient extent to occasion fears of a pro-French slave insurrection among Anglo-American colonists. The experience profoundly influenced the Maryland exiles, and having found a means of improving their lot and reestablishing their pre-dispersal standard of living, they and their descendants would ultimately establish a plantation economy on the Acadian Coast.[6]

The remaining Acadian immigrants, however, had no practical experience with slavery. Because tribes within Acadia and along the colonial borders were consistently French allies, intertribal disputes were rare, and unlike in neighboring New France, Indian slaves were unavailable. Most early Acadian settlers had also served as *engagés* for the colony's concessionaires and, having thus experienced prolonged servitude, apparently found the idea of bondage repulsive.[7]

Though compelled to tame the wilderness themselves, some Acadian pioneers, by virtue of personal initiative and unflagging industry, nevertheless managed to build modest fortunes. Like biblical patriarchs, these frontiersmen and their descendants measured their wealth in terms of real estate and livestock. The gradual expansion of their farming operations as well as the establishment of large-scale, seasonal fishing and trapping operations compelled the Acadian patriarchs to acquire at least part-time or seasonal employees.[8]

The birth of Acadian capitalism held profound, long-term social ramifications for the equalitarian and fiercely independent frontiersmen. No longer content or able to operate their farms and businesses

---

"*Cimarrones* and the San Malo Band in Spanish Louisiana," *Louisiana History*, XXI (1980), 237–63.

6. Sollers, "The Acadians," 11–14; Memoir on the Acadians, February, 1763, AC, C 11d, 8:242–51; Hoyt (ed.), "Contemporary View," 575; Wellington (ed.), "The Journal of Dr. John Sibley," 490–91.

7. Clark, *Acadia*, 361; Marcel Trudel, *L'Esclavage du Canada français: Histoire et conditions de l'esclavage* (Quebec, 1960); Rameau de St-Père, *Une Colonie féodale*, I, 147.

8. Census of Acadia, 1686, photostatic reproduction in Donald J. Hebert (comp.), *Acadians in Exile* (Cecilia, La., 1980), 478–521; Lauvrière, *Tragédie*, I, 179; Rameau de St-Père, *Une Colonie féodale*, I, 167, 224, 238–40, 247.

single-handedly, the new Acadian businessmen established themselves as a new elite whose social position, unlike that of their forebears, was based largely upon liquid capital and movable property.
The resulting socioeconomic stratification became more pronounced
in the waning years of predispersal Acadian life. It is thus hardly surprising that members of the emerging elite were the first to purchase
slaves as a means of restoring their lost prestige.[9]

Louisiana's first Acadian slaveholders were four Cabannocé residents, two of whom were descendants of the early patriarchs in the
thriving Beaubassin district. The remaining members of this select
circle were scions of prosperous pioneer families at the St. John River
and Cobequid posts. There are no extant slave conveyances for these
individuals, but their bondsmen were almost certainly purchased on
credit from New Orleans merchants in 1765. These black laborers
were quickly pressed into service, assisting their new masters in
clearing the dense hardwood forests hindering development of their
fertile riverfront properties.[10]

Few Acadians immediately followed the example of the first Cabannocé slaveholders. Most Acadians initially regarded blacks and
mulattoes as their social equals, working and traveling with them.
But by the early 1770s a handful of settlers in each of the Acadian
posts—usually young men with infant children—had purchased
young Negro women as nursemaids or simply as maids to assist
their wives after childbirth with household management. In the
Cabannocé and Opelousas posts, a majority of the slaves fit this
description.[11]

During the first decade of Acadian life in Louisiana, slave acquisitions were prompted by familial rather than economic considerations. Until the mid-1770s, when the exiles attained their former
standard of living, even the most ambitious immigrant was preoc-

9. Rameau de St-Père, *Une Colonie féodale*, I, 224, 238–40; Hebert (comp.), *Acadians
in Exile*, 512–13.

10. Census of Cabannocé, 1766, ASD, 2595:n.p.; Arsenault, *Histoire*, III, 875–79,
IV, 1474–79, VI, 2434–35; Arsenault, *History of the Acadians*, 38, 44; Rameau de St-Père,
Une Colonie féodale, I, 192; Moore, *Revolt in Louisiana*, 157; Sale, Jean-Baptiste Macarty
to Jean-Baptiste Broussard, June 10, 1778, SMOA.

11. LeDée to Unzaga, February 28, 1771, PPC, 188B:68; Judice to Ulloa, February
14, 1767, PPC, 187A:n.p.; Census of the Cabannocé post, 1766, PPC, 187A:n.p.; General census of the Attakapas post, 1774, PPC, 218:89–91; Census of the Opelousas
post, 1777, PPC, 2358:n.p.; Census of the Cabannocé post, 1769, PPC, 187A:n.p.

cupied with the demands of carving a new life from the wilderness. Moreover, the typical exile initially lacked the financial resources and the credit to acquire black laborers. Though the 1765 immigrants arrived at New Orleans with over 107,000 livres in French Canadian paper currency, the French provincial government and its Spanish successor refused to honor it. Penniless, like the waves of immigrants that followed, the exiles were compelled to bide their time, rebuilding modest estates by their own labors. By the late 1770s, however, ambitious Acadians wishing to acquire slaves had amassed sufficient funds—usually 300 to 350 piastres—to purchase them on an individual basis.[12]

The number of Louisiana Acadians owning slaves in the prairie settlements rose from only 5 percent in 1775 to 10 percent in 1785; meanwhile Acadian slaveowners in the river districts rose from 20 to 40 percent. The increased demand produced a corresponding increase in slave prices. Between 1775 and 1785, prices demanded and received by the traveling slave merchants (caboteurs) from New Orleans, and Creole planters seeking a profitable outlet for surplus laborers, nearly doubled, rising from around 350 to approximately 500 piastres.[13]

As the circle of slaveholders expanded slowly in the 1770s and early 1780s, the new elite emerged—based as before on land and livestock, but for the first time having rigid social boundaries that automatically elevated the slave owners above the workers they employed. The acquisition of slaves gave the slaveholder social stature, undoubtedly appealing to some upwardly mobile Acadian immigrants who aspired to join the colony's Creole aristocracy. Most of

12. Ulloa to Grimaldi, July 9, 1766, ASD, 2585:n.p.; List of the receipts issued by Mr. Maxent to the Acadians, April, 1765, AC, C 13a, 45:29; Charles Babin Estate, January 11, 1775, SMOA; Ledger of the paper currency given by the Acadians to their agent, St. Maxent, March 8, 1766, ASD, 2585:n.p.; Slave sale, Michel Isaac to Olivier Thibeaudot, November 24, 1777, SMOA; Slave sale, J. B. Macarty to J. B. Broussard, June 10, 1778, SMOA; Slave sale, Joseph Melancon to Amand Broussard, July 19, 1778, SMOA; Slave sale, Benoist de Ste. Claire to Joseph Broussard, June 14, 1780, SMOA.

13. Slave census for Ascension Parish of the Lafourche des Chetimachas post, December 3, 1775, PPC, 189B:294; Census of the Opelousas post, 1777, PPC, 2358:n.p.; Census of Ascension Parish, April 15, 1777, PPC, 190:173; Slave sale, Jacques Verret to Benjamin LeBlanc and Firmin Landry, May 10, 1787, SJOA; Slave sale, David Ross to Jean Bourgeois, May 29, 1787, SJOA; J. B. Rougiés to Michel Gaudin, May 24, 1787, SJOA.

the immigrant slaveholders, however, were eminently practical pioneers who realized simply that development of a *habitation* for commercial agriculture required amounts of labor far beyond the capacity of the family labor pool. As a consequence, in the late 1770s, many ambitious Acadians who, unlike the vast majority of the immigrants, were unhappy with the comfortable existence they had only recently attained, began to acquire young black field hands.[14]

Though median Acadian slaveholdings in many settlements ranged from only two to four slaves in the 1770s, the proliferation of the slave population—an increase of 1700 percent in some posts—necessitated changes in the Acadian life-style. Control of the slave population was initially very mild, with black laborers working shoulder to shoulder with their white masters. The presence of a large, alien, and subservient population by the 1780s nevertheless subjected the inexperienced slave owners to the constant specter of servile insurrection.[15]

This fact was emblazoned upon the minds of all Acadians—slave owners and yeoman farmers alike—by the abortive slave insurrection of 1785. While leading a slave patrol at Lafourche de Chetimachas in early November, 1785, Acadian Paul Foret discovered but failed to capture the notorious renegade freedman Philippe in the slave quarters on Veuve Landry's farm. When a subsequent investigation revealed that Philippe and his lieutenant, Pirame, were plotting a massive slave insurrection and, indeed, had already organized a "company" of fugitive slaves, the Lafourche district was placed on alert, and a reward of twenty piastres was levied on the chief insurrectionary's head.[16]

Philippe and his followers, however, with the assistance of Acadian-owned slaves, repeatedly eluded traps laid by the local slave patrol. Meanwhile, with intelligence supplied by his enslaved support-

14. Ulloa to Grimaldi, March 9, 1766, ASD, 2585:n.p.
15. Census of the Opelousas post, 1788, PPC, 2361:n.p.; Census of the Opelousas post, 1777, PPC, 2358:n.p.; Census of the Attakapas post, 1774, PPC, 218:89–91; Census of the Cabannocé post, 1769, PPC, 187A:n.p.; Census of Ascension Parish, December 3, 1775, PPC, 189B:294; Census of slaves and slaveholders at the Iberville post, 1775, PPC, 189B:245; "List of settlers whose slaves have become fugitives during the last several years," March 27, 1783, PPC, 196:304; Michel Cantrelle to Piernas, 1781, PPC, 198A:455–58.
16. Judice to Miró, November 13, 1785, PPC, 198A:455–58.

ers, Philippe's black insurrectionaries raided several Acadian farms, stripping them of provisions and arms. Within a week, Philippe had acquired enough muskets to outfit thirty men, and the situation in the Lafourche area had grown desperate for the white population. Militia patrols, driven by desperation to day and night duty, were completely exhausted; yet, because of the extensive black spy network in local slave quarters, the militiamen held little hope of capturing their elusive quarry. Of still greater concern, the fugitives were not only beginning to fire upon white travelers and couriers but were recruiting disaffected slaves from Bayou Lafourche and neighboring Mississippi River districts. A massive slave insurrection seemed imminent. As described earlier, Commandant Louis Judice secured the services of the local Houma tribe and raised the bounty on Philippe and each of his men to one hundred piastres.[17]

The Houmas soon located and ambushed Philippe and two of his men on the night of November 15, but the black leader escaped unharmed. Philippe's incredibly good fortune, however, came to an end later that evening, when Esther, a slave belonging to Nicolas Daublin, reported the black rebel had taken refuge in the slave quarters on the plantation. Daublin, assisted by one Manuel, quickly cornered Philippe and after a one-hour gun battle, killed him.[18]

Philippe's death brought the abortive servile insurrection to a swift conclusion. Three of Philippe's black collaborators and one white sympathizer were arrested, brought to trial, and punished. Intimidated by the rapid collapse of the uprising, the Lafourche slave community quickly displayed its former superficial docility.[19]

Though the crisis was resolved in the slaveholders' favor, the event served as an important watershed in Afro-Acadian relations, producing a spontaneous and radical change in Acadian attitudes toward blacks throughout Louisiana. No longer viewed as mere laborers, Negroes were now seen as inveterate schemers who posed an ever present threat to internal security. Both slaveholding and

17. Judice to Miró, November 15, 1785, PPC, 198A:459–62; Judice to Miró, November 13, 1785, PPC, 198A:455–58; Judice to Miró, November 19, 1785, PPC, 198A:463, 465–67; Judice to Miró, November 30, 1785, PPC, 198A:477–79.
18. Judice to Miró, November 19, 1785, PPC, 198A:465–67.
19. Judice to Miró, November 23, 1785, PPC, 198A:474; Judice to Miró, December 11, 1785, PPC, 198A:480; Miró to Judice, December 22, 1785, PPC, 198A:489; Judice to Miró, November 30, 1785, PPC, 198A:477–79.

nonslaveholding Acadians consequently demonstrated no hesitation in mounting a united and openly hostile front against threats, either real or perceived, from the slave community in subsequent years. When smallpox appeared in the slave quarters at Louis Judice's farm in 1787, for example, Lafourche Acadians, acting in defiance of the commandant's orders, imposed and enforced a quarantine and attempted to purchase the diseased slave in order to exterminate her. Similarly, in 1795 river and Lafourche Valley Acadians rallied to oppose deportation of slaves implicated in Pointe Coupée's recent abortive slave insurrection and to urge that the rebels be subjected "to the full rigors of the law." [20]

Like their Creole neighbors, Acadians in Louisiana's prime agricultural regions had developed a siege mentality by the late 1780s. The creeping paranoia of Acadian slaveholders was also reflected in the increasingly repressive regimens to which their bondsmen were subjected. Acadians now enthusiastically served in the local slave patrols, and their inspections of slave cabins became more frequent and more meticulous. Slaves resisting these periodic inspections were immediately flogged—in violation of the Black Code, the corpus of French law governing local slave administration since 1724 —and hauled before the local magistrate to face charges of insubordination. [21]

Abuses by the owners complemented abuses by the patrols. Sexual exploitation of Acadian-owned slave women became increasingly frequent in the late eighteenth century, and by the antebellum period, mulatto children of Acadian parentage had become commonplace in the river parishes. [22]

20. Pierre Richard to Michel Cantrelle, April 22, 1795, PPC, 31:463–63vo; Cantrelle to Carondelet, April 23, 1795, PPC, 31:462–62vo; Cantrelle to Carondelet, May 5, 1795, PPC, 31:468; Cantrelle to Carondelet, January 12, 1796, PPC, 33:352; Joseph Sorrel to Carondelet, June 7, 1795, PPC, 31:603; Procès-verbal of a meeting of the Iberville residents regarding the indemnification of the Pointe Coupée planters, May 17, 1795, PPC, 31:551–52; Brasseaux, "Acadians, Creoles, and the 1787 Lafourche Smallpox Outbreak," 55–58.

21. Judice to Miró, November 30, 1785, PPC, 198A:477–79; Judice to Miró, October 5, 1790, PPC, 203:152–53; General police regulations, 1791, PPC, 204:353; Judice to Carondelet, December 21, 1793, PPC, 208:293; Pierre Richard to Cantrelle, April 22, 1795, PPC, 31:463–63vo; Depositions of Olivier Landry and Simon Broussard, in Trial of Jean-Baptiste Broussard's negresse, October 11, 1786, SMOA.

22. See, for example, Deposition of Jean Doucet, 1780, SMOA; Pierre Landry Es-

SLAVE OWNERSHIP IN ACADIAN LOUISIANA, LATE EIGHTEENTH CENTURY

Settlement	Date of Census	Percentage of Households Owning Slaves
Attakapas	1794	3.5
Opelousas	1788	34.6
Baton Rouge	1795	19.3
Iberville	1777	26.9
Ascension	1777	39.0
St. James	1777	41.9
Lafourche	1789	2.2

SLAVE OWNERSHIP IN ACADIAN LOUISIANA, 1810

Parish	Percentage of Households Owning Slaves
Attakapas	56
Opelousas	51
West Baton Rouge	64
Iberville	83
Ascension	79
St. James	82
Assumption	30
Lafourche	12

Expansion of the miscegenation problem corresponded with the growth of the slave population in the Acadian parishes. Between 1790 and 1810, the slaveholding segment of the Acadian community increased significantly (see table). The causes were natural population growth, continued slave acquisition (apparently primarily from

tate, September 11, 1778, APOA; Joseph Broussard Estate, December 19, 1788, SMOA; Miró to Judice, May 16, 1788, PPC, 201:600–603vo.

smugglers), and the operations of Louisiana's forced inheritance laws, which required equal division of estates among the heirs. By 1810 a majority of the Acadians in the river and Teche Valley parishes owned black chattel.

The growth of slavery in the Acadian parishes signaled a fundamental change in the Acadian community itself. Prior to the late eighteenth century, Acadians had consistently refused to recognize the innate racial, cultural, or social superiority of any group, while simultaneously recognizing and abhorring the cultural and physical differences of their Indian neighbors. This double standard was reestablished in Louisiana following the Grand Dérangement, and ultimately applied to the refugees' newly acquired black laborers. Though initially uncomfortable with the institution, the Acadians were compelled by the threat of insurrection to protect and vigorously maintain Negro slavery. By identifying rigorous slave control with their own security, the exiles were tacitly committed to an unarticulated policy of white superiority. Thus, by 1810 what had been a nascent slave society had come of age.

Conclusion

Having reached an accommodation with the region's burgeoning slave system, the Acadians were by 1803 on the threshold of a new and significant period of sociocultural change, one that would transform them from transplanted Canadians into Louisiana Cajuns. The precise course of this general trend would be determined by the remarkable Acadian capacities for both adaptability and cultural conservatism. The interaction of these seemingly incompatible traits contributed both to the group's distinctiveness and to its ability to endure potentially destructive environmental forces and political developments.

In late 1803, when Louisiana was transferred successively from Spanish to French to American control, the residents of Nouvelle Acadie stood at the dawn of a new era, a period in which their beleaguered culture would face new challenges to its existence. Several developments appeared to augur the imminent collapse of Acadian culture: the growing cultural diversity within the Acadian community; the apparent erosion of traditional values as evidenced by their gradual acceptance of Negro slavery; the increasing contact between the exiles and rival groups; the broad geographic distribution of, and general lack of contact between, the region's isolated Acadian settlements; and the beginnings of Americanization. Yet, in the mainstream, Acadian culture differed only cosmetically from its pre-dispersal counterpart. Indeed, at the time of the Louisiana Purchase most of the immigrants and their descendants continued to share a common heritage and identity and common values.

The legacy of the Acadian pioneers permeated the world of my youth, the insular world of south-central St. Landry Parish in the 1950s. Of Acadian descent in both paternal and maternal lines, I grew up in a closed society in which nearly everyone was related, though the familial ties were often so ancient that no one was quite sure of the degree of consanguinity. It was precisely because it was such a closed society that its members paradoxically placed a premium upon personal independence, upon recognition of inherent personal dignity, and gauged a man's worth by his personal achievements, not by those of his long-forgotten ancestors. It was consequently an egalitarian society in which pretentious persons were reviled and children of all economic strata dated one another without anyone giving a second thought to the fact.

Yet, Acadian values extended only to the group's easily distinguishable cultural boundaries. That blacks were inferior was universally accepted, despite generally amicable personal relationships between the races, and segregation was deemed the foundation of an ideal society. In addition, other whites of French descent in the neighboring areas to the north were perceived as being somehow "different"; Opelousas, for example, occupied a higher rung on the region's social ladder, Evangeline Parish a lower one. In any event both groups were to be avoided. Finally, priests—usually European or Canadian missionaries who constituted the last major element of local society—were viewed privately with a mixture of suspicion and derision by many members of the Ladies' Altar Society and Knights of Columbus.

While Cajun friends and acquaintances from the southwestern prairies and "down the bayou" in the Lafourche-Terrebonne area shared my early life experiences, such was clearly not the case with many persons of Acadian descent who grew up in more affluent circles in Lafayette, in the bayou basin communities, and along the Mississippi River. Their families had long since denied their heritage and almost universally labeled their fellow Acadians who continued to identify themselves as Cajuns as "those old coonasses." Thoroughly Americanized, these so-called genteel Acadians placed a much greater value on material well-being, education, and social prominence than their less sophisticated country cousins. Only when Cajun identity became "respectable" following the creation of

CODOFIL (1968) would these *Acadiens cachés* come out of the cultural closet.

These sociocultural divisions were, and remain today, the living legacy of New Acadia. The evolution of emerging regional cultures within predispersal Acadian society was greatly accelerated by environmental factors in late-eighteenth-century Louisiana. For example, by the early nineteenth century, many Acadians in the original settlement areas joined their non-Acadian neighbors in forging a plantation economy, while many more tradition-bound small farmers and ranchers fled the onslaught of the slave regime by moving ever deeper into the lower Lafourche and Terrebonne swampland and into the southwestern prairies. Yet, it was not simply a matter of haves and have-nots, for within each area, social stratification grew increasingly complex as some ranchers began to build immense herds and consolidate public lands into vast *vacheries,* while east of the Atchafalaya, large numbers of Acadians created a niche for themselves in the region's burgeoning economy as artisans catering to the sugar industry.

The resulting complexity of Acadian society was compounded by the economic changes wrought by the transportation revolutions of the late nineteenth century and the technological revolutions of our own age. Today in Lafayette, the self-proclaimed cultural capital of Cajun Louisiana, one finds Acadians in all walks of life—doctors, lawyers, bank presidents, schoolteachers, university professors, engineers, computer scientists and technicians, realtors, welders, cooks, truck drivers, waitresses, offshore oil workers, television repairmen, video engineers, salesmen, religious leaders, and garbage collectors. Occupational pursuits of Acadians in the Hub City's rural hinterlands are equally diverse.

Outsiders, however, almost universally fail to view Acadian society in its totality and thus fail to comprehend its bewildering complexity. Indeed, burdened by the traditional stereotype of Acadians as primitive swamp dwellers, the outlander has come to view Louisiana Cajuns as an endangered cultural species destined to go the way of the forest primeval. Yet, Louisiana Acadian society has never been more vibrant; its indigenous cuisine and music are now exported throughout the United States, Canada, and Europe. But to survive, Cajun society and its base culture have been compelled to evolve, and the course of this evolution has often defied meaningful description because of the prevailing misconception of Cajun society as a monolithic entity. Though the published misconceptions of such researchers have inevitably elicited groans from the local Acadian readership, Cajuns nevertheless revel in their seemingly enigmatic mystique, which over the years has effectively minimized outside interference in their affairs. Traditionally regarded as aliens in their own land, they have survived by profiting from the lessons learned by their forebears in establishing New Acadia so many years ago.

APPENDIX A
The Peyroux-Terrio Feud

Though the story of the 1785 Acadian influx is well known, the subsequent careers of the two organizers of the migration—Henri Peyroux de la Coudrenière and Olivier Terrio—has remained obscure. Indeed, the poignant tale of Terrio's attempt to gain compensation for his unflagging efforts in France on behalf of the Spanish crown is largely forgotten.

Upon completion of the 1785 Acadian colonization project, Peyroux and Terrio sought remuneration for their services from Louisiana's Spanish colonial government. Peyroux had received partial compensation in France, where from 1783 to 1785 he had enjoyed a small salary from Aranda, and this income had been complemented, shortly before his departure aboard *Le Beaumont*, by a bonus of three thousand livres tournois. Upon arrival at New Orleans in mid-August, 1785, the immigration agent's annual salary of seven hundred livres tournois was resumed. Despite his generous pension, Peyroux was far from satisfied with the financial settlement. He insisted upon a commission both in the Spanish army and as commandant in Louisiana, which, he contended, had been promised him by Aranda. Unaware of the alleged Spanish commitments, Martín Navarro, intendant of Louisiana, sought instructions from Madrid. Reacting to Navarro's inquiry, the Spanish government issued, in April, 1786, commissions to Peyroux as captain in the Spanish army and as commandant of the Ste. Geneviève post in Spanish Illinois (present-day Missouri). The avaricious Frenchman assumed his new duties in 1787.[1]

Unlike Peyroux, Olivier Terrio received recognition only from his fellow Acadians. Shortly before departing France in May, 1785, the Acadian shoe-

1. Memoir on the transportation of 1,730 Acadians to Louisiana, 1792, PPC, 197:966; Navarro to Gálvez, September 6, 1785, PPC, 85:526vo–27vo; Notes on Henri Peyroux de La Coudrenière's arrival and sojourn in Louisiana, September 27, 1800, PPC, 217B:112.

maker, who had abandoned his business in 1783 to devote all of his attention to the Louisiana colonization project, requested funds from Peyroux in order to satisfy his French creditors. Peyroux, who no longer required Terrio's services, offered only insults and refused to write his subordinate a letter of recommendation to the Louisiana authorities. Terrio then turned to Asprès, but the Spanish consul could provide him only six francs. Growing desperate as the date of departure approached, Terrio sought and secured financial assistance from his *confrères*. The appreciation of his fellow exiles, upon whose behalf he had labored so tirelessly, was also reflected in his election as an Acadian "chief" aboard *La Bergère*.[2]

Unlike Terrio's fellow exiles, the Louisiana authorities failed to recognize the cobbler's critical contribution to the colonization project. This oversight was a direct result of the deteriorating relations between Terrio and Peyroux. Wishing to satisfy his Acadian creditors, Terrio confronted Peyroux at New Orleans one day after the latter's arrival from France and demanded funds on the basis of the Frenchman's promise to "share his last morsel of bread." Peyroux responded, "I have promised you nothing." He even refused to apprise Navarro of the cobbler's services to Spain. Terrio thus had no recourse but to suspend his claims against the Spanish government and to participate in the settlement of *La Bergère* passengers at Notre Dame de l'Ascension Parish, Lafourche des Chetimachas District.[3]

The intense bitterness born of Peyroux's ruthless exploitation was undiminished by the passage of time, and when in March, 1792, the Ste. Geneviève commandant appeared in New Orleans, Terrio filed a formal report of his activities in France and subsequent abandonment by Peyroux with Governor Carondelet. Apparently because he had just commissioned Henri Peyroux de la Coudrenière to recruit settlers for Louisiana in the United States, a project demanding the Frenchman's immediate departure from the Crescent City, Carondelet took no action upon Terrio's accusations. The incident is, nevertheless, crowned with poetic justice, for, returning from his mission in 1794, Peyroux received "neither the promised compensation, nor reimbursal for the cost of . . . [his] voyages."[4]

2. Memoir on the transportation of 1,730 Acadians to Louisiana, 1792, PPC, 197:966; Terrio to Aranda, 1785, PPC, 197:960; Proclamation by Asprès, May 12, 1785, PPC, 197:964.

3. Terrio to Aranda, 1785, PPC, 197:960; Memoir on the transportation of 1,730 Acadians to Louisiana, 1792, PPC, 197:966; Petition from Olivier Terrio, March 17, 1792, PPC, 197:973.

4. Petition from Olivier Terrio, March 17, 1792, PPC, 197:973; Memoir on the transportation of 1,730 Acadians to Louisiana, 1792, PPC, 197:966; List of events, 1792, PPC, 197:951–52; Notes on Henri Peyroux de La Coudrenière's arrival and sojourn in Louisiana, September 27, 1800, PPC, 217B:112.

Settlements and Settlers: Some Acadian Pioneers

Note: All spellings of names are from contemporary records.

West of the Atchafalaya River

Opelousas District

BAYOU DES CANNES Fabien Richard and Louis Richard.

BAYOU JONAS (present-day Egan) Valéry Bourque.

BAYOU MALLET Joseph LeJeune, J. B. David, and Joseph Landry.

BAYOU NEZPIQUÉ Paul Boutin.

BAYOU PLAQUEMINE BRÛLÉE (between present-day Crowley and the Mermentau River) Pierre Bernard, David Guidry, Pierre Guidry, André Martin, Jean Mouton.

BAYOU PLAQUEMINE BRÛLÉE (between present-day Estherwood and Crowley) Pierre Arceneau, *fils*, Frédéric Mouton.

BAYOU PLAQUEMINE BRÛLÉE (between Pointe Noire Gully and present-day Lewisburg) François Boutin, Michel Comeau, Jean-Baptiste Cormier, Joseph Cormier, Silvain Sonnier, Honoré Trahan.

BAYOUS BLAIZE LEJEUNE AND DES CANNES Blaize LeJeune, *fils*, Blaize LeJeune, *père*, Joseph LeJeune, Pierre Trahan.

GRAND COTEAU AREA Augustin Boudreau, Joseph Boutin, Paul Boutin, *fils*, Paul Boutin, *père*, David Guidry, Michel Leger, Paul Leger, Baptiste Richard, Mathurin Richard, Pierre Richard, Jean Savoy.

NORTH PLAQUEMINE BRÛLÉE AREA Jean-Baptiste Chiasson, Michel Comeau, Paul Doucet, Pierre Hebert, Louis Leger.

OPELOUSAS Charles Comeau, Michel Comeau, Joseph Cormier, Michel Cormier, Joseph Granger, Jean-Baptiste Hebert, Pierre Pitre, Pierre Richard, Victor Richard, Charles Jean Saunier, Joseph Saunier, Olivier Saunier, Silvain Saunier, Widow Marie Savoie, Pierre Savoie, Widow Marie Thibodeau, Pierre Thibodeau.

PRAIRIE BELLEVUE (south of present-day Opelousas) Augustin Comeau, Fabien Richard, Jean-Baptiste Richard, Louis Richard, Olivier Richard, Victor Richard, Cyrile Thibodeau, Pierre Thibodeau.

PRAIRIE DES COTEAUX Michel Comeau, Michel Cormier, Pierre Cormier, and Louis Richard.

PRAIRIE DES FEMMES (near Grand Coteau) Michel Cormier.

Attakapas District

BAYOU CARENCRO Ignace Babin, Augustin Boudreau, Silvain Broussard, Jean Comeau, Pierre Guidry, François Guilbeau, Jean Guilbeau, Jean Mouton, Marin Mouton, Pierre LeBlanc, Simon LeBlanc, Amant Préjean, Mathurin Richard, Jean Savoy, Paul Thibodeau.

BAYOU TORTUE Firmin Breaux, Amand Broussard, Athanaze Broussard, Claude Broussard, François Broussard, Joseph Broussard, Victor Broussard, Charles Dugas, Pierre Dugas, Raymond LeBlanc, Charles Melancon, Raymond Richard, Anselme Thibodeau, Michel Trahan.

BEAUBASSIN (due east of present-day Carencro) Louis Arceneaux, Alexandre Arceneau, François Arceneau, Pierre Arceneau, Joseph Breaux, Jean Guilbeau.

CHICOT NOIR Victor Blanchard, François Boudreau, Baptiste Duhon, Charles Duhon, Claude Duhon.

JEANERETTE AREA (above Jeanerette on both banks of the Teche) Amant Broussard, François Broussard, Charles Dugas, Jean Dugas, Jean-Baptiste Hébert, Baptiste La Bauve.

LAFAYETTE AREA Augustin Boudreau, Claude Broussard, René Broussard, J. B. Cormier, Joseph Castille, Widow Louis Cormier, Pierre Dugas, Charles Dugas, Joseph Guidry, Moÿse Hebert, Jean Mouton, Sr., André Martin, Joseph Sonnier, Olivier Thibodaux, Jr., Théodore Thibodeau, René Trahan.

LA MANQUE Widow Anne Brun, Victor Comeau, Michel Doucet, Simon LeBlanc, Bonaventure Martin, Claude Martin, Joseph Martin, Widow Marguerite Martin, Charles Pellerin, Georges Pellerin, Armand Thibodeau, Widow Marie Thibodeau, Olivier Thibodeau.

LA POINTE Charles Babineau, Michel Bernard, Jean Boudreau, Jean-Baptiste Broussard, Mathurin Broussard, Silvestre Broussard, Simon Broussard, Théodore Broussard, Joseph Guidry, Charles Guilbeau, Joseph

Pépin Hebert, Baptiste Thibodeau, Charles Thibodeau, Magdalena Thibodeau, Paul Thibodeau, Jean Trahan.

LOWER VERMILION VALLEY (area between present-day Lafayette and Abbeville) Claude Broussard, Joseph Broussard, Silvain Broussard, Théophile Broussard, Charles Comeau, Charles Dugat, François Dugas, Simon Grangé, Charles Guilbeau, Charles Hebert, André Martin, Joseph Melancon, René Trahan, Théodore Thibodeau.

East of the Atchafalaya River

1764 IMMIGRANTS Among the 1764 immigrants from New York were Jean Porrier and Magdelaine Richard. Joseph Blanchard, Firmin Giroir, Joseph Guilbeau, Charles Mouton, Charles Savoy, François Savoie, and their relatives were probably also among this group.

ABOVE BAYOU PLAQUEMINE—IBERVILLE AND WEST BATON ROUGE PARISHES Jean Babin, Widow Marguerite Comeau, Widow Auguste Landry, Augustin Landry, *père*, Augustin Landry, *fils*, Widow Magdeline Landry, Mathurin Landry, Amant Melancon, Blaise Rivet, Marie Rivet, Antoine Rodrigue.

ASCENSION PARISH Armand Babin, Charles Babin (I), Charles Babin (II), Ephrème Babin, Firmin Babin, François Babin, Jacques Babin, Joseph Babin (I), Joseph Babin (II), Olivier Boutin, Marie Bourg, Baptiste Braud, Firmin Braud, Paul Braud, Augustin Broussard, Saturin Brun, Etienne Bujeau, Joseph Bujeau, Mathurin Bujeau, Athanaze Dugas, Charles Dugas, François Dugas, Charles Duhon, Claude Duhon, François Duhon, Honoré Duhon, Jean Duhon, Firmin Dupuis, Pierre Dupuis, Anselme Forêt, Charles Forêt, Paul Forêt, Armand Gautreau, Joseph Granger, Widow Anne Dupuis Guédry, Joseph Guédry, Pierre Guédry, Jean Jeansonne, Abraham Landry, Armant Landry, Charles Landry, Etienne Landry (I), Etienne Landry (II), Firmin René Landry, Jacques Landry, Jean Landry, Joseph Landry, Mathurin Landry, Pierre Landry (I), Pierre Landry (II), Pierre Landry (III), René Landry, Simon Landry, Vincent Landry, Désiré LeBlanc, Widow Isabelle Boudreau LeBlanc, Jean LeBlanc, Jérôme LeBlanc, Pierre LeBlanc, Silvain LeBlanc, Simon LeBlanc, Charles Melancon, Widow Marie Thériot Melancon, Joseph Orillon, Armand Préjean, Charles Préjean, Joseph Préjean, Marin Préjean, Joseph Richard, Joseph Roger (I), Joseph Roger (II).

ASSUMPTION PARISH Charles Babin, Ephrème Babin, Baptiste Breaux, Etienne Bujeau, Pierre Bujeau, François Dugas, Charles Forêt, Paul Forêt, Joseph Granger, Abraham Landry, Pierre Landry, René Landry, Désiré

LeBlanc, Isaac LeBlanc, Pierre LeBlanc, Silvain LeBlanc, Amand Préjean.
CABANNOCÉ Jean Arceneau, Pierre Arceneau (I), Pierre Arceneau (II), Baptiste Bellefontaine (Godin), Barthélémy Bellefontaine (Godin), Bonaventure Bellefontaine (Godin) Jacques Bellefontaine (Godin), Joseph Bellefontaine (Godin), Charles Bergeron, Jean-Baptiste Bergeron, Pierre Bernard, Athanaze Braud, Widow Caissy Bergeron, Geneviève Bergeron, Germain Bergeron, Olivier Boudreau, Joseph Bourg, L'Ange Bourg, Michel Bourgeois, Paul Bourgeois, Pierre Bourgeois, Bujeau, Pierre Chiasson, François Dugas, Charles Claude Duhon, Claude Duhon, Honoré Duhon, Widow Anne Dupuy, Charles Forêt, Pierre Forêt, Charles Gaudet, Isabelle Gaudet, Jérôme Gaudet, Simon Gautreau, Firmin Giroir, Joseph Guilbeau, Joseph Hébert (I), Joseph Hébert (II), Pierre Hébert, Antoine LaBauve, Landry, Joseph Landry, Etienne LeBlanc, Marcel LeBlanc, François Melancon, Widow Melancon, Belony Mire, Simon Mire, Joseph Part, Olivier Part, Michel Poirier, Amand Préjean, Basile Préjean, Charles Préjean, Joseph Préjean, Joseph Richard, Bruno Robichaud, Claire Robichaud, Widow Anastasie Dugas Robichaud, Abraham Roy, Joseph Saunier, Charles Savoie, Joseph Savoie, Jean-Baptiste Thibodeau, Pierre Vincent.
LAFOURCHE DES CHÉTIMACHES, Napoleonville area—Louis Aucoin, Pierre Aucoin, Eloi Blanchard, Laurent Blanchard, Jean-Pierre Bourg, Widow Fabien Bourg, Jean-Baptiste Bourg, Pierre Bourg, Widow Jean-Baptiste Daigle, Widow Hyppolite Dugas, Pierre Gautreau, Joseph Hébert, Pierre Marie Thériot, Widow Mathurin Trahan.
Lafourche Crossing-Raceland area—Jean-Baptiste Babin, E. Boudreau, Joseph Boudreau, N. Boudreau, Jean-Baptiste Bourgeois, Paul Boudreau, Pierre-Paul Bourgeois, Jean-Baptiste Breau, Marguerite Breau, Achille Forêt, J. Forêt, François Gaudet, Guillaume Hebert, Jean-Louis Hebert, P. Gautreau, M. Labauve, Antoine Landry, Claude LeBlanc, Hypolite LeBlanc, Mathurin LeBlanc, F. Pitre, Basil Richard, Jean-Baptiste Robichaux (I), Jean-Baptiste Robichaux (II), Louis Robichaux, Pierre Robichaux, François Savoie, Joseph Savoie, Jean Thibodeaux.
PASSENGERS ABOARD THE BRIGITE Anne Marguerite Babin, Charles Babin, François Laurent Babin, Marie LeBlanc Babin, Mathurin Babin, Pierre Moïse Babin, Victoire Babin, Jean-Baptiste Boudrau, Magdelene Bourg, Jean Frédéric Gravois, Jean Hubert Gravois, Joseph Gravois, Magdelaine Blanche Gravois, Marguerite Angélique Gravois, Marie Félicité Gravois, Marie Susanne Gravois, Marie Thersille Gravois, Victoire Gravois.
ST. GABRIEL Pierre Allain, Ignace Babin, Jean-Baptiste Babin, Joseph Babin, Marie Babin, Pierre Babin, Anselme Blanchard, Joseph Blanchard, René Blanchard, Widow Elizabeth Brasseux, Pierre Brasseux, Joseph Castille, Charles Comeau, Joseph Dupuis, Jean-Baptiste Forêt, Pierre Forêt, Marie

Granger, Alexandre Hebert, Amant Hebert, François Hebert (I), François Hebert (II), Geneviève Hebert, Ignace Hebert, Joseph Hebert, Paul Hebert, Pierre Hebert, Anne Landry, Athanaze Landry, Augustin Landry, Hiacinthe Landry, Jean Landry (I), Jean Landry (II), Jean-Baptiste Landry, Joseph Landry, Pierre Landry, Bonaventure LeBlanc, Jean LeBlanc, Marie Josephe LeBlanc, Pierre LeBlanc, Amant Melancon, Amant Richard, Joseph Richard, Marie Richard, Mathurin Richard.

SAN LUIS DE NATCHEZ Widow Catherine Babin, François Babin, Joseph Babin, Widow Marguerite Babin, Olivier Babin, Anne Braud, Antoine Braud, Widow Cecilia Braud, Widow Clara Braud, Jean Braud, Jean-Charles Braud, Joseph Braud, Marguerite Braud, Widow Anne Derouen, Anne Dupuis, Jean-Baptiste Dupuis, Pierre Guidry, Augustin Landry, Basil Landry, Joseph Landry, Widow Marguerite Landry, Mathurin Landry, Rose Landry, Michel Rivet, Charles Trahan.

Bibliography

PRIMARY SOURCES

Manuscripts

Archives Nationales, Paris, France
Archives des Colonies
    Series B (Ordres du roi), Volumes 117–22. Microfilm copy on deposit at the Center for Louisiana Studies, University of Southwestern Louisiana.
    Series C 9b (Saint-Domingue, Correspondance générale), Volume 116. Microfilm copy on deposit at the Center for Louisiana Studies, University of Southwestern Louisiana.
    Series C 11d (Acadie, Correspondance générale), Volumes 1–10. Microfilm copy on deposit at the Center for Louisiana Studies, University of Southwestern Louisiana.
    Series C 13a (Louisiane, Correspondance générale), Volumes 36–50. Microfilm copy on deposit at the Center for Louisiana Studies, University of Southwestern Louisiana.
Archives du Ministère des Affaires Etrangères
    Political Correspondence, Series Angleterre, Volumes 47 and 450. Photostatic copy on deposit at the Jefferson Caffery Louisiana Room, Dupré Library, University of Southwestern Louisiana.
Archivo General de Indias, Seville, Spain
    Audiencia de Santo Domingo, legajos 2542, 2551, 2565, 2575, 2585. Microfilm copy on deposit at the Center for Louisiana Studies, University of Southwestern Louisiana.
    Papeles Procedentes de Cuba, legajos 25–35, 109, 110–12, 181, 187A–221B. Microfilm copy on deposit at the Center for Louisiana Studies, University of Southwestern Louisiana.
Ascension Parish Courthouse, Donaldsonville, Louisiana

211

Original Acts, 1770–1803. Microfilm copy on deposit at the Center for Louisiana Studies, University of Southwestern Louisiana.
Assumption Parish Courthouse, Napoleonville, Louisiana
Original Acts, 1770–1803. Microfilm copy on deposit at the Center for Louisiana Studies, University of Southwestern Louisiana.
British Museum, London, England
Judge Charles Morris' Papers on the Causes of the War of 1755 and the History of the Acadians, Folios 31–39, Brown Manuscript Collection, Add. MSS 19072.
Papers Relating to Nova Scotia, 1749–1790. Add. MSS 19073.
Canadian National Archives, Ottawa, Canada
Fort Ponchartrain Church Records, Series MG8, Subseries G8.
Centre d'Etudes Acadiennes, Université de Moncton, Moncton, New Brunswick
Placide Gaudet Collection.
Hall of Records, Annapolis, Maryland
Baltimore County Notary Public Record Book, 1744–1797, pp. 188–95.
Port of Entry Records, Inward for Patuxent District, 1745–1767. Port of Annapolis, October 24–December 31, 1755.
Iberville Parish Courthouse, Plaquemine, Louisiana
Conveyances, 1790–1803.
Louisiana State Archives and Record Service, Baton Rouge, Louisiana
Opelousas Colonial Records, 1765–1803.
Louisiana State Museum, New Orleans, Louisiana
Lists of Acadians Subscribing to the Spanish Oath of Allegiance, August 28, 1769–December 16, 1769, Document Numbers 176908201, 1769090901, 1769092801, 1769120901, 1769121601.
National Archives, Washington, D.C.
Third Decennial Census of the United States, 1810, Population Schedules, Louisiana. Microfilm copy on deposit at the Jefferson Caffery Louisiana Room, Dupré Library, University of Southwestern Louisiana.
Public Archives of Nova Scotia, Halifax, Nova Scotia
Governor M. Wilmot to Lord Halifax, December 18, 1764, Series RG 1, Volume 40.
Public Record Office, London, England
Record Group 585, Colonial Office. Microfilm copy on deposit at the Center for Louisiana Studies, University of Southwestern Louisiana.
Register of State Lands, Baton Rouge, Louisiana
Claims, Southwest District, Reels 253–58. Microfilm copy on deposit at the Jefferson Caffery Louisiana Room, Dupré Library, University of Southwestern Louisiana.
Pintado Papers, Opelousas District, Books I–II. Microfilm copy on deposit at the Jefferson Caffery Louisiana Room, Dupré Library, University of Southwestern Louisiana.

St. James Parish Courthouse, Convent, Louisiana
    Original Acts, 1770–1803. Microfilm copy on deposit at the Center for
    Louisiana Studies, University of Southwestern Louisiana.
St. Landry Parish Courthouse, Opelousas, Louisiana
    Probate Records, 1760–1803.
St. Martin Parish Courthouse, St. Martinville, Louisiana
    Original Acts, 1760–1803.
University of Southwestern Louisiana, Lafayette, Louisiana
    Alexander Mouton Memoirs, in Lucille Meredith Mouton Griffith
        Papers, Collection 26, Tablet 1, Southwestern Archives.
    Brand Book for the Opelousas and Attakapas Districts, Jefferson Caf-
        fery Louisiana Room, Dupré Library.
    "Copie d'un vieux registre de St. Martin de Tours." Typescript of the
        oldest St. Martin de Tours Catholic Church registers, Jefferson Caf-
        fery Louisiana Room, Dupré Library.
    Records of the States of the United States, 1754–1789: Louisiana. Film
        533, Louisiana Section A, Reel 2, Part 3, Jefferson Caffery Louisiana
        Room, Dupré Library.

Newspapers

Annapolis *Maryland Gazette*, 1753–1770.
Baton Rouge *Gazette*, 1828.
New Iberia *Louisiana Sugar Bowl*, 1873.
Opelousas *Courier*, 1853.
Pennsylvania Gazette, 1755–1765.

Interviews

Interview with Mathé Allain, May 12, 1980, Lafayette, Louisiana.
Interview with Father James Geraghty, June 10, 1981, Lafayette, Louisiana.
Interview with descendants of Catherine Pierre: Carolyn Stemly, "Attakapas
    Indian Healers." File 181, Acadian and Creole Folklore Collection, Univer-
    sity of Southwestern Louisiana.

Printed Memoirs and Documents

Akins, Thomas B., ed. *Acadia and Nova Scotia: Documents Relating to the Aca-
    dian French and the First British Colonization of the Colony, 1714–1758.* 2nd
    ed. Cottonport, La., 1972.
*American State Papers: Documents, Legislative and Executive, of the Congress of
    the United States.* Class VIII, *Public Lands Series.* 9 vols. Washington, D.C.,
    1832–73. Vols. I–III.
Antonio Barnabé v. *Bernard Dauterive.* In "Index to Spanish Judicial Records."
    Louisiana Historical Quarterly, VIII (1925), 529.

Berquin-Duvallon, Pierre-Louis. *Vue de la colonie espagnole du Mississippi, ou des provinces de Louisiane et Floride occidentale, en l'année 1802*. Paris, 1803.

Bolton, Herbert Eugene, trans. and ed. *Athanase de Mézières and the Louisiana-Texas Border, 1768–1770*. 2 vols. Cleveland, 1914.

Brasseaux, Carl A., comp. "A Report on Manufacturing and Manufactured Articles, 1810." *Attakapas Gazette*, X (1975), 153.

——, ed. "An 1810 Census Report on the State of Manufacturing in the Northeastern Section of the Attakapas District. *Attakapas Gazette*, X (1975), 102.

——, trans. and ed. *A Comparative View of French Louisiana, 1699 and 1762: The Journals of Pierre Le Moyne d'Iberville and Jean-Jacques-Blaise d'Abbadie*. Lafayette, La., 1979.

Browne, William Hand, Bernard Steiner, and J. Hall Pleasants, eds. *Archives of Maryland*. 59 vols. Baltimore, 1883–1953. Vols. III, VI, XIV, XXX–LII.

Carter, Clarence, ed. *Territorial Papers of the United States*. 28 vols. Washington, D.C., 1927–75. Vol. IX.

"Census by the Sieur de La Roque." In *Report Concerning Canadian Archives for the Year 1905*, II, 152–65. 3 vols. Ottawa, 1906.

Chandler, Richard E. "The St. Gabriel Acadians: The First Five Months." *Louisiana History*, XXI (1980), 287–96.

——. "A Shipping Contract: Spain Brings Acadians to Louisiana." *Louisiana Review*, VIII (1979), 73–81.

——, trans. and ed. "End of an Odyssey: Acadians Arrive in St. Gabriel, Louisiana." *Louisiana History*, XIV (1973), 81–87.

——, trans. and ed. "Odyssey Continued: Acadians Arrive at Natchez." *Louisiana History*, XIX (1978), 446–63.

Dalrymple, Margaret Fisher, ed. *The Merchant of Manchac: The Letterbooks of John Fitzpatrick, 1768–1790*. Baton Rouge, 1978.

Diocese of Baton Rouge. *Diocese of Baton Rouge Catholic Church Records*. 2 vols. Baton Rouge, 1978–80.

Folsom, George, ed. "Expedition of Capt. Samuel Argall . . . to the French Settlements in Acadia . . . 1613." New York Historical Society *Collections*, Ser. 2, I (1841), 335–42.

Fontaine, L. U., ed. *Voyage du Sieur du Dièreville en Acadie*. Quebec, 1885.

Gagnon, C.-O., ed. *Lettre de M. l'abbé Le Guerne, missionnaire de l'Acadie*. Quebec, 1889.

Ganong, W. F., ed. "Historical-Geographical Documents Relating to New Brunswick." *Collection of the New Brunswick Historical Society*, No. 5 (1904), 163–75.

——, ed. "The Cadillac Memoir of 1692." *Collections of the New Brunswick Historical Society*, No. 13 (1930), 77–97.

——, ed. "The Official Account of the Destruction of Burnt Church." *Collections of the New Brunswick Historical Society*, No. 7 (1907), 301–307.

Hale, Robert. "Journal of a Voyage to Nova Scotia Made in 1731 by Robert Hale of Beverly." *Historical Collections of the Essex Institute*, XLII (1906), 217–44.

Hebert, Donald J., comp. *Acadians in Exile*. Cecilia, La., 1980.
———, comp. *South Louisiana Records*. 4 vols. Eunice, La., 1978–80.
———, comp. *Southwest Louisiana Records*. 29 vols. Eunice, La., 1974–81.
Hoyt, William D., ed. "A Contemporary View of the Acadian Arrival in Maryland, 1755." *William and Mary Quarterly*, 3rd Ser., V (1948), 572–75.
Israel, Fred. L., ed. *Major Peace Treaties of Modern History, 1648–1967*. 4 vols. New York, 1967.
Kinnaird, Lawrence, ed. *Spain in the Mississippi Valley, 1765–94: Translations of Materials from the Spanish Archives in the Bancroft Library*. Annual Report of the American Historical Association for the Year 1945, Vols. II–IV. Washington, D. C., 1946.
Laussat, Pierre Clément de. *Memoirs of My Life to My Son During the Years 1803 and After*. Translated by Agnes-Josephine Pastwa. Edited by Robert D. Bush. Baton Rouge, 1978.
Le Page du Pratz, Antoine Simon. *The History of Louisiana Translated from the French of M. Le Page du Pratz*. 1774; rpr. Baton Rouge, 1975.
"List of Baptisms at St. Joseph's Church, Philadelphia, from August 29, 1758, to December 31, 1775." *American Catholic Historical Society of Philadelphia Records*, I (1884), 227–350.
Mandements, lettres pastorales et circulaires des évêques de Québec. 6 vols. Quebec, 1887–90.
Martin, Paulette, trans. "Ordinance Regulating Concessions and Cattle in Spanish Louisiana, 1770." *Attakapas Gazette*, XII (1977), 180–82.
———, trans. "The Kelly-Nugent Report of the Inhabitants and Livestock in the Attakapas, Natchitoches, Opelousas and Rapides Posts, 1770." *Attakapas Gazette*, XI (1976), 187–93.
Olmsted, Frederick Law. *A Journey Through Texas; or, a Saddle Trip on the Southwestern Frontier*. New York, 1857.
Pennsylvania Archives: Votes and Proceedings of the House of Representatives of the Province of Pennsylvania. 8th Ser. 8 vols. Philadelphia, 1931–35.
Pennsylvania Colonial Records: Minutes of the Provincial Council of Pennsylvania. 16 vols. Philadelphia, 1838–53.
Pittman, Phillip. *The Present State of the European Settlements on the Mississippi*. Bicentennial Floridiana Facsimile Series. 1770; rpr. Gainesville, 1973.
Pugh, W. W. "Bayou Lafourche from 1820–1825: Its Inhabitants, Customs, and Pursuits." *Louisiana Planter and Sugar Manufacturer*, October 29, 1888, p. 143.
Rees, Grover, trans. "The Dauterive Compact: The Foundation of the Acadian Cattle Industry," *Attakapas Gazette*, XI (1976), 91.
Reider, Milton P., and Norma Gaudet Reider, comps. *The Crew and Passenger Registration Lists of the Seven Acadian Expeditions of 1785*. Metairie, La., 1965.
Reinecke, George F., trans. and ed. "Early Louisiana French Life and Folklore, from the Anonymous Breaux Manuscript as Edited by Professor Jay K. Ditchy." *Louisiana Folklore Miscellany*, II (1966), 6–58.
Robin, Claude C. *Voyage to Louisiana*. Trans. Stuart O. Landry. New Orleans, 1966.

Rowland, Dunbar, comp. and ed. *Mississippi Provincial Archives, 1763–1766: English Dominion.* Nashville, 1911.

Sibley, John. "Historical Sketches of the Several Indian Tribes in Louisiana, South of the Arkansas River, and Between the Mississippi and River Grand." *Annals of Congress,* 9th Cong., 2nd Sess. (1852), 1075–88.

Sparks, W. H. *The Memories of Fifty Years . . .* 4th ed. Macon, Ga., 1882.

Thwaites, Reuben Gold, ed. *The Jesuit Relations and Allied Documents: Travels and Explorations of the Jesuit Missionaries in New France, 1610–1791.* 73 vols. 1896–1901; rpr. New York, 1959.

"Washington Square, Philadelphia, the First Burial Ground for Catholics— For Patriots of the American Revolution, and for Martyrs of the Faith, the Exiled Acadians—Their Petition to the King of Great Britain." *American Catholic Historical Researches,* XVIII (1901), 38–40.

Wellington, G. P., ed. "The Journal of Dr. John Sibley, June–October 1802." *Louisiana Historical Quarterly,* X (1927), 474–97.

Wroth, Lawrence C., ed. "A Maryland Merchant to the Friends in 1750." *Maryland Historical Magazine,* VI (1911), 213–40.

SECONDARY SOURCES

Allain, Mathé. "The Evolution of Acadian Cuisine." Address delivered in New Iberia, Louisiana, May 12, 1980.

Ancelet, Barry J., and Michael Doucet. "The Evolution of Cajun and Creole Music." Paper presented at the tenth annual meeting of the French Colonial Historical Society, Lafayette, Louisiana, 1980.

Arsenault, Bona. *Histoire et généalogie des Acadiens.* 6 vols. 2nd ed. Quebec, 1978.

———. *History of the Acadians.* Montreal, 1978.

Arseneault, Jeanne. *Rapport de recherche sur le costume historique acadien.* Caraquet, N.B., 1979.

Arseneault, Jeanne, and Lynn Losier. *Confectionnez vos costumes acadiens pour les fêtes du 375ᵉ.* Caraquet. N.B., 1980.

Baade, Hans W. "Marriage Contracts in French and Spanish Louisiana: A Study in 'Notarial' Jurisprudence." *Tulane Law Review,* LIII (1978), 1–54.

Baudier, Roger. *The Catholic Church in Louisiana.* New Orleans, 1939.

Bell, Winthrop. *The "Foreign Protestants" and the Settlement of Nova Scotia.* Toronto, 1961.

Bible, George P. *An Historical Sketch of the Acadians: The Deportation and Wanderings.* Philadelphia, 1906.

Billington, Ray Allen. *Frederick Jackson Turner: Historian, Scholar, Teacher.* New York, 1973.

———, ed. *The Frontier Thesis: Valid Interpretation of American History?* New York, 1966.

Boudreau, Marielle, and Melvin Gallant. *La Cuisine traditionelle en Acadie.* Moncton, N.B., 1975.

Bourgeois, Lillian C. *Cabanocey: The History, Customs and Folklore of St. James Parish.* New Orleans, 1957.

Bourgeois, Phileas F. *Les Anciens Missionnaires de l'Acadie devant l'histoire.* Shediac, N.B., n.d.

Brasseaux, Carl A. "Acadian Life Under the Spanish Regime." *Les Cahiers de la Société historique acadienne,* X (1979), 132–41.

————. "Acadians, Creoles, and the 1787 Lafourche Smallpox Outbreak." *Louisiana Review,* VIII (1978), 55–58.

————. "Administration of Slave Regulations in French Louisiana, 1724–1766." *Louisiana History,* XXI (1980), 139–58.

————. "Frontier Tyranny: The Case of Commandant Louis Pellerin, 1764–1767." *McNeese Review,* XXVII (1980–81), 15–24.

————. "*L'Officier de Plume*: Denis-Nicolas Foucault, *commissaire-ordonnateur* of French Louisiana, 1762–1769." M.A. thesis, University of Southwestern Louisiana, 1975.

————. "Opelousas and the Alabama Immigrants, 1763–1766." *Attakapas Gazette,* XIV (1979), 112–17.

————. "Petition of the *Habitants* for the Destruction of Stray Cattle." *Attakapas Gazette,* XI (1976), 78–79.

Brebner, John B. *New England's Outpost: Acadia Before the Conquest of Canada.* New York, 1927.

Brown, George W., *et al.,* eds. *Dictionnaire biographique du Canada.* 10 vols. Quebec, 1966–72.

Browne, Mary Nicholson. "The Acadians." *The Patriotic Marylander,* II (1915), 23–40.

Brun, Regis-Sygefroy. "Le Séjour des Acadiens en Angleterre et leurs traces dans les archives britanniques, 1756–1763." *Les Cahiers de la Société historique acadienne,* 32^{ieme} (1971), 62–68.

Bruns, J. Edgar. "Joseph Landry (1750–1814): Acadien exilé, sénateur de la Louisiane, homme politique à ses heures." *Les Cahiers de la Société historique acadienne,* 43^{ieme} (1974), 104–107.

Bujold, Nicole T., and Maurice Caillebeau. *Les Origines des premières familles acadiennes: Le Sud-Loudunais.* Poitiers, 1979.

"Cajuns Can Claim Status Under Equal Job Act." Lafayette *Daily Advertiser,* August 10, 1980, p. 17.

Calhoun, James, ed. *Louisiana Almanac, 1979–1980.* Gretna, La., 1979.

Casgrain, Henri-Raymond. "Coup d'oeil sur l'Acadie avant la dispersion de la colonie française." *La Canada Française,* I (1888), 115–34.

Caughey, John W. *Bernardo de Gálvez in Louisiana, 1776–1783.* 2nd ed. New Orleans, 1972.

Cazaudebat, Jane. "Grand Prairie, 1803–1853." *Attakapas Gazette,* XIV (1979), 174–83.

Clark, Andrew Hill. *Acadia: The Geography of Early Nova Scotia to 1760.* Madison, 1968.

Clark, John G. *New Orleans, 1718–1812: An Economic History.* Baton Rouge, 1970.

Comeaux, Malcolm L. *Atchafalaya Swamp Life: Settlement and Folk Occupations.* Baton Rouge, 1972.

Conrad, Glenn R., comp. *New Iberia: Essays on the Town and Its People.* Lafayette, La., 1979.

―――, ed. *The Cajuns: Essays on Their History and Culture.* Lafayette, La., 1978.

Corbett, Julian S. *England in the Seven Years' War: A Study of Combined Strategy.* 2 vols. London, 1907.

Couillard Desprès, Azarie. *Charles de Saint-Etienne de La Tour, gouverneur, lieutenant-général en Acadie, 1593–1666.* Arthabaska, Que., 1930.

Daigle, Jean, ed. *Les Acadiens des Maritimes.* Moncton, N.B., 1980.

Delanglez, Jean. *The French Jesuits in Lower Louisiana.* New Orleans, 1935.

Del Sesto, Steven L., and Jon L. Gibson, eds. *The Culture of Acadiana: Tradition and Change in South Louisiana.* Lafayette, La., 1975.

De Valigny, Pacifique. *Chroniques des plus anciennes églises de l'Acadie: Bathurst, Pabos et Ristigouche, Rivière St. John, Memramcook.* Montreal, 1944.

Din, Gilbert C. "*Cimarrones* and the San Malo Band in Spanish Louisiana." *Louisiana History*, XXI (1980), 237–63.

Doughty, A. *The Acadian Exiles.* Toronto, 1920.

Eccles, William J. *France in America.* New York, 1972.

Erlanger, Philippe. *La Vie quotidienne sous Henri IV.* Paris, 1958.

Foret, Michael James. "Aubry, Foucault, and the Attakapas Acadians: 1765." *Attakapas Gazette*, XV (1980), 60–62.

Fortier, Alcée."The Acadians of Louisiana and Their Dialect." *Publications of the Modern Language Association*, VI (1891), 64–94.

―――. *A History of Louisiana.* 4 vols. New York, 1904.

―――, ed. *Louisiana: Comprising Sketches of Counties, Towns, Events, Institutions and Persons, Arranged in Cyclopedic Order.* 3 vols. Atlanta, 1909.

Fontenot, Mary Alice, and Paul B. Freeland. *Acadia Parish, Louisiana: A History to 1900.* Baton Rouge, 1976.

Frégault, Guy. "La Déportation des Acadiens." *Revue d'Histoire de l'Amerique française*, VIII (1954), 309–58.

―――. *La Guerre de la conquête, 1754–1760.* Vol. IX of *Histoire de la Nouvelle France.* Montreal, 1955.

Gayarré, Charles Etienne Arthur. *A History of Louisiana.* 4 vols. 1854–66; rpr. New Orleans, 1965.

Gipson, Lawrence Henry. *The British Empire Before the American Revoluton.* 15 vols. New York, 1946–70.

Grégoire, Jeanne. "Les Acadiens dans une Seconde Patrie: La Louisiane." *Revue d'Histoire de l'Amerique francaise*, XV (1962), 582–93.

Griffin, Harry L. *Attakapas Country: A History of Louisiana Parish.* 1959; rpr. Gretna, La., 1974.

Griffiths, Naomi. *The Acadians: Creation of a People.* New York, 1973.

―――. "Acadians in Exile: The Experience of the Acadians in the British Seaports." *Acadiensis*, III (1973), 67–84.

―――, ed. *The Acadian Deportation: Deliberate Perfidy or Cruel Necessity?* Toronto, 1969.

Groulx, Lionel. *Histoire du Canada français depuis la découverte*. 2 vols. 4th ed. Montreal, 1960.

Hannay, James. *History of New Brunswick*. 2 vols. St. John, N.B., 1909.

Harvey, D. C. *The French Regime in Prince Edward Island*. New Haven, 1926.

Hawke, David. *The Colonial Experience*. Indianapolis, 1966.

Henige, David, comp. *Colonial Governors from the Fifteenth Century to the Present*. Madison, 1970.

Hilliard, Sam Bowers. *Hog Meat and Hoecake: Food Supply in the Old South, 1840–1860*. Carbondale, Ill., 1972.

Holmes, Jack D. L. *Gayoso: The Life of a Spanish Governor in the Mississippi Valley, 1789–1799*. 1965; rpr. Gloucester, Mass., 1968.

Hudnut, Ruth Allison, and Hayes Baker-Crothers. "Acadian Transients in South Carolina." *American Historical Review*, XLIII (1938), 500–13.

Hutton, J. A. "The Micmac Indians of Nova Scotia to 1834." M.A. thesis, Dalhousie University, 1961.

Huxley, Aldous. *The Devils of Loudun*. New York, 1952.

Jehn, Janet, comp. *Acadian Exiles in the Colonies*. Covington, Ky., 1977.

Johnson, Cecil. *British West Florida*. New Haven, 1942.

Johnston, George. *History of Cecil County*. 2nd ed. Baltimore, 1972.

Kemper, James P. *Floods in the Valley of the Mississippi*. New Orleans, 1928.

Kilman, Grady. "Slavery and Forced Labor in Colonial Louisiana, 1699–1803." M.A. thesis, University of Southwestern Louisiana, 1972.

LaBande, Edmond-René, ed. *Histoire du Poitou, du Limousin et des Pays Charentais*. Toulouse, 1976.

Lanctot, Gustave. *Histoire du Canada*. 3 vols. Montreal, 1960–63.

Lauvrière, Emile. *La Tragédie d'un peuple: Histoire du peuple acadien de ses origines à nos jours*. 2 vols. Paris, 1886.

LeBlanc, Dudley. *The Acadian Miracle*. Lafayette, La., 1966.

LeBlanc, Robert G. "The Acadian Migrations." *Proceedings of the Minnesota Academy of Science*, XXX (1962), 55–59.

Ledet, Wilton Paul. "Acadian Exiles in Pennsylvania." *Pennsylvania History*, X (1942), 118–28.

Lemann, Thomas B. "Forced Heirship in Louisiana: In Defense of Forced Heirship." *Tulane Law Review*, LII (1977), 20–28.

"Lifestyle of Early Settlers Reflected in Acadian House Museum and Acadian Craft Shop." *Acadiana Profile*, V (1975), 22.

McCloy, Shelby T. "French Charities to the Acadians, 1755–1799." *Louisiana Historical Quarterly*, XXI (1938), 656–68.

McGowan, James T. "Creation of a Slave Society: Louisiana Plantations in the Eighteenth Century." Ph.D. dissertation, University of Rochester, 1976.

Mamalakis, Mario. "Arceneaux Home Dates Back Almost 200 Years." Lafayette *Daily Advertiser*, May 18, 1980, p. 81.

Marchand, Sidney A. *The Flight of a Century (1800–1900) in Ascension Parish, Louisiana*. Donaldsonville, La., 1936.

———. *The Story of Ascension Parish, Louisiana*. Donaldsonville, La., 1931.

Martell, J. S. "The Second Expulsion of the Acadians." *Dalhousie Review*, XIII (1933–34), 359–71.

Martin, Ernest. *Les Exilés acadiens en France au XVIIIᵉ siècle et leur établissement en Poitou*. Paris, 1936.

Martin, François-Xavier. *The History of Louisiana from the Earliest Period*. 2 vols. New Orleans, 1827–29.

Massignon, Geneviève. *Les Parlers français d'Acadie, enquête linguistique*. 2 vols. Paris, 1962.

Moore, John Preston. *Revolt in Louisiana: The Spanish Occupation, 1766–1770*. Baton Rouge, 1976.

O'Neill, Charles Edwards. *Church and State in French Colonial Louisiana: Policy and Politics to 1732*. New Haven, 1966.

Papuchon, General. "La Colonie acadienne du Poitou." *Bulletin de la Société des Antiquières de l'Ouest*, (1908), 311–67.

Perkins, James B. *France Under Mazarin*. 2 vols. New York, 1886.

Perrin, William Henry, ed. *Southwest Louisiana, Biographical and Historical*. New Orleans, 1891.

Porter, Michael P. "Forced Heirs: The Legitime and Loss of the Legitime in Louisiana." *Tulane Law Review*, XXXVII (1963), 710–64.

Rameau de St-Père, François-Edmé. *Une Colonie féodale en Amérique: L'Acadie, 1604–1881*. 2 vols. Paris, 1889.

Raymond, William O. "Brigadier General Monckton's Expedition to the River Saint John in September, 1758." *Collections of the New Brunswick Historical Society*, No. 9 (1914), 113–65.

———. "The North Shore: Incidents in the Early History of Eastern and Northern New Brunswick." *Collections of the New Brunswick Historical Society*, No. 4 (1899), 81–134.

Reed, Revon. *Lâche pas la patate: Portrait des Acadiens de la Louisiane*. Montreal, 1976.

Reed, William. "The French Neutrals in Pennsylvania." *Pennsylvania Historical Society Memoirs*, VI (1858), 285–316.

Rees, Grover. *A Narrative History of Breaux Bridge, Once Called "La Pointe."* Lafayette, La., 1976.

Richard, Edouard. *Acadia: Missing Links of a Lost Chapter in American History*. 2 vols. New York, 1895.

Rushton, William F. *The Cajuns: From Acadia to Louisiana*. New York, 1979.

Scharf, John T. *History of Maryland from Earliest Times to the Present Day*. 3 vols. Baltimore, 1879.

Schmeisser, Barbara M. "La Vallée de Memramcook et la continuité du peuplement acadien." *Les Cahiers de la Société historique acadienne*, XII (1981), 143–46.

Sequin, Robert-Lionel. *La Civilisation traditionelle de l'habitant aux 17ᵉ et 18ᵉ siècles*. Montreal, 1967.

Solano Costa, Fernando. "Emigración acadiana a la Luisiana española." *Jerónimo Zurita. Cuadernos de Historia*, II (1954), 85–125.

Sollers, Basil. "The Acadians (French Neutrals) Transported to Maryland." *Maryland Historical Magazine*, III (1908), 1–21.

————, ed. "Party of Acadians Who Sailed from the Potomac, Bound for the Mississippi." *Maryland Historical Magazine*, IV (1909), 279–81.

Souvay, Charles L., "Rummaging Through Old Parish Records: An Historical Sketch of the Church of Lafayette, La." *St. Louis Catholic Historical Review*, III (1921), 243, 245–46.

Sprague, Marshall. *So Vast So Beautiful a Land: Louisiana and the Purchase*. Boston, 1974.

Stankiewicz, W. J. *Politics and Religion in Seventeenth-Century France*. Berkeley, 1960.

Stanley, George F. G. *New France: The Last Phase, 1744–1760*. Toronto, 1968.

Swanton, John R. *Indian Tribes of the Lower Mississippi Valley and Adjacent Coast of the Gulf of Mexico*. Washington, D.C., 1911.

Taylor, Gertrude C. *Land Grants Along the Teche*. 3 maps. Lafayette, La., 1979–80.

Texada, David Ker. *Alejandro O'Reilly and the New Orleans Rebels*. Lafayette, La., 1970.

Theriot, Marie del Norte, and Catherine Brookshire Blanchet. *Les Danses rondes: Louisiana French Folk Dances*. Abbeville, La., 1955.

Thomas, Daniel H. "Fort Toulouse: The French Outpost at the Alabamons, 1717–1763." *Alabama Historical Quarterly*, XXII (1960), 141–230.

————. "Pre-Whitney Cotton Gins in French Louisiana," *Journal of Southern History*, XXXI (1965), 135–48.

Tomkins, Frank H. *Riparian Lands of the Mississippi River . . .* New Orleans, 1901.

Treasure, G. R. R. *Seventeenth Century France*. London, 1966.

Trudel, Marcel. *L'Esclavage du Canada française: Histoire et conditions de l'esclavage*. Quebec, 1960.

Turner, Frederick Jackson. *The Frontier in American History*. New York, 1920.

————. "The Significance of the Frontier in American History." In *Annual Report of the American Historical Association for the Year 1893*. Washington, D.C., 1894.

Villiers du Terrage, Marc de. *Les Dernières Années de la Louisiane française*. Paris, 1904.

Vinter, Dorothy. "The Acadian Exiles in England." *Les Cahiers de la Société historique acadienne*, 30^{ieme} (1971), 388–402.

Voorhies, Felix B. *Acadian Reminiscences: The True Story of Evangeline*. 2nd ed. Lafayette, La., 1977.

Voorhies, Jacqueline K. *Some Late Eighteenth-Century Louisianians*. Lafayette, La., 1973.

————, trans. "The Attakapas Post: The First Acadian Settlement." *Louisiana History*, XVII (1976), 91–96.

————, trans. "The Promised Land? The Acadians in the Antilles, 1763–1764." *Attakapas Gazette*, XI (1976), 81–83.

Wallis, W. D. "Historical Background of the Micmac Indians of Canada." In *National Museum of Canada Bulletin No. 173: Contributions to Anthropology, 1959*. Ottawa, 1961.

Wallis, W. D., and R. S. Wallis. *The Micmac Indians of Eastern Canada*. Minneapolis, 1955.

Watson, John F. *Annals of Philadelphia*. Philadelphia, 1830.

Wedgwood, C. V. *The Thirty Years' War*. London, 1938.

Winzerling, Oscar W. *Acadian Odyssey*. Baton Rouge, 1955.

Wood, Gregory A. *The French Presence in Maryland, 1524–1800*. Baltimore, 1978.

Wright, Esther C. *The Petitcodiac: A Study of the New Brunswick River and of the People Who Settled It*. Sackville, N.B., 1945.

Zaslow, Morris. "The Frontier Hypothesis in Recent Canadian Historiography." *Canadian Historical Review*, XXIX (1948), 153–67.

Index

Abbeville, La., 95, 98
Abnaki Indians, 189
Acadia: dike system of, 11, 31;
  Huguenot pioneers of, 5–6, 150; livestock holdings in 1714, p. 121; neglected by France, 3, 6, 9; Scottish
  Calvinists in, 6, 8
Acadian Coast, 91, 106, 107, 113–15,
  125, 128, 131, 147, 181, 190
Acadian Reminiscences, 105
Acadians: and agriculture, 9, 11, 125–
  33; architecture, 139–42; at Belle-Ile-
  en-Mer, 59; and Catholic church,
  150–66; in Cayenne, 58, 60; characteristics of, 2–3, 9–10; costume, 127,
  136–39; cuisine, 133–36; dances, 138,
  147, 164; deportation and dispersal
  of, 23–34; diet, 75, 127, 128, 129,
  132–36; egalitarianism of, 3, 188; as
  engagés, 8, 9; in England, 45, 56–57,
  62; environment and, 9–10, 121–49;
  ethnic identity of, 1–2; ethos, 144–
  47, 164–65; in exile, 35–72; in Falk-
  land Islands, 59–60; in France, 55–
  72, 107, 141; French (precolonial)
  background of, 3–5, 8; frontier experiences of, before dispersal, 3, 5–19;
  furniture, 142–43; and gambling,
  148, 163; at Grand Ligne settlement,
  France, 63–65; and horse racing, 148,
  149; as hunters, 9; immigration to
  Louisiana, 73–89, 107, 109–14; individualism of, 8; industriousness of,
  3; kinship system of, 3; litigiousness
of, 8, 144; music, 147; and Negro
slavery, 41, 134, 135, 158, 163, 169,
173, 184, 188–97, 198; and oath of allegiance to Britain, 14, 15, 17–20, 24;
pragmatism of, 3; and ranching, 74,
75, 121–25, 132, 171, 172; relations
with Creoles, 96, 99–101, 112, 114,
121, 132, 142, 144, 148, 149, 157, 163,
167–76, 192; relations with Indians,
5, 9, 17, 129, 152, 153, 177–87; seasonal pursuits of, 9–10; settlement
patterns of, 76–78, 80–81, 90–115,
122, 145, 146; smuggling by, 16, 131,
132
Alexander, William, 6
Algiers, La., 83, 108
American Revolution, 112, 124, 131, 145
Amherst, Jeffrey, 29, 30
Amitié (ship), 109, 111
Andalusia, Spain: proposed coloniza-
  tion of Acadians at, 62
Andry, Louis, 75, 76, 168
Anglo-Americans, 99, 100, 149
Angoumois Province, France, 8
Annapolis, Md., 37, 38, 41
Annapolis *Maryland Gazette*, 36
Annapolis River Valley, 15
Annapolis-Royal, Nova Scotia, 14–16,
  24, 25
Anne I, 13
Anticlericalism, 150–66
Appalachian Mountains, 29, 36, 105, 180
Aranda, Pedro Pablo Arbaca de Bolea,
  condé de, 65–67, 69, 71